IN A CLOSET HIDDEN

Mary Wilkins

Conscience
At home
Always. New England

In a Closet Hidden

THE LIFE AND WORK OF
MARY E. WILKINS FREEMAN

Leah Blatt Glasser

University of Massachusetts Press

Amherst

Frontispiece: Portrait of Mary E. Wilkins Freeman. Mary Wilkins Freeman Collection (#7267), by permission of Clifton Waller Barrett Library, Special Collections Department, University of Virginia Library.

Copyright © 1996
The University of Massachusetts Press
All rights reserved
Printed in the United States of America
LC 95-46798
ISBN 1-55849-027-2 (cloth); 028-0 (pbk.)
Designed by Dennis Anderson
Set in New Baskerville by dix!
Printed and bound by Thomson-Shore, Inc.

Library of Congress Cataloging-in-Publication Data
Glasser, Leah Blatt, 1951–
In a closet hidden : the life and work of Mary E. Wilkins Freeman
/ Leah Blatt Glasser.
p. cm.
Includes bibliographical references and index.
"Selected bibliography of the works of Mary E. Wilkins Freeman":
p.
ISBN 1-55849-027-2 (cloth : alk. paper).
—ISBN 1-55849-028-0 (pbk. : alk. paper)
1. Freeman, Mary Eleanor Wilkins, 1852–1930.
2. Feminism and literature—New England—History—19th century.
3. Women and literature—New England—History—19th century.
4. Lesbians' writings, American—History and criticism.
5. Women authors, American—19th century—Biography.
6. Women authors, American—20th century—Biography.
7. Sex role in literature.   I. Title.
PS1713.G58   1996
813'.4—dc20
[B]   95-46798
CIP

British Library Cataloguing in Publication data are available.

The lines from "The Mirror in Which Two Are Seen as One" are reprinted from *Diving into the Wreck: Poems 1971–72* by Adrienne Rich, by permission of the author and W. W. Norton & Company, Inc. Copyright © 1973 by W. W. Norton & Company, Inc.

For Gerry, Rachel, and Benjamin

Of a summer afternoon,
In a parlor window there,
She would sit, her meek face showing
Delicately long and fair,
Sewing on some dainty garment, no one ever saw
  her wear.

To the last,

When she cried, poor, shy old maiden,
Her artless secret saw the sun: —
She had been with love acquainted,
Always, just like anyone: —
But had kept him in a closet hidden, as a
  skeleton.

"A Maiden Lady," Mary E. Wilkins Freeman

CONTENTS

❦

ACKNOWLEDGMENTS

I AM EXTREMELY grateful to Mount Holyoke College for the faculty fellowship I was awarded and for the subsequent faculty grants. These generous awards gave me the time and resources I needed to complete the book.

I was strongly encouraged by Claire Rosenfield, David Hirsch, and Mark Spilka at Brown University when I first began the project. Their faith in my ideas gave me the confidence to persist at a time when few were aware of the value of studying Mary E. Wilkins Freeman. David Hirsch's intelligence and insight on Freeman has always inspired me. I am indebted to him for his sensitive and careful reading of my book, for the breadth of his bibliographical knowledge, and for his helpful advice over the years.

At a time when I might have decided to put aside my work on Freeman, Sara Ruddick posed the crucial questions that made it possible for me to continue. Her quiet probing helped me recognize the issues at the heart of my subject in highly personal terms. She encouraged me to analyze the process of working on Freeman in the context of my own life. The essay I wrote for the anthology she was editing at the time, *Between Women,* became a turning point in my work on Freeman.

I am grateful to Gail Hornstein, chair of women studies at Mount Holyoke College, and the network of women scholars in the Five College Women's Research Studies Center for their support during my semester as research associate at Dickinson House. I am equally grateful to members of the Mount Holyoke College English department for their sustaining support and interest in the project, particularly William Quillian and Carolyn Collette in their capacities as department chairs. Their encouragement was invaluable and our conversations about teaching women writers figured significantly in my work on Freeman. My thanks for the help of the department research assistant, Sarah Provost. The enthusiasm of my students at Mount Holyoke College has made it possible for me to see Freeman come to life in the classroom and has helped me recognize her pertinence for women today.

I thank the academic deans with whom I worked most closely, Marilyn Pryor, Ruth Bass Green, and Mary Jacob, for their daily encouragement and compassion. I was fortunate as well to have the extended support of other members of the staff, and am particularly grateful to my administrative assistant, Aileen Bartels. I thank Karen Bourque-Werner for her excellent work as a research assistant and computer consultant.

I am grateful to Brent L. Kendrick for his extraordinarily useful letter collection, *The Infant Sphinx,* and for his generous permission to make use of his collection of photographs. My thanks to the Clifton Waller Barrett Library, Special Collections Department at the University of Virginia Library for permission to use materials and photographs from the Mary Wilkins Freeman Collection (#7407). My appreciation extends as well to the New York Public Library, Manuscripts and Archives Division, Special Collections, for permission to quote from the Anthony Collection. For permission to revise and reprint portions of my published essays, I thank Beacon Press, Routledge, and the *Massachusetts Review.* Finally my thanks to Andrienne Rich and to Norton Press for permission to quote from "The Mirror in Which Two are Seen as One."

This book could not have been completed without the benefit of extended loans from the Mount Holyoke College Library. I am especially grateful to the librarians who assisted me substantially in my research, including Anne Edmonds, Marilyn Dunn, and Kathleen Norton, and to the librarians in the Mount Holyoke College Archives, Elaine Trehub and Patricia Albright. I thank College Librarian, Susan Perry, for permission to quote from the recollections in the Mount Holyoke College Archives of students who attended Mount Holyoke Female Seminary in 1870.

My understanding of Freeman deepened as a result of fruitful discussions with friends and colleagues Sue Freeman, Beate Allert,

Chris Benfey, Martha Ackmann, Denise Knight, Alfred Bendixen, Marjorie Pryse, my running partner Kathy Dunn, and others. More recently, the questions posed by scholars in the Nineteenth-Century Women Writers Study Group helped me think about Freeman in the context of her contemporaries. Joan Hedrick's thoughts about the process of literary biography have encouraged me to consider the broader questions that my work on Freeman may raise. I thank Paul Lauter for our conversations about Freeman and the opportunity to introduce her work in the Heath Anthology. I am especially grateful to my colleague and friend Daniel Czitrom for his calm and brotherly advice since I began the book, for his helpful suggestions after reading portions of the manuscript, and for our frequent conversations about the process of writing.

The book could not have been written without the love and patience of my husband, Gerald Glasser, who has lived with me and with my "roommate," Mary E. Wilkins Freeman, for so many years. He has given me the necessary space for work, while drawing me back to realize and celebrate the beauty of our family. My thanks to my daughter, Rachel, who sat on my lap at six years old and asked me to tell her about Mary and whose passion for writing reminds me so much of Freeman's, and to my compassionate son, Benjamin, who understands the meaning of what it is to be a nurturing male and who served me breakfast in bed as a reward for late nights at the computer. I relied on the three of them for their reassuring words and their understanding of my need for the time alone to write.

I thank my sister Carole Gonshak for giving me perspective and for helping me laugh when I felt least able to do so, and my sister Marilyn Young, whose honest and insightful comments after reading portions of the manuscript were enormously helpful in the early stages of the book. I am grateful to my parents, Mollie and Aaron Blatt, for their unconditional love and support. Perhaps I found Freeman's bond with her mother so understandable because of my own relationship with my mother. I am especially grateful to her for the care she took to enrich the lives of my children while I was at work on the book.

Finally, I would like to express particular appreciation for the invaluable advice, encouragement, and support of my editor, Clark Dougan, and for Pam Wilkinson's careful, intelligent, and detailed editing of the manuscript.

PREFACE

Discovering Mary E. Wilkins Freeman

She is the one you call sister
you blaze like lightning about the room
flicker around her like fire
dazzle yourself in her wide eyes
listing her unfelt needs
thrusting the tenets of your life
into her hands

Adrienne Rich,
"The Mirror in Which Two Are Seen as One"

As we look to the history of women writers for an understanding
of our roots, it is tempting to create imaginary women to satisfy
longings for an unambiguous feminist heritage. But the heritage is
that much richer for its implicit ambiguities. Mary E. Wilkins Freeman, my hidden sister, has haunted me ever since I first read "A New
England Nun" in 1975. At the time, I was in graduate school at
Brown University and my interest in her work seemed odd to many
of my peers who were focused on the major male writers of the
American literary canon. I realize now that in the process of reconstructing the meaning of Freeman's work and imagining the dimensions of her life, I have been struggling to come to terms with my
own. I have had to move through stages of identification, idealiza-
tion, and evasion before I could look at Freeman's life and work with
honesty, write about her both caringly and accurately, stop "listing

her unfelt needs" by indirectly listing my own, and truly say "she is the one you call sister." [1] My attempt to reinvent Freeman's world has carried with it the challenge of considering, as honestly as possible, what this reinvention might suggest about myself. In some sense, a review of the stages of my work on Freeman is as much a study of my own development as a feminist as it is about Freeman's development as a woman writer.

When I first began to write a literary biography of Mary E. Wilkins Freeman, I was a selective listener. I felt I had a mission. Along with Harriet Beecher Stowe, Sarah Orne Jewett, Charlotte Perkins Gilman, Kate Chopin, Willa Cather, Zora Neale Hurston, and other long neglected women writers, Freeman was enriching my teaching of American literature courses, and yet few were aware of the scope of her work. Here was my chance to set the record straight, to redefine and reevaluate a New England woman who had been overlooked and misinterpreted. Freeman had been traditionally categorized as merely a local colorist, a "minor" American writer of the post–Civil War period whose primary talent lay in depicting the peculiarities of her New England region. I saw, however, that Freeman's work demanded feminist analysis, and I recognized that her subject in fact had little to do with regionalism. With her focus almost entirely on women's struggles and concerns, their intricate forms of repression and rebellion, Mary E. Wilkins Freeman explored the psychology of women's conflicts as she knew them. By giving voice to her silent "shy old maiden," Freeman opened a door to what the "spinster" of her time generally kept "in a closet hidden, as a skeleton." [2] I was drawn to her subversive strategies in her fiction, her understanding of the role of work in women's lives, her courageous portraits of aging women, and her depictions of the unique relationships that women form. I felt an obligation, a deep connection to a woman whose work had been so misunderstood.

"If a woman be at liberty to write," Freeman said, "let her write as if she were running a race in the sight of the world. . . . She must write above all things the truth as far as she can see the truth." [3] Her advice to "the girl who wants to write" suggested to me the sense of urgency, defiance, and freedom that she associated with her role as a turn-of-the-century woman writer. Writing granted her a form of "liberty" and yet it demanded that she "run a race" in the sight of the patriarchal values and judgments of nineteenth-century New England. Given my own struggles to balance writing and mothering at the time, these words naturally drew me to Freeman. Unlike Freeman, I had chosen the traditional path of early marriage and motherhood. The inevitable frustrations as I then attempted to create my own "liberty" through writing became the driving force behind my work on Freeman.

Initially, I wanted Freeman to satisfy my definition of writing as a form of self-affirmation for women. This was the only voice—assertive, defiant, and free—that I had wanted to hear in my earliest work on Freeman. And I *was* able to hear just this voice by reading selectively stories such as "The Revolt of 'Mother' " in which her lively heroines rebel, or by focusing only on the rebellious aspects of her life: her long resistance to marriage, her financial independence as she wrote to support herself. I was, after all, just recognizing my own capacity to pursue my work effectively while facing early motherhood. At the sight of my large belly and the folder with the notes for my first essay on Freeman, a colleague openly expressed his disappointment. "What have you done to your career?" he asked. Perhaps I turned to the refreshing rage of so many of Freeman's heroines as a way of indirectly expressing my own.

In my eagerness to identify with Freeman as a strong independent woman, able to support herself through the work she loved, I unconsciously evaded the dual nature of her work. Dismayed by her method of framing powerful psychological portraits with safe, sentimental beginnings and endings, I found myself longing to rewrite beginnings and reshape endings of her stories or to manipulate details to fit my notion of a feminist model. At the time, I could not confront the complexity of Freeman's work. In my fantasy, Freeman was wholly a rebel; but in reality, like Charlotte Brontë's governess Jane Eyre, she was both "rebel" and "slave," a "divided self."

Freeman wanted to rebel openly, but at the same time she sought shelter and acceptability, even at the price of enslavement to standards that she knew to be oppressive and unjust. When I first began my work, unable to acknowledge Freeman's ambivalence because of my need for a feminist model, I was troubled whenever the energies of both "rebel" and "slave" would appear in the same work and disturbed by inconsistent characterizations. As long as I was impelled to remake her fiction through my interpretation of her work, I avoided confronting the significant question of why, how, and where Freeman's work became an expression of self-division and conflict.

Looking in "the mirror in which two are seen as one," and looking at my own resistance to Freeman's more fearful and conventional self, I have come to realize that conflicting voices have shaped my life as well and are voices worth listening to. And I did learn to listen. I began to hear, understand, and appreciate Freeman's conflicting voices. Accuracy or balance came once I could explore Freeman's duality—and my own. The sister I came to see in Freeman was finally not simply a creature of my imagination, an unconflicted, unambivalent rebel. Once I could acknowledge that I was engaged in the process of telling a story about a life that was necessarily haunted by contradictions, I was able to arrive at a needed balance, able to listen openly to the voices I had initially blocked, both her voices and mine.

In the early stages of my work, I was struggling to carve out the time I needed for writing. I had yet to define my work as self-nourishing, pulled as I was by the needs of others—the new baby, the many students wanting feedback on their writing. By facing the complexity of Freeman's multiple voices, however, I have had to acknowledge the conflicting energies that have shaped my life as a mother, teacher, writer, and more recently, academic dean. While passionately protective of the autonomy available to me through writing, I am equally drawn to the maternal world in which I have thrived. Like Freeman, the bond I share with my mother and sisters has figured significantly in my life. The intensity of our relationships has made me especially sensitive to the depiction of mothers, daughters, and sisters in Freeman's work. My own approach to motherhood has been equally intense and has often left me with the inevitable tug between the pleasures of family life and the need for time to myself for my work. The more I began to appreciate Freeman's paradoxical characterizations of women and the fascinating contradictions buried in her work, the more I was able to recognize and accept my own.

Reading her letters and manuscripts, I began to see that writing offered Freeman the chance to express what she was never able to verbalize openly—her conflicts between defiance and submission, self-fulfillment and self-sacrifice, or more concretely, her conflict between the desire on the one hand for autonomous spinsterhood and on the other for acceptable marriage. In an interview of Freeman for *Harper's Bazaar* in 1900, Margaret Hamilton Welch suggested, quite unwittingly, this sense of Freeman's dualism. Referring to her appearance and manner, Welch described Freeman as a woman who belonged "physically, to that class of blond women whose type is represented wholly in the coloring of hair and eyes and complexion. . . . In conversation she has a straightforward simple manner that has a touch of mannishness in its directness, while at the same time her femininity is one of her most prominent characteristics."[4] I would suggest that both her appearance and her manner reflect the contradictions that were so apparent in her work: a combination of "simple" gentility and "mannish" self-possession, quiet acquiescence and fierce independence. Perhaps Welch's association of Freeman's "directness" with "mannishness" (and hence deviation from the norm of femininity) drove Freeman to do what she could to disguise her own capacity to be an assertive, self-employed woman writer. Photographs of Freeman capture exactly this contradiction, with both the softness in the curls lining her face, the scooped neckline, and the laced border of her dress and the firm determination of her jaw, the set of her mouth, the almost piercing clarity of her eyes.

I have had the luxury of working in a New England setting and of visualizing Freeman in the seclusion of her room on the second floor of her home in Randolph, the room she needed for writing. One of her biographers described it as a room full of windows that overlooked "the elms of Main Street and beyond . . . the coastal hills."[5] I have looked out of my own windows from my attic study and easily imagined Freeman sitting in this room at her "low table and amid the plainest things," writing just as I was writing. I sensed always that she would have sanctioned my choice to close the door to the study for my time alone with my work. At the same time, her work brought me closer to an understanding of the complexity of this process. Whether working in my study at home or in my haven at Mount Holyoke College, an office set apart from my administrative space on campus, I have been keenly aware of the very conflicts Freeman explored in her fiction. In order to write, I have had to balance the urge to place the needs of others above my own, whether they are the needs of my children, students, husband, or colleagues, with the need for the isolation required in order to pursue self-generated, autonomous work. Freeman's heroines similarly struggle for the recognition of the importance of their work while longing for the comforts of connectivity and love.

My study of Freeman's life and work is a study of unresolved and paradoxical polarities: repression and rebellion, submission and autonomy, heterosexuality and lesbianism, marriage and spinsterhood, the nurturance of others and self-nurturance, what Adrienne Rich refers to as the "energy of relation" and the "energy of creation." To describe the feeling of receiving her first acceptance and check for a short story, Freeman said "I felt my wings spring from my shoulders capable of flight and I flew home."[6] Feeling "capable of flight" because of the power of her capacity as a writer, Freeman nevertheless could only fly "home." Most striking in her life and work is the haunting echo of two inner voices: one that cries out for rebellious flight and another that clings to the safety of home and all its accompanying restrictions.

In order to capture the conflicting voices in Freeman's world, I have moved beyond her short stories to some of her frequently overlooked novels. In some of her work, the voice is defiant, unwilling to submit. In other works, we hear passive acceptance and internalization of oppressive standards for wives and daughters. In her most interesting though most uneven fiction, she pits one voice against another, creating then a dialogue between opposing selves, and in a very modern sense, ending with inevitable ambiguity. The psychology of self-division became the subject at the heart of almost all of her work. Freeman provides then a graphic example of the ambivalence shared by so many nineteenth-century women, caught between conflicting needs for acceptability and self-fulfillment. She often expressed this conflict through the use of psychological doubles, mirror selves; her rebellious heroines are shadowed by passive, socially acceptable characters whose actions or words influence, sometimes tame and even transform the actions of the more aggressive women characters.

Chapter 1, "Nurtured in Repression," focuses on the way in which the mixed messages Freeman received as a girl growing up in Randolph, Massachusetts, shaped her portrayals of childhood and adolescence in her short stories and novels. This chapter explores as well the nature of Freeman's relationship with her mother and the degree to which this informs so much of her work on women.

My second chapter, "The Art of My Work," turns to Freeman's discovery of her own voice, her growing awareness of "caring more in my heart for the art of my work than for anything else."[7] Freeman's depiction of the work of women in her fiction took many forms. Whether her characters are engaged in housework, gardening, quilting, storing the essences of roses, telling stories, or cultivating herbs, Freeman's portrayals captured her own understanding of her role as a woman writer and the complexities of the writing process itself, her need for the autonomy that writing provided.

Freeman began to recognize that the choice to earn her living as a writer was connected to her choice to resist marriage. Chapter 3, "Sometimes I Think I Am a Monster," explores Freeman's depiction of spinsterhood in her fiction and her own experience of unmarried life. Her letters as well as her published and unpublished prose suggest that she both enjoyed unmarried life and was ashamed of this pleasure.

Freeman began to express her resistance to marriage in her letters and fiction during the childbearing years. Her attempts to explore sexuality become especially interesting in this light. Freeman's most extensive study of sexual politics in nineteenth-century New England emerges in her longer works. Although critics have traditionally focused on her short fiction because of its obvious strength when compared with her novels, I turn in Chapters 4 and 5 to *Pembroke* and *Madelon* because they offer two of her most powerful portrayals of women's sexuality.

Freeman's vision of nineteenth-century women's communities as an alternative to married life is the focus of Chapter 6, "The Tenderness of One Woman for Another." The years in which Freeman lived with Mary Wales, soon after the loss of her mother, father, and sister, were the richest years of her literary career. She was in fact at her best when she wrote, often in highly sensual terms, about the bonds women form. Multiple voices emerge in her short stories and novels focusing on women's relationships: voices that both celebrate and deny the superior quality of life for those women characters who, despite the stigma of spinsterhood, choose to love and support each other in place of making a man the center of their lives.

Freeman's late decision to marry, after twenty years of living with Mary Wales, had a significant effect on her capacity to write effectively. Chapter 7, "If You Don't See the Old Me," captures Freeman's painful realization that she had taken the risk of losing "the old me" when she married Dr. Charles Freeman, and indeed there were many losses. The fiction she wrote at this time reflects her new understanding of the scope of her loss.

Discussions in my seminar on nineteenth- and early twentieth-century women writers, "Rhythms of Revolt," were especially helpful when I wrote my last chapter. Here I place Freeman's voice alongside the complementary voices of two of her New England contemporaries, Sarah Orne Jewett and Charlotte Perkins Gilman. Set in this context, Freeman's work provides an ambiguous voice of protest, carrying neither the boldness of Gilman nor the pastoral calm of Jewett, defiantly analyzing but also ultimately accepting the inequities, offering a feminist analysis but avoiding feminist conclusion.

Teaching at Mount Holyoke College, the very place Freeman attended in 1870 (when it was called Mount Holyoke Female Seminary), I have had the pleasure of working in a woman-centered community in which the voices of women of the past are especially resonant. I was able to write much of the manuscript in the serene setting of the Five College Women's Studies Research Center at Dickinson House, a place in which I felt protected from all the administrative concerns of my life as an academic dean. It offered a "room of one's own" in which I could consider Freeman's world, and it was here that I most fully understood her intense need for a similar haven.

IN A CLOSET HIDDEN

1

"NURTURED IN REPRESSION"

∞

IN A LETTER to Sarah Orne Jewett, Mary E. Wilkins Freeman wrote, "I suppose it seems to you as it does to me that everything you have heard, seen, or done, since you opened your eyes on the world, is coming back to you sooner or later, to go into stories."[1] It is especially illuminating to trace the way in which the past was continually "coming back" to Freeman in the form of her fiction about childhood. An analysis of this fiction suggests the dominant motifs that shaped Freeman's early development. The most striking examples capture her almost obsessive focus on the role of loss in the lives of children, the significance and complexity of the mother-daughter bond, the struggle toward sexual identity in early adolescence, the pull in late adolescence of heterosexual love and marriage, and the conflicting need for autonomy. If we set whatever concrete information is available beside Freeman's reconstruction of her past in her stories about childhood and adolescence, a pattern begins to emerge. It becomes possible to piece together the fragments of a youth that was haunted by duality: empowering and disempowering, nurturing and oppressive, liberating and imprisoning.

Mary E. Wilkins Freeman's early years reflect all of the contradictions of nineteenth-century New England girlhood. Fred Pattee refers to Freeman as a "daughter of the Puritans . . . one who was nurtured in repression."[2] The odd phrasing here—to be fed in the context of being repressed—does capture the qualities of Mary's experience as the child of Warren and Eleanor Wilkins. She was certainly a "nurtured child," but the nurturing was not unconditional. Expectations of passive conformity to contemporary stan-

dards of femininity and to the restrictions of religious orthodoxy
were an implicit part of her upbringing. Struggling always with the
longing to rebel against such limiting codes of behavior and the
need to suppress that impulse in order to win love, Freeman ultimately turned to her fiction to reconstruct the meaning of her
childhood and to channel her unvoiced revolt.

Very few details are available on Freeman's early life. The biographies by Edward Foster and Perry Westbrook supply largely anec-
dotal information, limited and speculative for the most part, which
can be useful only in conjunction with a closer study of her fiction.[3]
Brent Kendrick's letter collection provides some insight into the
scope of her letters about writing and her relationship to her work.[4]
Given the limited archival material, however, Foster, Westbrook, and
Kendrick rely primarily on the comments of friends and neighbors
as well as Freeman's rare references in her letters for some sense of
the first twenty years of her life. The paucity of primary source material leads Foster to speculate about the seeds in her youth for what
he labels as Freeman's adult "neurosis," a reading for which there is
no factual support.[5] As Elizabeth Meese explains, the absence of
specific evidence is often a problem for biographers of women writers. The "skeletal nature" of the materials Foster cites "frequently
requires his inventiveness, through which he constructs his subject
according to his image of Freeman-as-woman."[6] If Freeman kept a
journal, it was not preserved and her letters were strikingly silent on
the subject of her early years. She seems to have turned to writing as
a way of reliving and reconstructing the meaning of her childhood.
For this reason, an understanding of Freeman's youth can be best
achieved through analysis of her fiction.

Mary Ella Wilkins was born on 31 October 1852, in Randolph,
Massachusetts, a rural town near Boston. (Mary later changed her
middle name in memory of her mother.) Although Randolph became the setting for many of her stories and novels, her developing
fascination with New England had little to do with sense of place,
scenery, or region. Rather, from an early age, she was an almost
obsessive observer of human behavior, which often meant *female*
behavior. As Josephine Donovan writes, "rural life in nineteenth-
century New England had become predominantly matriarchal or
female-centered." With the loss of lives in the Civil War and the
numbers of young men migrating westward or to urban centers after

the war, "the world left behind was, so to speak, a world controlled by the mothers and their values."[7] In Randolph Freeman developed in what was primarily a women's community, gathering a wealth of oral histories, the source of much of her fiction, in the kitchens of her grandmother (who lived in the house adjacent to hers), her mother, and her childhood and lifelong friend, Mary Wales. On the one hand, the most positive dimension of Freeman's childhood was the ease and comfort that came with female bonding in a community largely populated by women. On the other hand, the particular nature of Freeman's bond with her mother as well as the messages indirectly conveyed about the necessity of female passivity make it impossible to categorize such an upbringing as a straightforward pathway toward feminist empowerment.

Before exploring the dimensions of her relationship with her mother more fully, it is helpful to consider the role Mary's father played in her early life. Trained by his father, Warren Wilkins was a housewright and carpenter and is said to have enjoyed his trade in the early years in Randolph. As an architect, Freeman's father received some recognition for the beauty of his architectural plans.[8] Freeman's eventual pleasure in the construction of a story resembles her father's attention to detail in his architectural drawings. Some of her fiction would later include details about the structure and construction of houses as though reworking the drawings she must have seen her father create.[9]

Perhaps the most dominant role Warren played in Mary's development, however, was his emphasis on religious obedience. Mary's father traced his ancestry to early New England settlers. Like Hawthorne, he had an ancestor, Bray Wilkins, who was involved in the persecution of women who were deemed to be witches in seventeenth-century Salem. The little that we know about Mary's parents suggests that as orthodox Congregationalists, their lives were shaped by the "old-time religion handed down from the Puritan forefathers."[10] Mary's father seems to have been particularly preoccupied with religious restrictions. Joseph Chamberlain (collaborator with Freeman on "The Long Arm") said of Wilkins, "the Puritan seemed to survive in him as it does in thousands of other Yankees of the finer unsordid type, merely in a sort of exaggerated nervousness, conscientiousness and general unworldliness." Foster states "something of Calvinism survived in . . . his exaggerated sensibility, his occasional black moods."[11] Any Sunday in Mary's childhood included a series of tightly scheduled religious lessons which began at 10:30 A.M. and concluded at 8:00 P.M. The time blocks of these Sundays never varied: 10:30–12:00, prayer; 12:00–1:00, Sabbath school; 2:00–3:30, preaching service; 4:00, young people's service; 7:00–8:00, prayer meeting.[12]

The Randolph Congregational Church, three years before Mary's birth, preached a rigid, only slightly watered-down Calvinism. Although Mary eventually turned to the comparatively moderate preachings of John Labaree, who took the pastorate at Randolph in 1865, she continued to receive rigid instruction from her parents. Even Dr. Labaree, although noted for his more liberal approach to religion, is chiefly remembered for his "emphasis upon the sacred duty of coming to meeting every Sabbath; his condemnation of cards, dancing and drink; his insistence upon the centrality of the Ten Commandments in the Christian way of life," an emphasis then upon denial and rules. Foster says "Mary never forgot the terrible Tables of Law."[13]

"Set About with Restrictions"

Although Freeman never confided openly, she later explored the impact of these early lessons in self-denial when she created the character of Ephraim in her novel *Pembroke*. Through her depiction of Ephraim's childhood, she returned to her own experience of daily instruction in religious restrictions. Ephraim's monotonous recitals of the "assembly's catechism" are similar to the dreaded recitals Freeman faced at school and at home. Far from restraining Ephraim as his parents intend, the rigidity of such religious training simply ignites his rebellion. The creation of Ephraim seems to have provided Freeman with a channel for her own unexpressed and unrealized childhood revolt.

Like Mary Wilkins, Ephraim "was set about with restrictions which made his life miserable" (97). In the mind of Ephraim's mother, Deborah Thayer, Ephraim needs to learn the catechism as a means of filling his mind with spiritual wisdom and "fitting him for that higher state to which he might soon be called" (150). But for Ephraim, the steady, daily droning away of the "wisdom of the divines" is the equivalent of not living. Freeman offers a harsh critique here of the effect of Ephraim's monotonous recitals, the cost of a "spiritual education" at the expense of life itself. Throughout the novel, Freeman's tone is full of delight whenever Ephraim rebels, whenever he eats the forbidden "sweet overhanging fruit." For the pleasure of breaking the diet that has been established for him, he feels both physical pain and "a sense of triumph in his soul." He is especially drawn to forbidden plums: "he dearly loved plums, although they were especially prohibited." Whenever possible he would "roll one quietly under his tongue" and hope that his mother, Deborah, wouldn't see (97).

"Stolen pleasures" become the focus of his young life, as for Freeman self-indulgence became something she associated with the act of stealing what was forbidden. Ephraim's "crowning act of rebellion and revolt" occurs when he escapes from the Thayer home, "like a captive from prison," and runs to the great hill to sled. The description of his sleigh ride, "the one unrestrained hilarity of his whole life," captures the degree of Mary Wilkins's harbored desires for such freedom (229). The only way that Freeman came to know the joy Ephraim experiences in his rebellion is through the imaginative recreation in her novel. Yet Freeman also feared such rebellion. It is as though she were attempting to show her New Englanders that their world allowed no room for Ephraim's sort of uninhibited joy; she found it necessary to annihilate Ephraim after his moment of ultimate freedom.

Her passage describing his act of rebellion is powerful. It contrasts dramatically with the scene of Ephraim's indoor religious worship.

> All by himself in the white moonlight and the keen night air he climbed the long hill and slid down over and over. He ignored his feeble and laboring breath of life. He trod upon, he outspeeded all infirmities of the flesh in his wild triumph of the spirit. He shouted and hallooed as he shot down the hill.
>
> His mother could not have recognized his voice had she heard it, for it was the first time that the boy had ever given full cry to the natural voice of youth and his heart. A few stolen races and sorties up apple-trees, a few stolen slides had poor Ephraim Thayer had; they had been snatched in odd minutes, at the imminent danger of discovery; but now he had the wide night before him; he had broken all his trammels and he was free. (229)

In the "white moonlight and the keen night air," Ephraim gives way to an adventure that will bring him life as much as it will lead to his death. It is interesting that Freeman mentions "his wild triumph of the spirit" for it is this very spirit that the religious discipline of his upbringing attempts to develop and control. With Ephraim's death and the grieving that follows, Freeman expressed her disdain for the conditional love which shaped her own religious upbringing and clearly blocked her capacity to rebel as a child. In this way, she was able to revisit and perhaps even come to terms with the damage of having been "nurtured" through "repression."

Sandwiched between Losses

Mary's early childhood was full of mixed messages which would influence her fiction and which were, in part, a result of the many disappointments in her mother's life. Since Warren spent much of his time working at his trade, it was Eleanor who had the greater influence on Mary's childhood.[14] Eleanor's father had died the year before Mary's birth and her marriage to Warren had failed to match her expectations of financial security. Mary was the baby sandwiched between losses. On many levels, she was to serve as a replacement, a compensation. A first child had died in infancy the January before Mary's birth. When Mary was three, Eleanor gave birth to a frail boy who lived for only three years. Edward Wilkins was born on 15 February 1855, and died in 1858. All the more did Eleanor turn to Mary and depend upon her survival. Mary quickly became the center of Eleanor's life and this in turn became a source of both pleasure and pain for Mary. Eleanor's response to Mary's delicate health throughout her childhood and adolescence was an understandable but excessive fight against the threat of loss. Although another daughter, Anna, was born in 1859 when Mary was seven, Mary's position as the first child to follow such profound loss determined a particularly protective and almost fearful approach to her upbringing. Eleanor created a protective environment, a place where Mary was frequently made aware of her fragility rather than her strength, of her dependence rather than her potential for independence. Her mother's devoted attention and protection contributed to Mary's developing sense of self-importance, but it also stripped her of any faith in her capacity to protect herself.

Long, cold New England winters were spent almost entirely indoors because Eleanor feared for Mary's health; Mrs. Wilkins saw skating and snow-balling as too dangerous for her daughter.[15] Mary was raised not only with restrictions based on the need to conform to religious expectations, but with further limitations based on the assumption of her poor health; the impact of this combination is clear in Freeman's portrayal of Ephraim whose presumed frailty further dramatizes his final act of rebellion.

The majority of the children in Freeman's fiction appear in a context similar to Ephraim's, with mothers fearing their possible illness or death. The understandable conflict Freeman experienced had much to do with her role as the child whose very existence was the center of her mother's life. To voice open rebellion against the life her mother had chosen was to risk hurting her most central source of love. Throughout her childhood, then, the impulse to rebel was muted; by creating children such as Ephraim she found a channel for the voice of the long suppressed child rebel.

The sense of loss haunted Freeman's childhood ever since she "opened her eyes on the world," and it figured significantly in her fiction. When her sister Anna died in 1876 at the age of seventeen, leaving Mary as the only surviving child, Mary would once again attempt to fill a void. Her reflection on the impact of this experience emerged years later, in her short story "A Gentle Ghost." In a letter to Sarah Orne Jewett written in 1889, about a dozen years after Anna's death, Freeman described having had in her mind the "forlorn little girl" at the center of her tale, "A Gentle Ghost," for "a matter of a dozen years."

The story reflects much about the shadow of perpetual losses in Freeman's childhood and her consequent role in relation to her mother. She described the story as a "departure from my usual vein," and as her "lapse into the mystical and romantic . . . for which I have a strong inclination, but do not generally yield to." Although Freeman and others considered the tale supernatural, it was in fact a psychological drama. Referring to the "forlorn little girl," Freeman conveyed to Jewett the need to write about her. "I felt that she must be disposed of, so about two years ago, I put her in the Gentle Ghost."[16] "Disposing" of the "forlorn little girl," the child within, was Freeman's way of coming to terms with the effect of loss, both the beauty and the burden of her mother's approach to nurturance.[17] The parallels between Freeman's experience and that of Flora, the child in the story, are many. Even the physical description of Flora's small figure matches descriptions of Freeman at a young age: "Her hair was beautiful, and she had a charming delicacy of complexion; but she was not handsome, her features were too sharp, her expression too intense and nervous."[18]

"A Gentle Ghost" works most effectively on that borderline between the supernatural and the psychological. By the end of the story, the supernatural ghost transforms into a psychological one. Flora and her mother, Mrs. Dunn, are haunted by a "low moaning sound" emerging from the room that Flora had shared with her young sister Jenny before she died because Jenny had been afraid to sleep alone. Every time they hear the moaning, a sound that Mr. Dunn does not hear, Flora becomes pale and her mother's grieving intensifies. Flora is then determined, even as she fears it, to return to the bedroom, to ease the ghost of the lost sister, the lost daughter. "You'll make yourself sick," Mrs. Dunn pleads. In a "long wail," she reminds Jenny, "you're all I got left" (241). The dialogue that follows captures both the bond and the dilemma:

> "I don't see as you're much better yourself, mother," said Flora, heavily.
> "I don't know as I am," sobbed her mother; "but I've got you to worry about besides—everything else." (241)

The sense of being all her mother "got left" was a vivid aspect of Freeman's childhood, even after the birth of her sister Anna. It was almost impossible for Mary to separate her existence from her mother's, so central was she to her mother's life. The story captures this dependence well as Mrs. Dunn turns from her husband to Jenny, feeling "as if set about by an icy wind of loneliness. Her daughter, who was after her own kind, was all the one to whom she could look for sympathy and understanding in this subtle perplexity which had come upon her. And she would rather have dispensed with that sympathy and understanding and heard alone those piteous, uncanny cries, for she was wild with anxiety about Flora." The bond then is built on "understanding" with suffering as its source. "It was as if they both had passed through one corroding element which had given them the similarity of scars" (242). While her mother nurtured and protected her, warding off the threat of another loss, Freeman's very existence was nurturance for her mother.

The restorative twist the story takes reflects Freeman's wishful recounting of the past. Flora and her mother question the moaning, and consider the possibility that it might not be Jenny. The sound of the moaning proves to be the sound of Nancy Wren, a ten-year-old girl, the lonely child who lives in the nearby poorhouse and visits the cemetery every day. Nancy becomes the child to fill the gap. Afraid of the dark, Nancy Wren comes to live with the Dunns now, finding "her place in the nest of living hearts." In this way, Freeman manages through her fiction to fill the void *her* mother experienced and her own loss as well through the newly invented child, and the burden is lifted. She revives Anna's life by creating a new child for her mother and herself. Flora will sleep with Nancy Wren and all is restored. Flora is no longer the survivor requiring excessive protection. Freeman's fiction, in this sense, takes away grief, restores and remakes a childhood dominated by the unquiet ghosts of her mother's losses.

In reality, there was no Nancy Wren to free Mary from her mother's ghosts. Her childhood was continually shadowed by reminders of her mother's fears, which triggered her own sense of fragility. At the age when most children in Randolph were beginning school, Mary was still at home. Eleanor felt Mary was not strong enough and delayed starting her in school until she was seven (1859), shortly after her sister's birth.[19] The advantages of staying at home were evident. School clearly represented a separation from her mother's intense protection and may have exaggerated whatever displacement accompanied the presence of another child at home. Furthermore, school at "old Number 1" involved long days of repeating the catechism and behaving, an extension of the pressures she experienced at home on Sundays. Mary's pleasures came in whatever hours she could find after school for reading. Not surprisingly, she was reading fairy tales at this time.

At school, Mary felt isolated and alienated; she had never had the opportunity to play with the other children because Eleanor had "considered her too delicate to roam down South Main Street" where the majority of children lived. She was called "teacher's partial," "little, dolly-pinky-rosy," and "stuck-up."[20] Against the mockery of classmates, who considered her strange for her frailty and her superior intelligence, she built a strong defense, a mask of reticence and indifference that influenced her considerably in her adult life.

Her one childhood friend was Mary John Wales who lived nearby on the Wales's hundred-acre farm. Wales offered her a continuation of the maternal protection she experienced at home, often fending off the attacks of schoolmates. The Waleses' farm was just across South Main Street from the school and just south of the Wilkins's house. After school, Mary would often go straight to the spacious farm. The time she spent with Mary John in her early years was her only source of freedom. She played outdoors at the farm, spent time in the kitchen listening to the chatter of the family, and developed a bond with Wales that was strong enough to last through adulthood when she chose to live with Mary Wales for the twenty most productive years of her career.

Parting with Childhood

Perhaps the most striking feature of Freeman's childhood was its paradoxical blend of freedom and constraint as well as its perpetuation. Unlike many women of her time who chose early marriage as an alternative to spinsterhood, Freeman lived with her family until she was thirty. Her early biographers viewed this extended familial protection as a sign of her dependence and exaggerated need for nurturance. But in fact such protection freed her from service to others and became the source of her ultimate independence. Imbued with correct codes of feminine behavior (though she would silently rebel against them), she was expected to remain passive and encouraged to fulfill her father's wish that she would "marry early and well"; at the same time she was pampered and protected by her mother, and in this sense ironically readied for a career as an unmarried writer who would be cared for by others and granted the liberty of solitude.[21]

Resisting the pressure to marry which began in early adolescence and represented the departure from home, Freeman would cling to the "intimate mother-daughter relationship" that "lay at the heart of this female world" cultivated in childhood.[22] She was attracted to physical images of women as children, and often she presented herself well into adulthood, along with most of her women characters, as childlike. A pattern of "childlike" voices runs through her letters, as Kendrick observes, suggesting "a person many years younger than Freeman's actual age" whose "childlike nature reveals itself repeatedly in her correspondence." The suggestion of Freeman's attraction to an image of herself as a child is especially apparent in her most personal letters to women friends, where she signed her name as

"Dolly." In light of her portrayal of Lily in "Old Woman Magoun," who always carries her "dolly" with her, this is a fascinating choice. What did Freeman gain through the child-mask? Why did she cling to it? As Kendrick notes, "the pattern established in her childhood, that of being catered to and sheltered by her parents, continued to a degree throughout her life and manifested itself largely through her dependence on others." [23] It was dependence, however, that was empowering rather than crippling, for it kept her safely within the domain in which she thrived, the world of women and nurturance, and this freed her to write.

The dilemma Freeman faced as she neared adolescence, whose impact she analyzed in "Old Woman Magoun," was the fear of parting with childhood. This fear was the consequence of the messages conveyed in her mother's overprotection. "Old Woman Magoun" best captures the source of Freeman's resistance in adolescence to the move away from the "female world of love and ritual." Daughters in nineteenth- through mid-twentieth-century America were "born into a female world. Their mother's life expectations and sympathetic network of friends and relations were among the first realities in the life of the developing child. . . . It was within this closed and intimate female world that the young girl grew toward womanhood" in "what might be described as an apprenticeship system." [24] This was very much the case for Mary Wilkins Freeman. In "Old Woman Magoun," Freeman traces back to her mother's early protectiveness and creates a grandmother who, recognizing the dangers of heterosexuality, succeeds in restricting the child to the female haven. The story allows Freeman to make a tragic statement about the crossing of that bridge between childhood and adolescence for nineteenth-century girls.

In "Old Woman Magoun," Freeman creates a visualization of gender division in her time, providing an analysis of the complexities she faced when she was expected to move beyond childhood into young womanhood. On one side of Barry River, Old Woman Magoun presides, caring for Lily, her childlike fourteen-year-old granddaughter whose mother died just after giving birth to her, and sharing ideas with Sally Jinks about how "men is different." [25] On the other side of the river, Nelson Barry presides, the man who made Lily's mother pregnant at sixteen and then deserted her; Barry, Lily's natural father, plays cards, drinks, and converses with other men in his "favorite haunt," the grocery store which the women must frequent for necessary goods. Protected from the sexual advances of such men by age and her capacity for "strenuous feminine assertion," the old woman shelters her more vulnerable granddaughter from the outside world. Like Freeman as a child, Lily (appropriately given this name for her purity, innocence, and virginity) "had never been allowed to run with the other children of Barry's Ford." Lily still looks to be "only a child." "She was very small, and walked like a child, with the clap-clap of little feet of babyhood. She might have been considered, from her looks, under ten" (250). Freeman's emphasis on Lily's innocence and size is the dramatic prelude to her interaction with the men of the village.

Freeman's opening paragraph reflects her capacity to create a context for the psychology of her characters through regional imagery. She describes the hamlet of Barry's Ford (a name that suggests male ownership of the land the women must inhabit), as a place "situated in a sort of high valley among the mountains. Below it the hills lie in moveless curves like a petrified ocean; above it they rise in green cresting waves which never break." The sense of motion frozen, of "cresting waves" which remain fixed and unbroken, already suggests Lily's fate, to be frozen in the natural and pure state of childhood. As Julia Bader suggests, "the valley is poised in arrested motion and development, threatened from all sides, marked by a turbulent river over which Old Woman Magoun has persuaded the decadent males of the hamlet to erect a fragile bridge, a link to civilization."[26] The story begins with Lily on the brink of adolescent sexuality, threatened by the possible turbulence womanhood will bring.

In order to have economic independence and autonomy, the old woman must cross to the other side of the river, to the world dominated by men such as Nelson Barry. Freeman learned that this was her dilemma as well whenever she took her trips with Mary Wales into Boston and returned, exhausted, but with a story sold. To sell the produce from her small farm, and yet remain in her female sanctuary, the old woman asserts that the men of the village must build a stronger bridge across the river. Spreading her "strong arms like wings," she manages to get the men to do so. Ironically, the bridge they build becomes the source of her granddaughter's potential destruction. While it allows the grandmother to remain autonomous, it opens the opportunity for her granddaughter to be viewed, seized upon, and manipulated, even sold, by men.

The rag doll Lily carries is her link to childhood. Sally, the old woman's friend, questions the wisdom of allowing Lily to carry the doll to the store. This will be Lily's first crossing of the bridge:

> "Some girls at her age is thinkin' about beaux instead of rag dolls," said Sally Jinks.
> The grandmother bristled, "Lily ain't big nor old for her age," said she. "I ain't in any hurry to have her git married. She ain't none too strong." (249)

Magoun's assumption of Lily's frailty seems illusory (Sally comments on her good color) and is similar to Freeman's mother's assumption about Freeman's weakness. It is her way of protecting Lily from the exploitation Lily's mother had experienced. For Freeman, however, there were conflicting messages, and it was clear that Eleanor Wilkins wanted her daughter to have the security marriage would offer. At the same time, by emphasizing her daughter's fragility, she also held her firmly in the realm of childhood, protecting her from the very steps that might lead to that goal. Like Freeman as a child, Lily "had in her the making of an artist or a poet. Her prolonged childhood went to prove it, and also her retrospective eyes, as clear and blue as blue light itself, which seemed to see past all that she looked upon" (248). Before taking her journey across the bridge, Lily is warned by her grandmother to avoid speaking to anyone. Lily makes her way to the store, carrying her doll as she might a baby. She carries then the symbol of her own maternal bond with her grandmother, protectively holding the doll when approached by Jim on her way to the store.

Lily's interaction with Jim captures her dilemma, a dilemma Freeman must have experienced in her own early adolescence. She is clearly drawn to his "compelling" smile, notes his handsomeness, even allows him to hold her hand as "the road was lonely here" (251). All of the early stirrings of sexuality are apparent in her initial response, and she speaks of him later to her grandmother in a "wishful fashion" (265). At the same time, the child in Lily resists, recognizes danger, remembers her grandmother's warnings. She is challenged first by Jim, and then by Nelson Barry, about her love for her doll. And it is this challenge that becomes her signal to cross back over the bridge into the realm of maternal protection and childhood. "Suppose you throw away your doll," Nelson Barry suggests after handing her some candy, urging her then to replace her own childish possession with his gift. Her facial response "became the reproach of a woman" and Nelson's face is then "sobered." When Nelson kisses her, "Lily involuntarily started and shrank away from him. Then she rubbed her mouth violently with her little cotton handkerchief, which she held gathered up with the rag doll" (253). Her description of what occurred fills her grandmother "with a sort of despair" and with the "realization of a long-expected blow" (256). The grandmother's determination to keep Lily a child becomes still stronger.

A critical dialogue with Nelson Barry precedes Magoun's decision to take a drastic measure in order to prevent Lily from succumbing to the male manipulation which her movement into adolescent sexuality would ensure. Nelson Barry's visit to the old woman after he has seen Lily makes a strong statement about gender politics. Imposing more dramatically than ever before Lily's status as a child, she sends her to bed early with the comment "children ought to." Barry's comment precipitates the conclusion:

> Barry laughed. "You are keeping her a child a long while," he remarked in a soft voice which had a sting in it.
> "She is a child," returned the old woman defiantly. (260)

Restricting her granddaughter to the realm of childhood, Magoun manages to defy the patriarchal goal. Barry insists that he wants Lily and asserts male ownership: "I am going to have the girl, that is the long and short of it," he said, "and it is for her best good too." Although Magoun attempts to argue, language is not a tool that works in Barry's world. It only has value on Magoun's side of the river, among women. As Barry states, "there is no use talking. I have made up my mind . . . and you know what that means. I am going to have the girl" (260). It becomes clear, in fact, that Barry's statement is an insistence upon the sexual objectification of the young woman. She will become his commodity, now that she has attracted Jim, a way of paying back a debt from card-playing. Leaving Magoun one week to get things in order, Barry crosses the bridge and reminds himself that Old Woman Magoun must understand "better than her sex in general the futility of withstanding the inevitable" (263). Lily's death becomes Magoun's only means of "withstanding" the loss of her granddaughter to the oppression which Barry represents.

In the most powerful scene in the story, the grandmother watches her granddaughter eat poisonous berries and then nurses her into death. Freeman's imagery suggests an association of freedom and power rather than darkness and finality. To bring her child character no further than the age of fourteen is to spare her subjugation. Just as the child notices that the berries look good enough to eat, her grandmother looks "into the ineffable blue of the sky, over which spread at intervals great white clouds shaped like wings" (271). (Freeman associated the freedom of "wings" with autonomy when she described receiving her first check for a story.)[27] Here, without the option of a channel for her artistry, Lily's wings come with death. The painful death scene is beautifully rendered as an entry into the realm of the imagination, of fiction-making, and of eternal maternal protection. Old Woman Magoun lulls Lily through her delirium into death, creating a story within Freeman's story. She describes to Lily where she is going and the story she tells calms Lily in her pain. The place she will go to, Magoun chants, is a "beautiful place, where the flowers grow tall."

> "A blue color. . . . A beautiful blue color and as tall as your knees, and the flowers always stay there, and they never fade . . . and all the houses are built of silver and gold, and the people all have wings, so when they get tired walking they can fly, and—all the dolls are alive. . . . Dolls like yours can run, and talk, and love you back again." (273–74)

When Lily moans "it is dark," Magoun's description of the female heaven to which she is sending Lily builds in detail and becomes an elaborate fiction that offers freedom, peace, asexuality in a world of purity and whiteness, with Lily's mother there to lead her from the gate to a home in which no men can intrude.

> "There where you are going it is always light," said the grandmother, "and the commonest things shine. . . . You will come to a gate with all the colors of the rainbow . . . and it will open, and you will go right in and walk up the gold street, and cross the field where the blue flowers come up to your knees, until you find your mother, and she will take you home where you are going to live. She has a little white room all ready for you, white curtains at the windows, and a little white looking-glass, and when you look in it you will see—a face like yours, only it's an angel's; and there will be a little white bed, and you can lay down an' rest." (274–75)

Freeman's conclusion makes a devastating statement about her own transition from childhood into adolescence in the nineteenth-century New England village. Were she to cross that bridge and yield to her sexual desires as well as the desires of men, she would have to part with the maternal bond that had sustained her.

"Marry Early and Well"

At fifteen, Mary moved with her parents and sister to Brattleboro, Vermont. The family moved in the hope of bettering their financial situation. Instead they found themselves in a small, cramped cottage. Warren Wilkins's original plan was to build a spacious home on a site purchased in Eleanor's name when they first moved to Vermont. Eleanor had envisioned this new house as a better work space for her and a more comfortable environment for the family.[28] One of Wilkins's surviving architectural drawings shows the front elevation of a grand house on an Oak Street lot in Brattleboro. As Kendrick indicates, this drawing is likely to have been for the home Eleanor had hoped to have, but that house was never built.[29] It was to have been on a "superb residential site in a new section high above Brattleboro's business district."[30] Mary watched the optimistic plan fail as their first few years in Brattleboro went by and Warren's finances worsened. Her father gave up the work he loved and entered the dry goods business, but returned to his work as a builder and architect by 1879, presumably disillusioned with his efforts to improve their financial status. Clearly, her mother had no option but to succumb to circumstances, to accept the defeat, to remain in a space that ill suited her domestic life and made it difficult for her to maintain the pride she wanted to take in her work.

Her father expressed his hope that Freeman would marry early, seeing marriage as the most viable economic option, but Mary was well aware of how marriage had disappointed her mother. Lacking a means toward autonomy, dependent upon her husband's income, Eleanor's circumstances were determined by Warren's financial situation. The move to Brattleboro at the very point that Freeman was expected to begin considering marriage and domesticity was timely. She was crossing the bridge which her adolescent character Lily in "Old Woman Magoun" would never cross, living beyond the age of fourteen and facing the obvious option of preparing for marriage at the same time that she was observing the limitations her mother had had to accept.[31] This message came at a time when Freeman was just beginning to recognize her own potential as a writer, an alternative to marriage that could win her the autonomy her mother never had. Just before their move to Brattleboro in 1867, she had written a poem which her father proudly recited when he visited some nearby relatives. The recital was met with disdain from her uncle Edward Everett who noted "lot of good that will do—letting that child write poetry."[32]

As an adolescent, Freeman was increasingly caught between the need for her mother's love and her instinct to avoid becoming her mother and subsiding into her mother's forms of passivity. Despite continuous pressure from her mother to participate in domestic chores, no amount of discipline could pull Mary away from her reading to the reality of hated kitchen work. According to Foster, "disliking her household duties, she avoided them, nor could she be moved by disciplinary tactics."[33] It is clear that a growing tension between Mary and her mother centered on her resistance to undertaking the tasks expected of a "good girl." As the years passed, the contrast between Anna and Mary became apparent. While her sister Anna willingly undertook domestic work and increasingly met her parents' expectations, Mary quietly began to reject them. She would resist her mother's world of domesticity throughout her life. Her story "The Revolt of 'Mother' " is especially significant in this context, for the story seems to have been written as a tribute to her mother's work, a form of work she had never valued in her mother's lifetime.

As she observed the limitations of her parents' marriage just after the move to Brattleboro, particularly her mother's disillusionment and powerlessness, Freeman began to explore alternatives. Certainly by continuing her education she might find some autonomy in the profession of teaching. Resisting early on the attraction to young men and hence the inevitable conclusion of a marriage similar to her parents, Freeman attempted to satisfy the other expectation apparent in messages from both parents: religious devotion.

In 1870, after attending Brattleboro High School, Mary agreed to enroll at Mount Holyoke Female Seminary. She was so eager to satisfy her parents, who had scraped together whatever money they could to send her there, that she walked six miles to and from the home of Mrs. Gulliver (then principal of the Seminary and living in Brattleboro) to inquire about acceptance.[34] Like Emily Dickinson, however, she lasted at Mount Holyoke for only one year. Her description of this year, 1870–71, rests on the metaphor of appetite or its denial:

> I was very young . . . and went home at the end of the year a nervous wreck, so I fancy I may be somewhat confused about the whole. What I am sure of is that I ate so much beef in different forms and so many baked apples that I have never wanted much since. I have often wondered why they looked out so beautifully for our young morals, and did not vary our menu more. As I remember I did not behave at all well at Mount Holyoke and am inclined to attribute it to monotony of diet and too strenuous goadings of conscience.[35]

In much of Freeman's fiction there are images of food, particularly forbidden food. Here, her description of the experience at the Seminary is placed in the context of a menu. Freeman desired a varied diet, and the diet I think she indirectly refers to here is what Henry James would call "the feast of life." Her humor in the letter lightly camouflages a critique of her society. Mount Holyoke busily looked after the "young morals" of the women but failed to "vary our menus," and consequently deprived them of life's "menu." Her inability to "behave at all well," to accept a life of rules and restrictions, reflects Freeman's rebellious spirit. Yet such behavior worried her and she returned home after one year, as though defeated by her own inability to work effectively at self-denial.

Most troublesome for Mary were the explicit restrictions at Mount Holyoke. At home, she might close the door to her small room and read what she wished to read. There was no such space for private revolt at the Seminary. "Rules were serious matters in those days, and not lightly to be broken," M. D. E. Morse recalls in the *Mount Holyoke Alumnae Quarterly*. The list of rules was endless. There were first-class exceptions such as absence from church, from recitations, or from meals, as well as tardiness. According to Morse:

> Second class exceptions comprised minor offenses such as breaking study hours, walking over wet floors, . . . having room or wardrobe out of order. Once a day each girl was required to report any infractions of rules to her designated teacher. Either she was excused or told to "report to the front seat." This ordeal was faced on Saturday mornings when the entire Seminary gathered in Seminary Hall.[36]

In "Reminiscences of the Early 'Seventies,' " Morse recalls that until 1873, students were forbidden to speak "above a whisper" in the halls. "Sinners" who broke Seminary rules stood before the entire Seminary to make a "public confession of their misdeeds."[37] Freeman attributed her failure at Mount Holyoke to the effects of such externally imposed "goadings of conscience."

A glance at how other students at the Seminary responded to Mary gives some idea of the degree to which she withdrew while there. Recollections on file at the Mount Holyoke College Archives of the few students from the Seminary who remembered Freeman point to her seemingly deliberate isolation. From Anna L. Hufford, for example, we learn only that "she was rather small, and had light auburn hair and the delicate pink and white complexion that goes with it. By nature she seemed diffident and was rather reticent."[38] All classmates who speak of her remember her striking silence, her aloofness. None of the students felt they "knew" her.

The "watchwords" at Mount Holyoke were "duty and self-sacrifice." Freeman initially accepted these watchwords as moral necessities for women; by the end of the year, however, she felt the need to reject them and to retreat to the privacy of her room at home where she could increasingly indulge in the freedom of her imagination. Twenty-two of the thirty-five women who graduated the year Freeman would have graduated went on to early marriages or careers in teaching.[39] Freeman was a rare example of a New England woman who made the conscious choice of self-nurturance through the career of writing, a career that essentially served the needs of Mary Wilkins Freeman rather than the needs of husband, children, or pupils. Like Emily Dickinson, her inability to remain at Mount Holyoke may in some sense be linked to this desire to "shut the door" to society and its demands.

When she returned to Brattleboro after her year away, Mary was already on the path to rejecting the conventional options for women. She would not become a teacher or missionary as so many of her classmates would, although she did attempt a year of teaching at a school for girls in Brattleboro. At home, she explored the possibilities of romantic love but she avoided marriage.[40] In 1873, at the age of twenty-one, Freeman met Hanson Tyler, a navy ensign who had been on tour duty in Havana and was at home on leave in Brattleboro. The appeal of the distant sailor, a figure who enters some of her most interesting fiction, must have been strong for a young woman whose life was so sheltered by the narrowness of village life. The world of action, of escape from the village, was open to Tyler in a way that it would never be for Freeman. The romance with Tyler was brief and most of the feeling seemed to be Mary's. When he returned to duty, he never wrote to her and seemed to have dismissed the entire romance as mere flirtation. According to Foster, Hanson was known in the navy for "courage, humor, hard drinking and bad health."[41] In saying goodbye to Mary, he gave her a photograph and promised to write. A letter to his mother, however, indicated something of the lightness of his feelings:

> I hardly know whom to write to; I have not heard from anybody for ages and don't think I owe anybody any letters. As "leaf by leaf the roses fall," so one by one the girls have fallen off whom I used to be friendly with when last at home.[42]

There is no record of correspondence between Hanson and Mary, but it seems clear from the above letter that she was just one of the "girls" he was "friendly with when last at home." Yet for Mary, Hanson was extremely significant. The process of waiting for letters from a man figures importantly in "A Patient Waiter," a story that mirrors her frustration almost exactly. Here the character waits an entire lifetime for letters that never arrive from a man she loves. Freeman nursed her unrequited love just as so many of her characters do, well into middle age and even after her marriage to Charles Freeman. Records show that she kept the photograph of Hanson and buttons from his military uniform to the end of her life.[43] It is easy to see the role Hanson played in her fantasies of freedom and escape. By dwelling on the unattainable love with Hanson, Freeman was protected from a real marriage and the subsequent, inevitable submission to the circumstances her mother faced. Sexuality could thrive in fantasies of Hanson which might be dashed in an actual marriage. Believing in its impossibility, Freeman's selection of Hanson was a safe focus for her desires. Whether consciously or unconsciously, she made a choice that allowed her to maintain her autonomy, as her mother had not managed to do.

As is evident in her stories "Old Woman Magoun," "A Symphony of Lavender," "The Hall Bedroom," and many others, submitting to sexuality was fearful to Freeman for a range of understandable reasons. Sexual fulfillment worked against the lessons of self-denial that were so significant in the religious training she received. Furthermore, heterosexual love carried with it the expectation of marriage. As she watched her mother's numerous disappointments, she recognized the cost. Interestingly, she attempted in "The Revolt of 'Mother,'" one of the best examples of her restorative prose, to create the possibility of rebellion and fulfillment within marriage, to give her mother the voice she never had, the kitchen she had envisioned when they moved to Brattleboro, the opportunity to win some degree of recognition for her work.

"Land Beyond Circumstances"

In light of her mother's mixture of disappointment in married life and pride in her domestic arts, Freeman's story about a rebellious mother, "The Revolt of 'Mother,'" is intriguing. Soon after her sister Anna died in 1876, Freeman's parents were forced to give up their little cottage because her father's financial position had worsened. In 1877, the family moved into the home of the Reverend Mr. Tyler, the father of Hanson Tyler, Freeman's unrequited love. Freeman's mother was hired to serve as housekeeper for the invalid minister and his wife.[44] It is easy to imagine Freeman's response to her mother's suddenly subservient position. In addition to the dream of the elegant home never built, Eleanor had also now lost the little she actually had. As Michele Clark explains in her afterword to *The Revolt of 'Mother' and Other Stories,* "Eleanor, the wife, the mother, was now deprived of the very things which made a woman proud—her own kitchen, furniture, family china; and she had lost the one place in which it was acceptable for her to be powerful: her home."[45] Certainly Sarah Penn's desperate determination to win a decent work environment in the form of a fine kitchen reflects the need Freeman must have sensed in her own mother. The spirit of the story conveys the pleasure Freeman took in transforming her mother's subservience into revolt and creating the home her mother never had. In a rare moment of candid self-expression, Freeman mentioned that she wished her parents "might have been spared" to her, that she "longed to make some return to them for their love and care, but that now as they were gone" she would have "to pass it on to someone else."[46] This story was Freeman's vehicle for "passing it on."

Freeman was able to invest her fictional mother with the spirit, self-determination, and self-knowledge that her own mother never openly exhibited. Perhaps the mother she created is the mother she wished she could have had. In a letter of 1893, about a decade after her mother's death and two years after she wrote "The Revolt of 'Mother,' " Freeman expressed a longing to go to a "land where there are no circumstances." [47] In this story, she created such a land by granting "Mother" the right to overthrow those circumstances that most oppress.

Freeman's loving depiction of Sarah Penn as the "masterly keeper of her box of a house" was a way of acknowledging her mother's unacknowledged gifts, a delayed response to her mother's life story:

> Sarah Penn washed the frying-pan with a conclusive air. She scrubbed the outside of it as faithfully as the inside. She was a masterly keeper of her box of a house. Her one living-room never seemed to have in it any of the dust which the friction of life with inanimate matter produces. She swept, and there seemed to be no dirt to go before the broom; she cleaned, and one could see no difference. She was like an artist so perfect that he has apparently no art. Today she got out a mixing bowl and a board, and rolled some pies, and there was no more flour upon her than upon her daughter who was doing finer work.[48]

The passage stresses the seriousness with which Sarah approaches her job. She has created an art out of daily chores.

It is interesting that just after this description of Sarah as artist, Freeman inserts commentary which reflects her ambivalence about the source of her mother's art. Much as Sarah Penn is an artful creator of pies, the pies are designed to please her husband, Adoniram, although he fails to acknowledge the value of his wife's work:

> She was making mince-pies. Her husband, Adoniram Penn, liked them better than any other kind. She baked twice a week. Adoniram often liked a piece of pie between meals. She hurried this morning. It had been later than usual when she began, and she wanted to have a pie baked for dinner. However deep a resentment she might be forced to hold against her husband, she would never fail in sedulous attention to his wants. (298)

As the story makes clear, her "attention to his wants" is not reciprocated, hence a "deep resentment" builds until it fires the central action of the story, Sarah Penn's revolt.

"The Revolt of 'Mother' " is one of Freeman's most frequently anthologized stories. It reflects Freeman's understanding of her mother's world as much as it does her disappointment in its limitations. Her family had moved to Brattleboro because of her father's needs, and the move failed to bring her mother the one thing she had hoped it would achieve: a better home in which to assert her creative energies, energies that of necessity had been channeled into mothering and homemaking. Freeman's fictive mother in the story, Sarah Penn, has a similar experience as she watches her husband build a new barn for the animals and witnesses his refusal to build a much needed new home instead. Sarah's response is the positive response Freeman must have wished her mother could have made. Sarah defiantly moves into the barn and creatively redesigns it. By the end of her intensive labor, the barn is virtually a work of art—a comfortable new residence for Sarah Penn and her family. The spirit and determination of Sarah's actions capture the rhythm of domestic revolt with such energy that students reading the story today are moved by its power and see it as a feminist tale for women of any period.[49]

Freeman's representation of gender communication in this story suggests her understandable resistance to leaving the comforts of Eleanor's nurturing to become someone's wife. Sarah's battle to be heard was one Freeman preferred to wage symbolically in the context of her writing. In her fiction she was assured an audience and could create an Adoniram who, in the end, had to hear and see his wife's art. Even after her battle, however, Sarah has won the right to a space in which she can serve Adoniram more effectively. Freeman honored the fight but recognized this irony and avoided such a fate by resisting marriage for many years.

In presenting Sarah Penn's rebellion, Freeman manages to break through most of the barriers of gender differences in the domestic realm. She creates, in effect, a utopia in which the work of women must be recognized, valued, and embraced by men. Even the landscape is utopian at the end of the story, "an ideal one of peace," where "the air was very cool and calm and sweet" (313). Peace comes when Adoniram sees the meaning and power of Sarah's creativity, her capacity to envision and then transform the barn he had built into the home she had wanted so that she might better nurture those she loves. Adoniram embraces feminine values by the end of the story and his muttering has changed to weeping. He becomes a "fortress whose walls had no active resistance, and went down the instant the right besieging tools were used" (313). "Besieging tools" were available to Freeman's fictive heroine. They were tools her mother never used. The lessons Freeman learned from her mother are more like those voiced by Sarah in an early speech to her daughter, Nanny:

> "You ain't found out yet we're women-folks, Nanny Penn," said she. "You ain't seen enough of men-folks yet to. One of these days you'll find it out, an' then you'll know that we know only what men-folks think we do, so far as any use of it goes, an' how we'd ought to reckon men-folks in with Providence, an' not complain of what they do any more than we do of the weather." (296–97)

Sarah's fight for self-definition and for recognition of the value of her work begins verbally. Sarah "talks plain" to Adoniram as Freeman's mother never did to Warren Wilkins, and Freeman gives voice to her mother's unexpressed rage:

> "You see this room father; it's all the one I've had to work in an' eat in an' sit in sence we was married. . . . I want to know if you think you're doin right an accordin' to what you profess. Here when we was married, forty year ago, you promised me faithful that we should have a new house built in that lot over in the field before the year was out. . . . Father, I want to know if you think it's right. You're lodgin' your dumb beasts better than you are your own Flesh an' blood." (300–302)

Freeman's magnification of Sarah's revolt is what tempted her early biographers to call this simply a "comic folk tale." Freeman has Sarah Penn march "across the room as though it were a tragic stage." If not classic tragedy, the drama was one familiar to most New England women. As Sarah pleads her case, Freeman equates the power of her speech and its shift "from severity to pathos" with the eloquence of Daniel Webster; in this sense, she redefines oratory and heroism in women's terms. Exposing the inadequacy of her working headquarters, a small ill-lighted pantry, Sarah's "little" argument becomes larger than life. She shows that this "is all the buttery I've got—every place I've got for my dishes, to set away my victuals in an' to keep my milk-pans in." The passion of Sarah's argument is a passion about work that has value. "Father, I've been takin' care of the milk of six cows in this place an' now you're goin' to build a new barn an' keep more cows, an' give me more to do in it" (301).

Adoniram's response captures the dilemma of gender communication. Women's words are lost on Adoniram: "I've got to go off after that load of gravel. I can't stan' here talkin' all day." "Talkin' " then is not a means for transformation. As Martha Cutter stresses, the failure of language to open communication between the sexes is an important element in the story.

The aggressive actions, actions that are described in terms of male battlefields, but that have at their center female rather than male values, become the source for breaking through the barrier and enabling a genuine "talk" between Sarah and her husband at the end of the story.

> During the next few hours a feat was performed by this simple pious New England mother which was equal in its way to Wolfe's storming of the Heights of Abraham. It took no more genius and audacity of bravery for Wolfe to cheer his wondering soldiers up those steep precipices under the sleeping eyes of the enemy, than for Sarah Penn, at the head of her children, to move all of their little household goods into the new barn while her husband was away. (307–8)

Comparing Sarah's actions to those of heroic males, Freeman redefines heroism, equating Sarah with Wolfe on the marital battlefield. Had Freeman seen such a battle when her family moved to Brattleboro, had such a battle been realizable in the New England she knew, she might have considered the possibility of an early marriage. Through her fiction, she could win the battle, write stories about seemingly small battles and determine a female victory. As a woman writer in a tiny New England village, Freeman shared in Sarah's battle. Just as Sarah struggles to have her work recognized, Freeman fought to be taken seriously as a writer. For decades, critics categorized her subject matter as small, insignificant. Yet like Sarah Penn's vision of great possibility in ordinary things—a barn, for example—Freeman's work explores the largest questions through small incidents. Freeman's description of Sarah's artistic architectural feat is a symbol for her own work as an artist. When Sarah looks at the large barn, "she saw at a glance its possibilities."

> Those great box-stalls, with quilts hung before them, would make better bedrooms than the one she had occupied for forty years, and there was a tight carriage room. The harness room, with its chimney and shelves, would make a kitchen of her dreams. The great middle space would make a parlor, by the by, fit for a palace. . . . With partitions and windows, what a house would there be! Sarah looked at the row of stanchions before the

allotted space for cows, and reflected that she would have her front entry there. (308)

Sarah's creativity, generally lost or unexpressed in the endless tasks that occupy her days, is at last given full voice with this opportunity for rebellion. Her visions of possibilities hint at what Freeman must have felt as architect of her stories. In one day, the barn is transformed to match Sarah's artistic visions.

The village reaction to Sarah's aggression becomes an index for the courage her rebellion requires. "Some held her to be insane, some, of a lawless and rebellious spirit." Female rebellion and madness were commonly equated in Freeman's time. But Sarah's response to the local minister strengthens her capacity now to combine gesture and language, to be heard in a male world. She insists upon the justice of her actions:

> "I think it's right jest as much as I think it was right for our forefathers to come over from the old country because they didn't have what belonged to 'em," said Mrs. Penn. She arose. The barn threshold might have been Plymouth Rock from her bearing. . . . "I've got my own mind an' my own feet, an' I'm goin' to think my own thoughts an' go my own ways, an' nobody but the Lord is goin' to dictate to me unless I've a mind to have him." (310)

Sarah's revolutionary language invests creative domesticity with a sense of purpose and strength. As it builds in power and as she translates her words into actions which are now visible to the male eye, her language must be heard, can no longer be met with patriarchal silence. Sarah turns to physical action to overthrow the ideas of "men-folks," to defy the patriarchal system of valuing commodities over a woman's capacity for love and creativity.

"The Revolt of 'Mother' " offers, as Martha Cutter suggests, a vision of gender and language. Cutter's analysis of Sarah's initial dilemma is useful: "Sarah Penn lacks more than just a home for her family, more than just a place to maintain what Carol Gilligan would call a web of relationship between individuals. Sarah Penn also lacks a language; she cannot become a speaking subject." From the very start of the story, Adoniram's inability to hear Sarah stems from the degree to which "language is patriarchal, and it illustrates that women, marginalized by frontier values, are also marginalized in this other sense: they cannot speak; they are excluded from a discourse that is patriarchal in intent and meaning." Sarah Penn's most poignant battle was the battle Freeman was fighting in her fiction as she struggled to "redefine a linguistic frontier which has excluded her as a speaking subject."[50] Domestic power can only be recognized in Freeman's story when Sarah finds a language with which to communicate that power to her husband. The story then explores conflicting value systems. Adoniram wants to build another barn because he values the fact that the barn provides for cattle, cattle provides money, and money provides the opportunity to build another barn.

Sarah Penn's value system is clear in her conversations with her daughter. As Freeman's mother must have wished, Sarah longed to have a home large enough to accommodate Nanny and the man she is about to marry, along with their future offspring—a desire then to ensure familial closeness and continued nurturance. This was never possible for Freeman's mother; Freeman's marriage would have required a parting from home. Sarah's desire to continue to protect Nanny, however, does resemble Eleanor's protection of Mary. Sarah says of Nanny "She wa'n't ever strong. She's got considerable color, but there wa'n't never any backbone to her. I've always took the heft of everything off her an' she ain't fit to keep house an' do everything herself. She'll be all worn out inside of a year. I can't have it so, noways, father" (302). Interestingly, then, Sarah's motivation for revolt is continued protection of her daughter. The conflicting priorities of mother and father, are clearly drawn: "father's are for animals; mother's are for the human and relational."[51]

Freeman's story begins to create a new means for communicating differing gender values so that long overlooked feminine principles can begin to receive some recognition. It is only when Mother "creates a system of signs," in place of earlier attempts to "tell" Father, that the breakthrough begins.[52] Moving the house into the barn "she dumps all the 'value' of 'Home' into 'Barn,' and thereby takes an action which indicates that to her 'Home' is as important if not more important than 'Barn.' And Adoniram finally understands; where words cannot communicate, gestures succeed."[53] Cutter calls this moment "renaming," for it is Sarah's gesture to rename the "barn" as "home" and hence to shift the values by which Adoniram will live.

The feminizing of Adoniram in the end is poignant. He becomes "pale and frightened," parts with authority, agrees to put up the partitions, and genuinely pleads for explanation from Mother: " 'What on airth does this mean mother?' he gasped." When Sarah tells him that "we've come here to live, an' we're going to live here," Adoniram must recognize a new form of living with a new source at its center, the power of his wife, Sarah Penn. What Sarah wins in the end is recognition that "her focus on home nurturance, connectivity and generativity is valid."[54]

Had Freeman believed such a revolutionary breakthrough in language between the sexes were possible, her own choices might have been different. Sarah's impassioned description of the importance of her work and the inadequacy of her work space was a speech Freeman's father never heard, one that most likely her mother never had the opportunity to make. Furthermore, Eleanor was never able to move into the home Warren planned to build when they first moved to Brattleboro. Perhaps when Freeman harshly rejected the story years later, she was remembering these discrepancies between her own mother and the one she clearly took such pleasure in creating:

> In the first place all fiction ought to be true and "The Revolt of 'Mother' " is not true . . . there never was in New England a woman like Mother. If there had been she certainly would have lacked the nerve. She would also have lacked the imagination. New England women of the period coincided with their husbands in thinking that the source of wealth should be better housed than the consumers.[55]

Not "lacking the imagination," Freeman's story creates an alternative to her choice as an unmarried writer: rebellion within the context of conventional marriage. Yet her own rejection of the story helps explain the choice she made in her twenties to bury her longings for sexual fulfillment, to resist the pressure to marry, and to begin a career in writing. By observing her mother's world during her own early stages of sexual development, Freeman could see that heterosexuality and marriage constituted a threat to autonomy. From the start, the idea of entering heterosexual relationships carried the association of parting with the love of women, the community in which she had flourished in her mother's kitchen in Randolph and in the home of Mary Wales. While Sarah Penn's rebellion was, after all, to create a home in which to better serve her family, Freeman's choice was to thrive in the "female world of love and ritual" and to inhabit a home in which she would serve herself through her writing.

2

"THE ART OF MY WORK"

My muse is but a sorry thing,
With scarce a feather to a wing;
And when to sing she doth essay,
Alas! she's often shoed away.
She is so often off the key,
Her music wearies even me,
And I can have no cause for wrath
If others scare her from her path.

Mary E. Wilkins Freeman to Henry Mills Alden, 1906

As FREEMAN MADE clear in her advice to young women writers, expressing the "truth" about the conflict she shared with women of her time, the need to both rebel and belong, was like "running a race in the sight of the world."[1] The consequent "liberty" she promised to young women writers was the liberty to rebel through their writing against the limitations of which she was so acutely aware, a liberty that she urged women to seek aggressively, a liberty that she felt had been unavailable to her until she began to write. Her fiction often focuses on the role of work in women's lives and offers a context for understanding her own struggles toward autonomy through self-fulfilling work.

It is difficult to establish when Freeman began to write seriously, but Kendrick traces it to the winter of 1874 and includes a letter Freeman wrote to the editor Everett Edward Hale in 1875 in which she thanks him for his critique of her work. She described his letter to her about her fiction as "cold water to a thirsty soul." Interestingly, she equated her subjectivity about her work to a mother's "concerning her own children."[2] From the start, she saw her work metaphorically as her offspring.

The years between 1876 and 1883 were Freeman's most difficult, a time of both loss and discovery, death and birth. Within this seven-year period, she lost her sister, mother, and father. Eleanor was only fifty-three when she died unexpectedly in 1880. Given the nature of Mary's relationship with her mother, this was perhaps the most devastating blow. With the pain of loss, however, came the birth and full realization of the writer within. In 1881, at the age of twenty-nine, she received her first monetary reward, ten dollars in payment for the ballad "The Beggar King" which was published in *Wide Awake,* a children's magazine.[3] It was not until 1882, however, when her father had moved to Gainesville, Florida, because of his health and Mary was completely on her own in Brattleboro, that she was able to publish her first major story, "Two Old Lovers." The story reflects an important theme in Freeman's early work, perhaps reflective of her own choice to resist marriage in favor of a writing career. The prolonged relationship of the "two old lovers" in her story never reaches the stage of marriage. With the publication of this story, Freeman began to recognize her power as a writer of fiction.

Freeman described the experience of receiving her first acceptance and a twenty-five-dollar check in imagery that suggests both the thrill of flight and the awareness of entrapment: "I felt my wings spring from my shoulders capable of flight and I flew home."[4] The paradox expressed here is significant. She was certainly now "capable of flight," but she could only fly "home." Wanting both rebellious flight and the safety of acceptance at home in her New England village, Freeman wrote fiction that seemed to satisfy both needs.

Just a few months after the acceptance of "Two Old Lovers," Freeman's father died in Florida and was buried in Randolph beside her mother and sister. In 1883, Freeman returned to Randolph to live with her childhood friend Mary John Wales on the farm she had come to love as a child. Although there is no record of correspondence between Mary Wales and Mary Wilkins through the Brattleboro years, the bond had lasted. Freeman found an opportunity in her return to the Wales homestead for sustained support and respect, an ideal environment for her life as a writer. As children,

Mary Wales had often protected Freeman when she was frightened by other children.[5] Now that sense of strong, maternal nurturing would continue to protect Freeman through the critical years of her writing career. Mary Wales managed the household and shielded Freeman from a range of daily responsibilities that might have interfered significantly with her writing.

Freeman came to live with Mary Wales at a time of deep mourning. After the death of her family, she experienced a sense of isolation so severe that even as late as 1892 (nine years after her father's death, twelve years after her mother's) she wrote the following passage for *Harper's:*

Only the living know grief
Only the living.
Then, then the tombs be not for the dead,
  but for the living.
I would, I would that I were dead, that I might be free from the tomb,
  and sorrow, and death.[6]

Foster says that Freeman would often "wake in terror and call across the hall to Mary," and "they would talk until the terror passed." He describes Wales as "strong, practical, partly emancipated from the code."[7]

At the Waleses' farm Mary found "a room of her own" in the seclusion of the second floor, the space she needed for writing. Freeman wrote short stories and novels almost feverishly. Her letters describe ten-hour work days and the painful exhaustion that followed. Mary Wales served as her primary audience, listening to and reading drafts. One of Freeman's letters refers specifically to Wales's influence. "I have just finished a story which I do not dare send as yet," she explained in one letter to an editor. "It is so very tragic. Mary Wales who always giggles at my pathetic points, has just burst into a flood of tears much to my alarm."[8] The two women lived together from 1883 to 1902, and these years with Wales were the richest in Freeman's literary career. She found herself increasingly relying upon Wales's responses to her fiction, her love, her companionship. Living with Mary Wales, Freeman had the chance to develop a sense of herself as a writer most fully.

While she had always observed women in her community whose work rarely seemed self-directed and whose lives centered around the needs of others, Freeman began to see her own work as the center of her life. Looking back at her career in an autobiographical sketch (1921), she gave herself "the tardy credit of being perfectly conscious, whether or not I have succeeded, in caring more in my heart for the art of my work than for anything else."[9] Much as she valued "the art of her work," however, Freeman's commitment to a writing career was not unambiguous. Her choice to write necessitated a considerable struggle against the expectation of marriage. In many of her stories, women struggle alone to define their lives in terms of their work. Once Freeman determined that she would earn her living as a writer, a central question began to absorb her and to inform her fiction. What were the psychological effects of living with the stigma of spinsterhood, of wanting acceptance in her small New England community yet enjoying her autonomy? For Freeman the effect was twofold. She associated married life with security and acceptability, and part of her longed for this. But she also saw marriage as a threat to her hard-won independence, to her sense of herself as a woman writer whose work satisfied her own need to create.

When we turn to Freeman's fiction for a better understanding of her concept of work in the lives of women, we hear a multiplicity of voices: voices that are proud and independent, submissive and pleading, rebellious and spirited, obsequious and self-pitying, enraged and self-righteous, forgiving and sentimental. These voices capture Freeman's awareness of the ambiguities that arise for women who make their work rather than men the center of their lives. Writing was that center for Freeman and she saw it as a source of self-nurturance.

"A New England Nun"

In "A New England Nun" (1891), Freeman seems to be addressing her choice to remain unmarried in order to protect her work life. Although it is a story about spinsterhood and the suppression of sexuality, it is also a story about freedom, autonomy, and work in women's lives. It captures the threat that marriage represented for women in nineteenth-century America. For most of Freeman's unmarried heroines, living alone meant burying the sexual self; marrying meant burying the creative, independent self.

Ever since David Hirsch's pioneer essay in 1965 on "A New England Nun," a critical piece that brought the power of Freeman's prose to light, this story has become widely recognized as one of Freeman's most significant contributions to the canon. Although Hirsch's analysis has been questioned or challenged by several feminist critics, it is important to note that his essay was the first to reveal the value of giving Mary E. Wilkins Freeman's work the same attention that had been given to Nathaniel Hawthorne, Herman Melville, Mark Twain, or Henry James. Hirsch's analysis of Freeman's language demonstrates that Freeman transcended the label of local color, that she had invested "the minutest and most ordinary details with deeper psychic significance." [10] His interpretation of the conclusion of the story, when set beside more recent feminist criticism, suggests the remarkable ambiguity of Freeman's work.

Is Louisa, the heroine of "A New England Nun," the "uncloistered nun" who has rejected the possibility of sexual fulfillment, as Hirsch suggests? Or is she the victorious, autonomous woman described by so many recent feminist critics (Susan Allen Toth, Martha Cutter, Marjorie Pryse, Lorne Feinberg, and others), a brave woman who has in fact chosen her singular definition of self-fulfillment through defiant spinsterhood? [11] An alternative feminist reading (which I first suggested in my essay "She Is the One You Call Sister") views Freeman's construction of Louisa's world as a fine example of her analysis of the tension between these two possibilities. The strong relationship between these radically different constructions of fulfillment can be best addressed by studying the story in the context of its focus on Louisa's work as well as on her sexuality. The story helps illuminate Freeman's view (and her own choice) of independent work as it stood in direct opposition to the alternative of marriage.

Not unlike Freeman in her wait for Hanson Tyler, Louisa Ellis waits fourteen years for her sailor fiancé, Joe, to return from sea. Freeman's years of waiting for Tyler far exceeded Louisa's, and Tyler's failure to return was a source of unspoken relief; it enabled her to pursue her craft without interruption. By waiting for Tyler instead of marrying another, she could preserve order, maintain her focus on her craft, and live a self-directed life. Seen from the perspective of her contemporary Hamlin Garland, Freeman's was a narrow world which allowed no room for disorderly male conduct. Garland recalls a visit to Freeman:

Her home might have been used as a typical illustration for her characters. Its cakes and pies, its hot biscuits and jams were exactly right. I felt
large and rude like that man in one of her tales, "A New England Nun,"
who came into the well-ordered sitting room of his sweetheart with such
clumsy haste that he overturned her workbasket and sat down on the cat.[12]

Garland was right to feel out of place, for both Louisa and Freeman
passionately protected their self-made territories of order. The
tipped workbasket suggests the danger Freeman associated with the
prospect of marriage. To ward off the invasion of privacy which
marriage in nineteenth-century New England would bring, Louisa
builds cloistered walls behind which she both buries her sexuality
and celebrates her autonomy. When Joe Dagget returns, the thought
of marrying him terrifies Louisa and she brings the relationship to
an end.

Freeman begins her story by describing the pleasure Louisa takes
in being alone as she works "peacefully sewing at her sitting-room
window all the afternoon." The emphasis is on the precision in each
gesture as Louisa "quilted her needle carefully into her work, which
she folded precisely, and laid in a basket with her thimble and thread
and scissors." While Louisa's need for order may seem extreme (and
Foster sees the story as a portrait of neurotic spinsterhood), Freeman's story actually captures the isolation and quiet that attention
to one's craft requires. Every gesture of Louisa's work is described
lovingly and quietly, as though her work is an extension of the landscape described in the first paragraph in its "premonition of rest and
hush and night." The world Louisa occupies is untinged by the
needs of others. Unusual for her time, she takes pleasure in herself
and in the world she has created. She dines, literally, "with" herself.
A close study of her preparation for tea reveals Freeman's brilliance
in depicting the self-love that attention to a husband might destroy:

Louisa was slow and still in her movements; it took her a long time to
prepare her tea; but when ready it was set forth with as much grace as if
she had been a veritable guest to her own self. The little square table
stood exactly in the centre of the kitchen, and was covered with a starched
linen cloth whose border pattern of flowers glistened. Louisa had a damask napkin on her tea-tray, where were arranged a cut-glass tumbler full
of teaspoons, a silver cream-pitcher, a china sugar-bowl, and one pink
china cup and saucer. Louisa used china every day—something which
none of her neighbors did. They whispered about it among themselves.

Their daily tables were laid with common crockery, their sets of best china stayed in the parlor closet, and Louisa Ellis was no richer nor better bred than they. Still she would use the china. She had for her supper a glass dish full of sugared currants, a plate of little cakes, and one of light white biscuits. Also a leaf or two of lettuce, which she cut up daintily. Louisa was very fond of lettuce, which she raised to perfection in her little garden.[13]

Louisa is a "veritable guest to her own self"; this is similar to how Freeman describes her attention to her own work in her early letter to Edward Everett Hale: "Myself is an object of such intense, vital interest to myself."[14] Using her best china, Louisa bears the stigma of spinsterhood suggested by her whispering neighbors who marvel at her self-indulgence. She nourishes the self she has cultivated methodically, lovingly, with silver cream pitcher, pink china cup, and damask napkin. In contrast to Sarah Penn's renovated barn in "The Revolt of 'Mother,' " the home becomes a workplace in which to serve the self rather than others.

What makes "A New England Nun" so illuminating as it relates to Freeman's life is its celebration of the unrecognized joy and worth of Louisa's autonomy and its simultaneous analysis of the costs involved. Louisa looks at her "solitary home" with "almost the enthusiasm of an artist." For Louisa, her home and her capacity to care for it provide her with a clear identity. "She had throbs of genuine triumph at the sight of the window-panes which she had polished until they shone like jewels"(117). All of her tasks, gardening and picking currants for her tea, collecting the stems "carefully in her apron," occupying herself "pleasantly in summer weather with distilling the sweet and aromatic essences from roses and peppermint and spearmint," "drawing her needle gently through the dainty fabric," combine to capture the meaning of Louisa's work as her source of serenity; the major function of her work, similar to Freeman's work, is to offer her time for self-reflection, time for self-love. Her work, for the most part, is not done out of necessity or to achieve any specific purpose. Freeman described playing with sentences, doing and undoing them. Similarly Louisa "dearly loved to sew a linen seam not always for use, but for the simple, mild pleasure which she took in it . . . more than once she had dropped a seam for the mere delight of sewing it together again" (117). Although the world she describes may seem narrow, it is Louisa's creation. Louisa watches Joe track in "a good deal of dust"; he is a "coarse masculine presence

in the midst of all this delicate harmony" and she sees his power to
erase what she has constructed.

In "A New England Nun," Freeman offers a brilliant analysis of
the autonomy the single woman can achieve through her work, whatever form it takes, the self-fulfillment it brings, and its fragility in the
face of marriage. All of the images of Louisa's work are deliberately
delicate and on the brink of vanishing. Louisa's fears, contrary to
what Foster and other early critics have described, are far from neurotic. Her fantasies of disruption and subjugation are founded in the
realities Freeman had observed in the kitchens of her neighbors.
Louisa knows that "sitting at her window during long sweet after-
noons, she was peace itself." She anticipates that Joe "would laugh
and frown down all these pretty but senseless old maiden ways."
Marriage would require the loss of her own home. Her "maidenly
possessions" would be "robbed of their old environments" when
moved to Joe's home where "they would appear in such new guises
that they would almost cease to be themselves," just as Louisa senses
she will cease to be herself in her role as Joe's wife.

Is "A New England Nun" then simply a celebration, a victory of
spinsterhood and "the art of one's work" over marriage? To Freeman's credit, her story captures contradictory voices, the victory and
the loss involved in the choice to remain a "nun," faithful to oneself
and to one's work. Freeman's story also explores Louisa's buried
sexuality and the necessity of that burial. Her hobby is to distill the
essences from rose petals, and she stores the oils in vials for no
apparent use. This small detail indicates Louisa's stored-up though
ultimately unrealized and useless sexuality. Similarly, birdlike Louisa
locks up the wild flutterings of her canary in a tight little cage. When
Joe enters the room, the canary "fluttered wildly beating his little
yellow wings against the wires" (111). Although she may inwardly
"flutter wildly," Louisa is careful to keep the wires of her cage firmly
shut whenever Joe visits. She anticipates in marrying Joe that her
dog will be unchained. Ever since the dog had playfully sunk its teeth
into a neighbor's hand fourteen years ago (the exact time span of
Joe's absence), Louisa has locked the dog away. Indeed, the hermit
dog becomes Louisa's double. When she feeds him, directly after
her own dinner, we hear the "clank of a chain." Louisa denies the
dog "innocent canine joys," as she must deny herself sexual joys.[15]
Avoiding marriage, she will never release the passions her impris-

oned animals represent. These visions of the sexual release that marriage might bring accompany all of Louisa's fantasies of losing her own domain, losing selfhood. For many women of her time, denying one's sexuality was the price of autonomy.

In Louisa, we see a contradictory set of fears. On the one hand, Louisa fears the inevitable loss of independence in her required service to Joe. He upsets the order of her world much as he "fingered the books on the table" and "disrupted the order in which Louisa had placed them." Simultaneously, she recognizes the release of sexual energies that she has learned to suppress after years of living alone. The victory she wins in rejecting Joe brings with it a different form of imprisonment. Louisa's passionate self, the sexual "monster," will remain locked within her nunnery. Her canary will turn itself "into a peaceful yellow ball night after night and have no need to wake and flutter" because of a disturbing male presence; her dog's little "hermit hut," like Louisa's home, will be safe as "the snow might fall on its roof year in and year out, but he never would go on a rampage through the unguarded village" (124). Freeman's story leaves us with both the acknowledgment of loss and the wisdom of the choice. "All alone by herself," Louisa weeps a little; "but the next morning, on waking, she felt like a queen who, after fearing lest her domain be wrested away from her, sees it firmly insured in her possession" (124). Self-possession returns and the "uncloistered nun" feels "thankfulness."

The sacrifices that were necessary in her decision to devote herself to a career in writing were indirectly addressed in "A New England Nun." Freeman knew that she would lose a degree of social acceptability; Louisa, after all, heard the whispering of her neighbors. Freeman's trips to and from the post office rather than to and from the market were considered odd and unconventional. Although she would be queen of her own "domain," she also knew that in order to maintain such a victory, she would most likely need to part with visions of sexual fulfillment much as so many of her heroines did. What then did writing mean to Freeman? What were the complexities of this choice and what fulfillment did she find in such a commitment to work?

Freeman's comments on her profession stressed self-discovery and self-possession. She advised young women writers to trust their own intuitions and observations of life, to be independent:

A young writer should follow the safe course of writing only about those subjects she knows thoroughly, and concerning which she trusts her own convictions. Above all, she must write in her own way, with no dependence upon the work of another for aid or suggestion. She should make her own patterns and found her own school. . . . The keynote of the whole is, as in every undertaking in this world, faithful, hopeful and independent work.[16]

Her commitment to the independence she discovered as a writer is critical, although such independence did not come easily for Freeman. In order to win it, she had to make compromises at times to satisfy editors. She had to offer some degree of sentimentality while simultaneously incorporating the spirit of rebellion into her creation of lively, subtly unconventional heroines.

"Sentiments and Uplifting Ones"

When Freeman was at her weakest, she did allow "others" to "scare her from her path," as her playful poem to Henry Alden suggests.[17] Freeman was earning her living at writing, and knew what her editors sought. Her most viable source of income was women's magazines. The market Freeman found in *Harper's Bazaar* (and later, *Harper's Monthly*) was certainly a community of women readers, and with her emphasis on women's lives, this must have been very appealing to Freeman. Publishing primarily in *Harper's Bazaar,* however, she found that she could not ignore the requirement that there be a "certain degree of gentility" in her prose.[18] Henry Alden, editor of *Harper's* at the time of Freeman's publications, spoke of his "pledge" to the reading audience, and in her lesser works, Freeman honored this pledge at the expense of her own artistry.[19] Her concern for acceptability is apparent in the letter she wrote to one of her editors, Elizabeth Jordan: "I am very sorry but I do not understand . . . just what you and Mrs. Harvey want. Whatever it is, I shall be glad to respond if you will explain. I *do* see that sentiments and uplifting ones are in demand, and I cannot be quite sure of meeting your needs in that direction. . . . But I will be more than glad to do anything I am able. . . ."[20]

The letter expresses her recognition of the demand for sentimentality and acknowledges her willingness to meet this expectation; it also suggests the difficulty that she had with this requirement because "I am not exactly in an uplifted state myself." Her letters continually reveal both a willingness to compromise her standards for her public, as defined by her publisher, and a commitment to her own sense of "truth." At times, through elaborate and perhaps even unconscious subversion, she was able to satisfy both extremes.

The magazines in which Freeman published strove to appeal to and promote a particular image of womanhood. The advertisements in *Harper's*, analyzed at length by Monika Elbert, suggest that its women readers were expected to be intensely interested in fashion and male approval. Elbert comments on the contrast between the content of many of Freeman's most subversive stories, with their focus on impoverished women fighting for equity in a male world, and the objectives of *Harper's*. One of Freeman's methods of subversion was to couch her radical content in acceptable, domestic scenes of seeming female submission, thereby satisfying *Harper's* goals while subtly defying them. Many of Freeman's stories cleverly undermine the very fashions the magazine was promoting. With an emphasis on the value of work in women's lives—work pursued for the sheer pleasure of the work itself as well as for the satisfaction of independent self-support—Freeman simultaneously set these quests in the context of supreme femininity and delicacy; in this way she was able to inoffensively defy *Harper's* concept of women as merely consumers completely dependent upon men, consumers whose primary interest was to select the items the magazines advertised in order to win male attention and, ultimately, the financial security that came with marriage.[21] Such efforts at subversion could not have been easy, and there were times when Freeman simply wrote with an aim to please. Elbert's observations are pertinent for the stories she cites ("A Mistaken Charity," "A New England Nun" and "Old Woman Magoun"), but some of Freeman's weakest work demonstrated merely the compromise: sentimentality without the suggestion of subversion. Her reasons for succumbing were largely economic but she was also influenced by her need to be accepted and by her ambivalence about rebellion.

Her letter to her favorite editor at *Harper's Bazaar*, Mary Louise Booth, indicates her struggle to present "things . . . as they are":

> I suppose the trouble is, the uncomfortable feeling I have that I am not
> telling things exactly as they are, and making everything clear, if I don't
> mention everything. The more I write, the more I see that there is a great
> deal to writing. A story seems to me now, more of an undertaking than it
> did, and the feeling will grow on me.[22]

The candor of her comment captures the nature of Freeman's relationship with Mary Louise Booth, the editor and mentor who began
to work with Freeman soon after her mother's death, and who was
active in publishing her fiction in *Harper's Bazaar* through the 1880s.
It was Booth who was tempted to reject "Two Old Lovers" when she
glanced at Freeman's childish scrawl. But it was also Booth who
gave the story a second reading and who recognized the potential
Freeman had to "tell things as they are."[23]

Marjorie Pryse has suggested that the relationship Booth formed
with Freeman was almost maternal. Booth was Freeman's "main
critic and supporter, as well as an editor with an affinity for regionalism."[24] Most important, Booth invited Freeman to recognize her
strength as a writer and to define her life as an unmarried woman in
the context of her profession. In this sense, Booth helped Freeman
think of relationships in the context of work rather than in the more
conventional context of marriage. Freeman wrote Booth about the
nature of their relationship in these terms: "I begin to see that there
is one beautiful thing which comes from this kind of work, and the
thing I have the most need of, I think. One is going to find friends
because of it; and when one has no one of their very own, one does
need a good many of these, who come next."[25]

In "The Girl Who Wants to Write," Freeman states that the writer
"must not write to please an editor or a public incapable of being
pleased with the best, because in that very long run of the world she
will by so doing defeat her own needs." Yet Freeman struggled with
a necessary ambivalence. Recognizing in the same essay that the
young author is "in danger if she places too much stress upon the
opinions of others," she adds a phrase that captures her own uncertainty: "even the truth must be held back unless it is of a nature to
benefit and not poison."[26] Her sentimentality, which often works as
a frame for the volatile center of a story, was her attempt to "hold
back," for fear of the "poison" that the truth of women's struggles
often revealed. When Freeman applied her method of framing powerful psychological portraits of women with safe, sentimental begin-

nings and endings, she was writing subversively, but at the same time, she was creating a frame within which she could safely rebel, holding back and releasing rebellion simultaneously.

Freeman's fiction reveals a multiplicity of conflicting voices, and her comments on her fiction shift from the seriousness and self-awareness of the comments I have reviewed to self-mockery and self-deprecation. She made light of her own artistry in descriptions of her work that often sounded deceivingly frivolous, dismissing the weight and power of what she did so that its implicit rebelliousness might go unnoticed by editors and unfriendly readers. There was a strategy to almost every word she uttered about her work and in her fiction about the role of work in women's lives. In her essay "The Girl Who Wants to Write," for example, she speaks of writing as something a woman may do *not* out of "some seething of the central fire of genius" but "for money with which to buy a French hat." [27] On the surface, the comment seems to show Freeman's acceptance of a view of her work that had little to do with rebellion or assertiveness. She flippantly presents a "female" perspective on writing as a way of buying a stylish hat, as though her work were merely a means toward greater femininity and therefore acceptability. Yet, as with many of Freeman's statements, there is a double message here. The French hat itself reflects the very "seething fire" that her own statement satirically rejects and has nothing to do with the woman's concern for style. In her village community, someone wearing a foreign hat would have been considered extravagant and rebellious. By mentioning such a hat, so different from the caps or bonnets of the village spinsters she often wrote about, Freeman is suggesting that she associated her work with the possibility of attaining all that the hat represented—freedom, exoticism, a chance to break out of the village boundaries.

Freeman's disguise for her "seething fire" reflected not only her ambivalence about pleasing editors but her ambivalence about rebellion as well. To an extent she did internalize the standards of her time and fear the "monsters" her prose sometimes unleashed in the form of spinster-rebels. She frequently referred to her work as a collection of "little stories" and she said that what she did to reveal the "features of will and conscience" characteristic of "the village people of New England" had "been done with the best results by other American authors." [28] Her urge to undermine the power of her work is a theme in many of her letters and comments. As Hamlin Garland put it, Freeman's "succinct, low-voiced comment was often lost in the . . . clamor of less important voices."[29] Indeed she presented her own voice as "less important." Her later dismissal of one of her finest stories, "The Revolt of 'Mother' " is a good example of this impulse to self-deprecate, to deny the rebellion of "Mother" and feel safe within the strictures of New England morality.

Freeman, like many of her heroines, studied the attitudes of others in response to her work. One can easily imagine her reaction to the almost comically misplaced comments of Margaret Hamilton Welch, the woman who interviewed her for *Harper's Bazaar.* Welch came away from her visit to Freeman's writing haven in Randolph with an innocent but fairly harmful observation that minimized the power of Freeman's work by placing it in a rather peculiar context: "If the guest will linger he may be regaled with some chafing-dish confection, for in this cooking Miss Wilkins delights, and with ardor she pursues its development. It is whispered among her friends, indeed, that more than she prizes a fresh plot does she value a new receipt: certainly her rites as priestess of the alcohol shrine she makes a fair picture, and to watch her in this role 'composing' an original creation is to see her in one of her most interested and interesting moments." As proof that Freeman took greater pleasure in a new recipe than in a "fresh plot," Welch was then sure to include actual recipes she had obtained from the author.[30]

Freeman was continually diminished by others. Her self-image was a direct response to her perception of the attitudes of those who judged her. In the autobiographical piece she contributed to "My Maiden Effort," Freeman described the reaction she sensed when she received her first prize for a short story: "The story won a prize of $50 and when I went with a friend to claim it, the Prize Committee thought the friend must have written the story because I did not look as if I knew enough."[31] Although she was aware that they misjudged her, she couldn't help allowing their judgment to influence her vision of herself. Freeman goes on in the essay to describe the initial reaction to her story "Two Old Lovers": "It was accepted after being nearly turned down because the editor at first glance at my handwriting thought it was the infantile effort of a child not worth reading." Again she was reduced to the child's size (a size she interestingly attributed to almost all of her rebel heroines) and was considered unworthy of serious attention.

Because Freeman had to support herself through her writing, as Kendrick explains, "the dollar sign and the lure of the marketplace loom large in the letters." The monetary concern intensified when she realized that she did not intend to marry and gain the economic stability that would come with such a step. But, as Kendrick continues, "she did not write for money alone. She was as faithful to her art as circumstances allowed her to be."[32] In essence, Freeman was always uncomfortable with whatever compromises she might have made. One letter describes her discomfort: "Today I have written a little tale, concluding with a neat allusion to church, for the Congregationalist. I wouldn't write these if I did not like the money. . . . But it does not seem to me just right to write things of that sort on purpose to get money, and to please an editor."[33]

Although she watched the sales of her work closely and discussed payment in letter after letter, she worried deeply about the quality of the work itself: "aside from the financial aspect, [there] is more: the life of my work. I feel that is all I came into the world for, and have failed dismally if it is not a success."[34]

Her work did become "her life" and her comments on her approach to writing indicate that she was obsessed with the "life of her work" daily. A review of her more self-conscious statements about writing reveals the intensity of her self-criticism. In the first known letter about her craft, she describes the process, similar to childbirth, as both painful and exquisite:

> All the pleasure for me lies in the first knowledge of the conception, it is torture to touch it, to handle it, as I am obliged to do in order to express it, if I could only let the *Beauty* lie in my heart and not look at it, only feel that it was there, I should be happy, but to take it in my hand and put into a rhythmical frame is like handling a butterfly. I rub all the gloss off and it is never what it was at first to me.[35]

She recognized the delicacy of each "conception" and the danger of missing the mark. In this early letter, she also expressed a lifetime commitment to her work: "There is all eternity to work in and if one can only make patience immortal some time my fingers may grow so supple and gentle that they can touch Beauty without harming her and show her unspotted to people to make them happier."

The intensity of Freeman's concern about the quality of her work comes across in painfully vivid detail in "A Poetess." At the center of the story, Betsey Dole, a woman of fifty who was "born with the wantin' to write poetry," discovers that her admittedly sentimental poems have been judged to be "worth nothin' " by the local published poet, a young minister.[36] The minister's words are harsh and unfeeling. He is unable to recognize that Betsey's goal in writing her poems is to offer comfort and love to her neighbors through the written word (her most recent poem is written as a tribute to commemorate the death of her neighbor's child). Freeman experienced similarly unfeeling dismissals of her work by those who misunderstood its intent. Charles Miner Thompson, for example, complained that her style lacked elegance because it was "uneducated and uncultured," and "frequently ungrammatical"; he noted with great condescension that she belonged "to the noble army of the self-made."[37]

In light of Freeman's comments on her writing as "all that I came into the world for," Betsey's dramatic response to such misjudgment is poignant. Speaking out loud, but alone in her home, she articulates her rage against both the male dismissal of her work and her own internalization of this negative assessment. After she is told by her neighbor that the minister said "you had never wrote anything that could be called poetry, an' it was a dreadful waste of time," Betsey sits alone with the canary who has come to signify her own attempts at song and speaks "as if she recognized some other presence in the room."

> "Had I ought to have been born with the wantin' to write poetry if I couldn't write it—had I? Had I ought to have been let to write all my life, an' not know before there wa'n't any use in it? Would it be fair if that canary-bird there, that ain't never done anything but sing, should turn out not to be singin'? Would it, I'd like to know? S'pose them sweet-peas shouldn't be smellin' the right way? I ain't been dealt with as fair as they have, I'd like to know if I have." (194–95)

Similar in tone and energy to Sarah Penn's outcry against inequity, the vehemence of Betsey's monologue is soon matched by the energy with which she destroys all of the poetry she has written. In the brilliant passage in which Betsey burns her poems in the stove that she has just carefully cleaned, Freeman seems to be summing up the nature of her own relationship to the work that she had described in her letters as almost "torture to touch": "She stood watching them as their edges curled and blackened, then leaped into flame. Her face twisted as if the fire were curling over it also. Other women might have burned their lovers' letters in agony of heart. Betsey had never had any lover, but she was burning all the love letters that had passed between her and life" (195). The stories and novels over which Freeman labored were indeed "love letters . . . between her and life," and in this story she offers an analysis of both the sacrifices involved and her recognition of the danger of caring too much about the "opinions of others."

With Betsey's final action, Freeman depicts one sort of revenge against the obstacles she faced as a woman writing in the nineteenth century. Almost willing her own death, Betsey calls for the young minister to come to her bedside. She hands him the ashes of her poetry and asks him to be sure to bury them with her. While the young man is clearly oblivious to the implications of her last words, Freeman knew that her readers were not. Betsey asks him to write "jest a few lines" about her after her death: "I've been thinkin' that —mebbe my—dyin' was goin' to make me—a good subject for— poetry" (199). As Linda Grasso explains, "in this request, Freeman shows Betsey Dole's transformation from the writer to the written about, from the subject of her own life to the object in another's rendering. The only way Betsey can continue to exist is by becoming the subject matter of a male-authored text. . . ."[38] Yet through the "self-destructive revenge" of her heroine, Freeman managed to reach her audience, to get across a powerful statement about the damaging effect of male judgment on self-conception for women writers of her time. The conclusion suggests the idea that to become the *subject* of a male creation rather than to *be* the active creator is in fact to will one's own death. The caged canary, not unlike the bird in "A New England Nun," functions significantly in the story. Its sounds return at the conclusion, as if to remind readers that in fact Betsey's song must continue to be heard, for the bird "chirped faster and faster until he trilled into a triumphant song" (199).

Luckily Freeman's dissatisfaction with her own work did not lead her to Betsey's fatal conclusion. Instead, she expressed her hope that somewhere along the way she would achieve the quality to which she aspired. In her letters about her work, there is always the sense that she was striving for more, hoping to arrive at a level of depth in her prose that could surpass the compromises she was often compelled to make in order to get published. She sensed that this larger goal was something she might have to wait to reach, as if it were a matter of patience and then readiness:

> I am wishing more than I have done, to undertake some larger work, and have an uneasy feeling because of it. Lately the conviction grows on me, of heights and heights, and depths, and depths, which I have never dreamed of, and I doubt more and more my own proportion with regard to them. I do not want to undertake any work for which I am unequal, and if waiting can make me equal to it, I want to wait. I have a feeling that with anything of this sort, it is more a question of natural growth, than of deliberate effort, though I suppose that is against all the rules and precepts.[39]

Recognizing her potential, Freeman was able to get beyond negative criticism, to believe in the worth of her work, and to keep on with it. As she put it in her early letter to Edward Everett Hale, "I have never yet said of a limping line or of any line that 'it is good enough'; when I do, it will be time for me to lay by my pen."[40]

Rather than burn the drafts of her stories, Freeman submitted them for publication, and then agonized. Like Betsey Dole, everything else in her life was secondary to her writing. Freeman's descriptions of Betsey's approach to writing a poem are not unlike her description of her work on a draft. Writing her poetry on the backs of old letters and scraps of paper (with no money to buy fresh paper), Betsey works until her limbs are stiff, from morning until night, forgets to eat, emerges from the process with "red spots on her cheeks" and "unsteady" knees, gives up sleep as "she lay awake nearly all night, thinking of her poem" and "altered several lines in her mind" (188–89).

Like Betsey's, Freeman's focus was completely one-dimensional and unbending, and there is a consistent theme in her letters of "dodging everything I can" in order to keep her focus on her work. In many of her letters, Freeman turns down invitations that might distract her. In the midst of writing *Pembroke* she wrote in a letter: "one cannot kill a boy with heart disease and . . . at the same time lunch and dine with one's friends."[41]

Most of Freeman's letters to her editors at *Harper's* contain some discussion of payment for her work. She recognized when she was receiving less than she should, and she turned down, for example, an offer of eighty dollars as payment for a story which she said should easily get three hundred dollars, feeling "my work ought to count." While her letters suggest she was confident of her ability to negotiate her rates, she constantly struggled against self-doubt. Noting in a letter in 1884 that she was getting acceptances and enjoying them, she admitted that "it is odd how my own distrust of every story I write grows. I never was very self-confident but I am worse and worse." [42]

"To Tell Things Exactly as They Are"

The greatest struggle for Freeman was to "tell things exactly as they are." [43] As she wrote to Hamlin Garland: "the idea of being true is always with me. . . . Yes, I do think more of making my characters *true* and having them say and do just the things they *would* say and do, than anything else, and that is the only aim in literature of which I have been really conscious myself." [44] Of course her ability to release the "true" voices of her characters (as she did for Sarah Penn but later regretted) was sometimes colored by her own mixed feelings. This is what makes her characterizations of women and their understanding of the role of work in their lives so challenging to current feminist critics.

Freeman's friend from her years in Brattleboro, Evelyn Sawyer Severance, described Mary as "shy and shrinking," but also spoke of the odd combination, so evident in her most interesting prose, of "audacity and timidity." This is the mixture that best describes Freeman's depiction of women in the context of their work lives. Severance makes an interesting connection to a story that presents a contradictory analysis of the meaning of work in the life of the heroine Sally: "The little heroine of the 'Humble Romance' [Sally, a kitchen maid] might have been Mary herself at times. I always thought of her when I read the story." [45]

Freeman offers a conflicted description of the importance of Sally's work that captures this combination of "audacity and timidity." "A Humble Romance" is on the surface just what the title indicates, a humble love story: peddler meets maid. But couched within the conventional framework, Freeman offers us Sally, a subtle rebel whose "finger joints and bones were knotty" and who "from head to foot . . . was a little discordant note." Her expression, like Freeman's, "was at once passive and eager." [46] The story speaks to the issue of women and work quite directly. Jake convinces Sally to leave her job as maid to marry him: "I owns a cart and horse and disposes of the rags and sells the tin all on my own hook" (5). His work is independent, unlike Sally's jobs as either maid or prospective wife. He asks Sally to leave her dishes, to "ride like a queen and see the countryside," but her new "job" would essentially match the old one by providing just another form of dependence. Jake suddenly abandons Sally, leaving her his cart and a note asking her to "bear up." She takes over the role of peddler, which was considered a man's job, and takes pride in her work for the first time. She becomes active, assertive, independent. As Freeman reminds us, "a woman running a tin-cart was an unprecedented spectacle" (19). But the ambiguities are many. Freeman creates in Sally a "rebel slave" whose contradictions are at the center of the story. The rebel Sally carries a pistol to protect her property. But the passive Sally explains her role to the public carefully, with "meek dignity," an odd pairing of words. The dignity reflects an active pride; the meekness, her apologetic passivity. This is the duality that shaped Freeman's descriptions of her own "little stories."

Sally trades well, gives good bargains, and proves to be an exceptional peddler. In fact, she improves Jake's business through her bold trading with town dealers. Applying shrewd business sense, she transforms his trade into one that reaches out to women as well as men, adding "pins, needles and notions" to the stock. (It is this addition that accounts for the improvement.) In the end, Freeman allows her rebel to go only so far. She reminds her readers that all Sally's peddling was done in the interest of her "bearing up" until her prospective husband returned. When he does return, he tells "little un" the complicated circumstances that motivated his departure and Sally explains: "Jake, I did bear up. . . . Oh Jake, my blue silk dress an' the white bonnet is in the trunk of the cart . . . an' I can git 'em out an' put 'em on under the trees . . . an' wear 'em to be married in" (24).

Revoking the freedom she had granted Sally in her work—the work of a woman for herself—Freeman seems to push her character back to the role of "little un," little wife. In the end, Freeman leaves her readers with the "timidity" rather than the "audacity" that Severance noticed in Freeman's own character. Nevertheless, the echo of her pride is evident, and we are left with conflicting voices that express the author's desire both to celebrate Sally's talent and superiority and to have her win acceptability.

Freeman's motive for taming Sally's assertiveness was complex. Certainly she was at her weakest when, as one critic put it, she was "willing to add sentiment and morality to her stories like sugar to a cake recipe."[47] At the same time, she lived with and understood the reaction of her community to her decision to excel independently, to defy the established path of marriage in favor of a life devoted to her work. Perhaps pushing Sally back to the level of obedient wife at the end of "A Humble Romance" helped Freeman moderate her own rebellion and make it acceptable. By granting Sally, Sarah Penn, and other heroines their rebellions Freeman was able to express her need to defy the "gentility" required of her by the "young girls' " magazine in which she published. But in the end she limited their rebellion, and this enabled her to meet accepted standards by maintaining a safe, domestic arena.

The story that most vividly reflects Freeman's understanding of the struggle women faced when their work was not taken seriously is "A Church Mouse." The heroine, Hetty Fifield, battles against a hostile community for the right to choose her own form of work. Whenever Freeman wrote stories that drifted away from acceptable standards for "lady readers," she was engaged in a similar battle. In "A Church Mouse," the heroine rejects her community's assertion that the job of tending the local church can be held only by a man.[48] The male authorities in the village present Hetty with their objections: now that she has lost the room she had kept as a domestic, where will she live? How can she do the jobs that require men's strength such as tending the fires or working to ring the bell? Hetty's revolt is energetic, aggressive. She creates a room for herself in the church gallery. When a boy comes to ring the bell, she sends him away with pride and vigor: "I'm goin' to ring the bell; I'm sexton." She is proud of her new identity and refuses to give up the role. Finally, with community rage intensifying, Hetty barricades herself inside the church, making "her sacred castle impregnable except to violence."[49] She peers out the window and confronts the now growing crowd below with the "magnitude of her last act of defiance." In her "small, lofty room," Hetty will finally win the battle. Yet despite this victory, Hetty still manifests Freeman's ambivalence.

Freeman allows Hetty to win, but in the form of a mixed message. Recognizing that Hetty risks losing the love of her community if she fights for the right to personal fulfillment through work, Freeman suddenly deflates Hetty's heroism by shifting her from aggressive confrontation to timid pleading. After she successfully bars masculine intrusion into her self-claimed territory, Hetty appears meek and begins to plead to receive permission to remain in the church from the very authorities she had earlier dismissed. It is only after such pleading that she wins the fight. She never asks to earn a salary equal to her less competent predecessor, nor does she ask for the right to a decent room inside the church instead of in the gallery.

In the last scene, she appears timidly at the window to beg for "nothin' any better." She covers her face with her hands so that "her words end in a weak wail" (159). But then Freeman offers another mixed message. Hetty's shift in strategy is a matter of survival. It was what Freeman did when she at times added a sentimental ending to an otherwise sharply realistic story so that it would sell. Beside this weak image of Hetty—"small and trembling and helpless before them . . . like a little animal driven from its cover"—Freeman places the *women* in the village, who now demand that the men submit to Hetty's will (159). In this way, Freeman shows that Hetty's war is every woman's war. The story moves from an individual plea to a collective demand. Moreover, Freeman achieves what Hetty does— she rebels, but she does so safely and she is heard. Her story was published in a woman's magazine where it reached a similar audience composed largely of women.

Most striking in this story is Hetty's position in the church. It suggests a context for Freeman's feelings about the role of work in her life. Hetty's room is in a corner of the church gallery behind a sunflower quilt she has made. Freeman thus places her character in the nineteenth-century woman writer's predicament: Hetty is both trapped within the boundaries of the narrow congregation (ultimately answerable to its rules) and set apart by the quilt she hangs —her art form—to announce the significance of her separateness, her individuality, her ability to assert.

Although Freeman's letters show her awareness that writing was her only source of income and that this situation necessitated Hetty's style of strategic negotiations, they also indicate she was unhappy about what her limited options required. She told Fred Pattee in

1919 that she wanted "more symbolism, more mysticism" in her work, but that she found she often "left that out" because "she was forced to consider selling qualities."[50] None of her letters captures the anger she must have felt when she found herself driven toward sentimentality to please her public and to earn the money she needed to live. Yet in the range of her stories, in the mixture of conventional sentimentality in some and the "symbolism" or "mysticism" in others, we can see her uneasiness and even her anger at the limitations imposed upon her.

Her story "Sister Liddy" best captures Freeman's fictional exploration of the artistic process that might have been at work when she wrote her most sentimental stories or added the sentimental conclusion to "A Humble Romance."[51] Sharing her fictive creation, a sister called Liddy, with other women in an insane asylum, Polly paints a portrait of an imaginary sister in a "flood" of rich details that matches Freeman's least readable and most sentimental fiction. At the same time, a madwoman, Sally, wildly runs down the hallway and acts out all of Polly's repressed anger at the need to create an idealized sister who thrives outside the asylum in a happy marriage with a baby and a silk-lined cradle. As her story "Sister Liddy" makes clear, Freeman was strategic; she was able to win her public (hence earn a living) while subtly expressing her inner rage at the necessary compromises.

3

"SOMETIMES I THINK I AM A MONSTER"

∞

FREEMAN BECAME INCREASINGLY conscious that her choice to place work at the center of her life was a deviation from the norm. Living as an unmarried woman through her childbearing years, Freeman experienced and analyzed the complexities of nineteenth-century spinsterhood, using that single state as a focus for much of the fiction she wrote. Spinsterhood required a conscious rejection of the more acceptable forms of relationships—wife and mother—in favor of self-fulfilling work and friendship with women. Such a rejection was not unconflicted. In her fiction, Freeman brilliantly expressed the consequent feelings of social exclusion and misrepresentation. The spinsters in her stories have a range of voices: some were fulfilled in their work or in their bond with another woman; some remembered an unrequited love or a missed marriage, or craved a life of acceptability; some were defiant and rebellious; some oscillated between joyful rebellion and passive apology. As a single woman, Freeman could speak with all these voices.

Although nineteenth-century rural New England was largely matrifocal, Freeman still had to face the reality that she was being trained to part with this female world as soon as possible.[1] While it is true that, as Josephine Donovan suggests, the world left behind with the loss of men to the Civil War and migration westward was a world largely shaped by maternal values, there were certainly mixed messages. Like most young women, Freeman was expected, pressured in fact, to marry; from her mother's perspective, this step would ensure Mary's economic survival and masculine protection. Devoted to her mother and dependent on the bond they had, Freeman found their conflict very painful. She realized that, on some level, to resist the life her mother wanted for her was to reject the woman she loved and for whom she had become the primary source of fulfillment. Nonetheless, she rejected domesticity in her adolescence, and, ultimately, marriage in her early twenties.

In contrast to the messages Freeman received from magazines and advice books for women about the specific dangers of the spinster's life and the certain bliss of marriage and domesticity, she had her own observations of her mother's life as a source for skepticism about the benefits of heterosexuality and marriage. How did she weave these threads together to make some sense of things, to make the choices she needed to make as a woman and as a writer? And what concept of women's sexuality and autonomy did Freeman convey in the stories and novels she wrote both during her many years of unmarried life and in her short-lived marriage? To what extent did her fiction become restorative—a way of remaking or coming to terms with the past and a channel for her confusion and rage?

In 1877, Susan B. Anthony described the single woman as a model for all women to emulate: "single women are not halves, needing complements, as are the masses of women; but evenly balanced well rounded characters; therefore are they models to be reached by the average women we everyday meet";[2] clearly, Freeman was not prepared to assert openly a position that was so contrary to public opinion. She was far too conflicted to have become active in the early feminist movement. It is interesting, however, that even at its most ambiguous, her work and her life fully support Anthony's manifesto and continually defy the negative cultural stereotyping of the spinster or "old maid."

The attraction to spinsterhood began for Freeman in her adolescence. At the height of her own developing sexuality, she was becoming aware of her mother's lack of autonomy and subservience in marriage. In "The Revolt of 'Mother' " it is easy to see the delight Freeman took in giving "Mother" a strong, autonomous voice within marriage, giving her power by granting her the assertiveness she wished her mother had had, giving her the house her mother had only seen as a floor plan, giving her some acknowledgment for the value of her work. It is clear, however, from her own criticism of the story in the *Saturday Evening Post* that Freeman came to believe that such autonomy was not possible for those who chose heterosexuality and marriage.

Freeman's response to the pressure to marry was strategic. By picking the unobtainable Hanson Tyler to worship long after his departure, Freeman had created an effective excuse not to marry.[3] She concocted a way of choosing spinsterhood without appearing to have chosen it, without acknowledging unmarried life as an active choice. Yet her choice was synonymous with her choice to become a writer—a move toward rather than away from something. In nineteenth-century New England, however, spinsterhood was considered a stigma rather than an affirmation, a lamentable fate rather than a positive choice. In describing the whispering about Louise's extravagant use of china for her solitary meals in "A New England Nun," Freeman showed she was acutely aware of the stigma of spinsterhood.

When her father died in 1883, Freeman was thirty, still unmarried, living in Brattleboro with her cat, Augusta, and focusing increasingly on her writing. Aware that she was circumventing her father's hope that she would marry in order to pursue her own passion for writing, Freeman made the decision to move back to Randolph to live with her childhood friend, Mary Wales, on the farm she remembered fondly. At this point, she began writing steadily for *Harper's Bazaar* and *Harper's New Monthly*. By 1887 the stories she had been sending to *Harper's* were collected in the volume *A Humble Romance and Other Stories*. Freeman received increasing recognition for her prose with this publication, and her career was effectively launched. Yet at the height of her career in the late 1880s, Freeman knew that her success as a writer was set against and directly dependent on what others saw as her failure to marry. Much of Freeman's work reveals the degree to which she both internalized this judgment and rejected it, both enjoyed unmarried life and was ambivalent about her pleasure.

In an unfinished, unpublished short story, Freeman expressed what spinsterhood had come to mean for her. The voice of the narrator, Jane Lennox, is full of rage, fear, and disillusionment, but also of pleasure:

> I am a rebel and what is worse a rebel against the Overgovernment of all creation. . . . I even dare to think that, infinitesimal as I am, . . . I, through my rebellion, have power. All negation has power. I, Jane Lennox, spinster,

as they would have designated me a century ago, living quietly, and apparently harmlessly in the old Lennox homestead in Baywater, am a power. ...I often wonder if I might not have been very decent, very decent indeed, if I had laid hold on the life so many of my friends lead. If I had only a real home of my own and a husband and children in it. That was my birthright, but I was deprived of it, with neither trade nor barter. ... And another thing which was my birthright: the character of the usual woman. I am a graft on the tree of human womanhood. I am a hybrid. Sometimes I think I am a *monster,* and the worst of it is, I certainly take pleasure in it.[4]

While Jane feels "pride which intoxicates like forbidden stimulants," pride in her autonomy, she also expresses ambivalence. Her pride is based on what is in fact "negation" to her society, and although, as Jane asserts, "all negation has power," it is nevertheless a power dismissed by her society. Jane speaks in two voices. When she speaks longingly of a husband and children as a "birthright," Jane indicates that she has internalized the very view of those who have ostracized her. She sees herself as an anomaly: "I am a graft on the tree of human womanhood. I am a hybrid." In Jane, Freeman gave expression to the need for isolation and rebellion as well as the desire to be "very decent." While she expresses "glory" in her rebellion, she simultaneously fears such forbidden power. Seeing herself through the lens of her society, Jane begins the most perplexing sentence in her self-portrait with an apology: "Sometimes I think I am a *monster*"; but another voice in Jane emerges within the same sentence: "and the worst of it is, I certainly take pleasure in it." Taking pleasure in her "monsterhood" further stigmatizes the spinster. Freeman never finished this story. Perhaps Jane Lennox carries too much force and is too willingly the "monster" Freeman feared in herself. Edward Foster interprets the above passage as a reflection of Freeman's "tormented mood," the voice of a "troubled woman." He asks, "Was Miss Wilkins indeed a 'monster'?" Foster misinterprets the gist of the passage and reduces Jane's sense of herself as a "rebel," a "power," to an assessment of Freeman as "simply a troubled woman, prone on occasion to looking hard at herself, much harder than is customary among most troubled women."[5] The voices of Jane Lennox offer, in essence, an interpretation of spinsterhood; they seem to echo Freeman's vision of spinsterhood as both exhilarating and terrifying.

Freeman saw spinsterhood as an opportunity for freedom from

obligations that would distract her from her work. In a letter to Kate Upson Clark, she wrote "I suppose the first thing you'll want me to tell you is that I am *not* going to get married, and as far as the signs of the time go, I do not see any reason to apprehend that I ever shall be married. I simply cannot support a family yet, and just now all my powers are engaged upon the great American Drama." Her letter indicates her fear that marriage would work in exact opposition to what all of her powers were channeled toward. It would appear that despite the stigma of spinsterhood, Freeman was making a conscious choice. She fully recognized that the requirements of marriage would become impediments to her success as a writer; yet it must have taken some courage to continue her resistance. In the same letter, she describes feeling "blue and not getting any sleep" as she struggled to complete a manuscript. But her concluding comment is quite telling: "It is so much trouble to run one's self in all the departments! Talk about getting married! If I had to see to a man's collars and stockings, besides the drama and the story and Christmas and the new dress, in the next three weeks, I should be crazy." [6]

"Trouble" though it might be, Freeman was working at "running" her own life "in all departments." She knew that marriage would mean seeing to the trivialities of someone else's life, his "collars and stockings" rather than to her own "new dress," his needs rather than her own compulsion to complete "the drama and the story." Although she is clearly facetious when she says "I should be crazy," her comment is revealing. In "A Church Mouse," as in many of her other stories about elderly single women, Freeman suggests her society's association of craziness with the choice of spinsterhood. What enrages the male villagers most about Hetty's behavior is her self-sufficiency and independence, her satisfaction in living and working alone in the church. The deacon tells her "it ain't fit for an old woman like you to be alone in the church." To the male eye, as Charlotte Wolff explains, "women by themselves appear to be incomplete, as if a limb were missing." [7] The deacon's response to Hetty's actions is to assume that she has lost her senses, that she is mad. In this letter, however, Freeman reverses such an assumption; the duties associated with being married would make her "crazy."

Freeman's feelings about spinsterhood can be understood by studying her fictional spinsters and by considering her own long-delayed marriage. Her work and her comfortable life with Mary

Wales played a significant role in the delay. Submitting, as Jane Lennox wished she could have, to the need for a "decent" life, Freeman's long engagement reflects the depth of her hesitation. Although she met Charles Freeman in 1892, she did not marry him until 1902, and the marriage was announced and denied many times in that interim. A letter written in 1900 to a friend who was about to marry is poignant. She assures her friend that despite the marriage, "I shall find the old you. It will never be lost." In the same letter, Freeman reveals her own fears of losing autonomy in marriage:

> I don't proclaim it from the housetops yet for the date has been already postponed twice, but I am to be married myself before long. I shall live in New Jersey, Metuchen, so we shall be sort of neighbors. If you *don't* see the old *me,* I shall run and run until I find her. And as for you, no man shall ever swallow you up entirely, you beautiful thing, you, and he needn't think he can. But I am so glad for you, dear, and here's to a life like a fairy tale![8]

The assurance to her friend that "no man shall ever swallow you up entirely" expresses her own fear of being swallowed up in the life she will soon lead, as the doctor's wife. Her lighthearted reference to a "life like a fairy tale" is a recognition that the life of a "wife" is idyllic only in fairy tales and is more likely to lead to that "run" she describes at the thought of losing the "old me" because of her marriage.

Freeman's fears were quite justified. In her marriage to Charles Freeman, she did in fact lose the sense of control and connection with her autonomous self, what she has Jane Lennox describe as "womanly pride," her "powerful tonic" for having "missed" marriage. Marriage required poignant losses: with the move to Metuchen, New Jersey (where she found "I have not a blessed thing to write about"), she left Randolph and the companionship of Mary Wales.[9]

As is evident in "Old Woman Magoun," Freeman associated heterosexual relationships with a separation from the love of women. The gateway to death for Lily is her grandmother's utopian vision of an asexual world in a maternal heaven. Freeman turned to a concept of independence in asexual spinsterhood, an option to Lily's fate, when she wrote "A New England Nun." The extremes of Lily and Louisa, however, do not capture the full range of Freeman's exploration of spinsterhood. They simply underscore the spinster's dilemma when the only context for defining satisfaction is measured in standard, patriarchal, heterosexual terms.

In "Some Reflections on the Spinster in New England Literature," Barbara Johns explores the image of the spinster in American literature, and raises the critical questions which must be addressed in such an examination:

> A study of the spinster should confront the popular notion of spinsterhood precisely on its own grounds: Does the spinster regard herself as unattractive? Is she afraid or unresponsive to her own sexuality? Is she afraid of men and their sexuality? What choices regarding men and marriage does the society offer her? What choices does she make? Is she neurotic or repressed? Is she dour and obsessively neat? What does she do with her time and how is that time rewarded? Is there, in the fictive world she inhabits, the possibility of a healthy spinsterhood? Are there spinsters who are not simply or easily stereotyped?[10]

A review of the major works by Nathaniel Hawthorne, Harriet Beecher Stowe, William Dean Howells, Henry James, Sarah Orne Jewett, Edith Wharton, and Mary Wilkins Freeman reveals that these authors do not offer any single stereotype of spinsterhood. In comparing Freeman's spinsters to those in works by these other writers, Johns notes that Freeman's spinsters are unique: "Aware of their sexuality and alive to the possibility of romance, these women regard personal integrity as an essential value that marriage ought not to violate. Spinsterhood for them is an act of moral heroism."[11] While this image of the spinster is evident in much of her fiction, the "moral heroism" does not come without considerable struggle and ambivalence. It was difficult to ignore social expectations. One of the most popular books of the time was *The Physical Life of Woman: Advice to the Maiden, Wife and Mother;* this text urged its readers to avoid spinsterhood at all costs and outlined the proper behavior for women, dictating that "love and marriage are the only normal conditions of life."[12]

As Susan Koppelman sums it up, the term spinster in the nineteenth century "took the form of making the lot of women who did not marry appear so loathsome, so ridiculous, so pathetic, so unnatural or unhealthy, so empty and cold, that the assumption was no one would willingly choose such a life."[13] Studies of spinsterhood in nineteenth-century America provide a context for interpreting Freeman's approach to the subject. Lee Chambers-Schiller's study clarifies that whereas spinsters were initially acceptable *if,* in keeping with maternal ideology, they devoted their lives to caring for others, this perception of their role changed:

> As the century wore on, spinsters were increasingly defined as unacceptable childcare providers, guardians, or even teachers. Their spinsterhood took on an ominous cast, their celibacy no longer evidence of pure Christian love, but now suggestive of physical, emotional and intellectual degeneracy. In the post-Civil War period, physicians, biologists, and psychologists came to believe in the prominence of the womb. According to the articles on women's hygiene the woman whose reproductive organs went unused would experience their atrophy and derangement, together with a painful menopause and general physical and mental deterioration. A spinster could look forward to a shortened life span and quite possibly insanity.[14]

Freeman's fiction continually rejects such theories. Most of her spinsters survive and even thrive in their single states. To work against such sharp dismissals of the worth of the spinster, Freeman had to come to terms with her own internalization of the prevailing judgments.

Freeman's developing understanding of spinsterhood coincided with a historical transition. According to Ruth Freeman and Patricia Klaus, between approximately 1870 and 1920 "a change in attitudes toward spinsterhood can be discerned, both on the part of society toward spinsters and in the spinsters' attitude toward themselves. People contrasted the unmarried women of earlier times with this 'new spinster.' No longer reclusive, useless, and embittered, the new spinster led an outgoing, productive life."[15] As their lives became more productive, many women began to see spinsterhood as a positive state and the decision to remain unmarried in a male-dominated society became an active response to long established gender inequality. Because of this, spinsterhood grew as a threat and the stigma attached to it became more subtle, but also more intense. At the same time, the bonding between women became stronger. Freeman's relationship with Mary Wales, which I discuss in Chapter 6, is a good example of this pattern.

Freeman at least partially believed the propaganda—some of her letters indicate that she associated married life with happiness, security, and acceptable sexuality, and she sometimes longed for these.

But other letters and many of her stories and novels indicate that she also saw marriage as a threat to independence. Her reactions were never one-dimensional.

In her portrayals of spinsters, Freeman looked back to the period that had shaped her own growth into womanhood, a period in which the term "old maid" was widely used to characterize single women and carried the connotation of "an unattractive, malicious, prudish, petty, narrow, simpering, drab, gossipy, barren, shallow, trouble-making, envious, withered, characterless, bossy, snoopy, selfish, unsuccessful and impoverished woman."[16] She created spinsters who defied such caricatures. At the same time, she recognized that although the stereotype was flawed, many single women did long for whatever wholeness seemed to be contained in the idyllic concepts of marriage and motherhood. She knew that to many people, probably the vast majority, "the new spinster, rejecting marriage and motherhood as it existed in late Victorian society, was perceived as a threat to men and the family."[17] She also knew, as Ruth Freeman and Patricia Klaus explain, that at the prospect of aging and living alone, "spinsters worried and dreamed. Although they regarded themselves as 'rebels to a great command,' they suspected something important was missing in their lives. Unable to describe accurately the loss, some embellished it. As one spinster admitted in a revealing statement about their lives and conversations: 'This great realm of human experience from which we are shut out occupies our minds almost morbidly.' "[18]

With Lily's premature death at one extreme ("Old Woman Magoun") and Louisa's isolation at the other ("A New England Nun"), most of Freeman's stories about spinsterhood explore the alternatives of bonding with other women, of strengthening their relations with other than husband and children (mothers, sisters, friends, neighbors). Just as Freeman saw, in her words, "the art of her work" at the center of her life, her fictional spinsters find their greatest fulfillment in their work, whether it is gardening, singing, writing what turns out to be bad poetry, storing essences, growing herbs, quilting, or sewing.

Freeman's stories offer a range of voices, from that of the woman in a "Patient Waiter," who longs for a missed marriage all her life and makes this loss the focus of her energies, to that of the completely contented "Christmas Jenny," who longs for nothing more than to continue the rich life she is leading. The two women reflect Freeman's duality, her conflicting desires to rebel and to belong. Almost all her spinsters, though, defy in one way or another the concept of the unhappily isolated old maid. They have established new forms of self-definition through work, through relationships with other women, through their sense of unity with nature.

In exploring her wide range of spinster tales, it is useful to begin with stories in which she analyzes the choice itself, a young woman's conscious decision to resist marriage. "A Moral Exigency" and "Louisa" are good examples of Freeman's understanding of the pressure to marry, the conflicts that arise, and the motivation for choosing spinsterhood. Her analysis of the choice itself is indicative of all that Freeman considered in her own early decision against marriage.

"A Moral Exigency"

Like Eunice, her heroine in "A Moral Exigency," Freeman fought against externally imposed definitions. As Sandra Gilbert and Susan Gubar explain in *The Madwoman in the Attic*, for the woman artist "the essential process of self-definition is complicated by all those patriarchal definitions that intervene between herself and herself." [19] Freeman was consistently ambivalent about her own seeming deviance as an unmarried woman who worked to support herself, who broke away from the role her mother offered of subservient wife and mother. She was aggressive about getting her works published and resistant to marriage for many years, but she was apologetic about spinsterhood and finally, nearing fifty, became resigned to a marriage that would end in divorce. The heroine in "A Moral Exigency" voices the dissatisfaction and the repressed longings that Freeman herself lived with as a woman who craved power and autonomy yet needed to conform. Through the consciousness of Eunice, Freeman analyzes the conflicting needs of women in the nineteenth century —needs that women today may still recognize as their own. [20]

Of all Freeman's rebels, the twenty-five-year-old Eunice Fairweather most clearly reflects the contradictions and conflicts that shaped Freeman's early life. Like Freeman, Eunice is ambivalent, a mixture of fiery rebel and dutiful slave. Just as Freeman did, Eunice initially submits and then subtly rebels. Eunice agrees to attend "the seminary for which money had been scraped together," but she stays

for only one year. When Freeman described her own experience at
Mount Holyoke to Helena Todd, she acknowledged that she had
"not behaved at all well." And "not behaving at all well" worried
Freeman. As she says of Eunice, "she was a conservative creature," at
least on the surface.

The central question which "A Moral Exigency" raises is crucial
to an understanding of Freeman's concept of spinsterhood as a complex choice. When a woman faces the expectation that she will shape
her life to fit the social norm, that she will remain essentially passive
or adopt the role of mother and wife as her primary activity, what
conflicts arise? More important, what happens to the hidden, aggressive self, the shadow within? How does the woman cope with a volcano of buried energies? What sort of courage does this coping
require and what is the price or the possible resulting damage to the
woman's sense of self.

In this story, Freeman returns to her own sense of entrapment as
a daughter of orthodox Congregationalists. Brought up within the
confining boundaries of strict Puritan tradition, Freeman focuses
here on a minister's daughter whose duties seem endless and whose
social acceptance depends upon submission, obedience, and moral
"goodness." Through Eunice, Freeman touches on the terrible confinement she must have felt and the struggle involved in attempts at
breaking away. Eunice must perform a range of tedious domestic
tasks which stifle her creative and aggressive energies. The story
opens with Eunice's preparations for Christmas:

> She took it, as usual, loyally and energetically, but there had always been
> seasons from her childhood—and she was twenty-five now,—when the
> social duties to which she had been born seemed a weariness and a bore
> to her. They had seemed so today. She had patiently and faithfully sewed
> up little lace bags. . . . She had taken her prominent part among the corps
> of indefatigable women always present to assist on such occasions, and
> kept up her end of the line as minister's daughter bravely.[21]

Freeman indicates that submission of the kind Eunice experiences
requires an ironic bravery, the bravery needed to survive the range
of tasks expected of them, despite their desires for an end to the
"weariness." In some respects, Eunice resembles the heroine of Freeman's novel *Madelon,* who also feels stifled by "social duties" but who
initially struggles to conform in order to win the acceptance of the
"Puritan stock" around her. Inwardly, Madelon longs to have

"backed her heavy load of tenting through the snow on wild hunting parties, and broken the ice on the river for fish."[22] Outwardly, wanting the love of her community, she follows the prescribed "domesticity," buries the inner "fire." This is the duality that Freeman explores in so much of her fiction about women. It is similar to what the narrator of George Eliot's *The Mill on the Floss* describes, a plight tracing back to the days of Hecuba and Hector with the women "inside the gates . . . watching the world's combat from afar, filling their long empty days with memories and fear; outside, the men in fierce struggle with things divine and human."[23]

Barred from the "outside" as she is, trapped "inside the gates," Eunice strives to discover some means of fulfillment, some inkling of what life "outside" might be if she could release the buried self. Because she lived in small New England villages most of her life, Freeman too felt herself to be trapped "inside" and longed as well for some undefined freedom. She wrote to her friend Evelyn Sawyer, "I have a constant longing to go to a land where there are no circumstances."[24] She invests Eunice with this same "constant longing." In the painful detail of her description of Eunice's room, Freeman seems to ask her reader to recognize the "circumstances" that restrict and shape the life of a "good girl." Indirectly, the description also asks us to understand, even share in, Eunice's longing for escape.

> It was small, and one side ran in under the eaves; for the parsonage was a cottage. There was one window, with a white cotton curtain trimmed with tasselled fringe, and looped upon an old porcelain knob with a picture painted on it. That knob with its tiny bright landscape, had been one of the pretty wonders of Eunice's childhood. She looked at it even now with interest, and the marvel and the beauty of it had not wholly departed from her eyes. . . . There were a few poor attempts at adornment on the walls; a splint lettercase, a motto worked in worsteds, a gay print of an eminently proper little girl holding a faithful little dog. (20–21)

At first the interior of the room gives only the sense of feminine entrapment. Pretty tasselled fringes and white cotton trimmings seem to be the boundaries of Eunice's life; a permanent, inescapable enclosure. The picture of the "proper little girl holding a faithful little dog" is an image Eunice has been trained to adopt and she "believed in it." Yet the tiny landscape on the porcelain knob holds a fascination for Eunice. As in her supernatural story "The Hall

Bedroom," Freeman's character gazes at the landscape as though gazing at a possible doorway out of the imprisonment of her little room. [25] The knob increases our sense of how tiny and limited Eunice's world is and, with her fascinated gaze, emphasizes that her longing for freedom is equal in strength to the degree of confinement. Freeman creates a sense of sterility in Eunice's surroundings. The room was "drearily cold." Indeed Eunice has "never had a fire in her bedroom"; it "would have been sinful luxury" (21). Even in this small detail, the polarities of Eunice's life emerge. "Sinful luxury" of bodily warmth and pleasure is what Eunice secretly desires, while everything in her environment prevents such fulfillment. Her attitude toward her life is that of "resigned disapproval." Survival in the role of minister's daughter requires resignation; but the seeds for Eunice's revolt appear in this phrase since "disapproval" accompanies her resignation.

Eunice undertakes the numerous responsibilities in the hated parsonage and plays the role of a poor country minister's wife because her mother is ill. Freeman fills her pages with the breeding dissatisfaction of her heroine: "She was a church member and a good girl, but the role did not suit her. Still she accepted it as inevitable and would no more have thought of evading it than she would have thought of evading life altogether." The analogy is important and intentionally ironic. The role she has reluctantly but obediently accepted *determines* her evasion of life itself.

Having established the limitations of Eunice's world, Freeman presents her reader with revolt. Mr. Wilson, a widower with four young children, arrives to ask Eunice to marry him. Despite her father's promptings, Eunice firmly refuses. Wilson is a younger version of Eunice's father with "something of the same cast of countenance," and with a "ministerial affability" (23–24). To marry Wilson would be to duplicate the life she has led under her father's domination for twenty-five years. Her refusal is the first step toward rebellion. Eunice's verbal confrontation with her father is something Freeman never experienced. Yet it is probable that Freeman's decision to write and to remain single throughout her father's lifetime created a difficult, unspoken conflict. The concern Eunice's father takes in Eunice's marriage, his sense that she should accept her first offer, echoes Warren Wilkins's fear and distress when Freeman showed no signs of marrying. He is quoted as saying "Mary has no

talent and I don't know what she will do to make a living." The only
option Mary's father and his fictional counterpart could perceive,
given the realities of the New England village and the family's finances, was for her to marry as soon as possible. But while her sister
was out attending parties and bringing friends to the house, Mary
was "withdrawn" and "curled up in a big chair with a book or gazing
out the window."[26] Freeman seems to be expressing her own harbored resentment for her father's and her society's expectations
through Eunice. Eunice's father urges her not to respond "too hast-
ily" to the proposal and his argument reflects what Freeman would
have faced under similar circumstances as unmarried daughter: "Mr.
Wilson is a good man; he would make you a worthy husband, and he
needs a wife sadly. Think what a wide field of action would be before
you with those four children to love and care for. You would have a
wonderful opportunity to do good" (25). Eunice is instantly aware of
the irony of this "wide field of action": action must be translated for
the woman into service and service must be seen in the context of
doing for others rather than for oneself.

Eunice's refusal is harsh and outspoken, giving full voice to Freeman's unvoiced rebellion. To her father's argument of financial security, she responds astutely: "There would be six hundred a year and
a leaky parsonage for a man and woman and four children, and
nobody knows how many more" (25). When her father imposes an
even higher authority on Eunice—"The Lord would provide for his
servants," Eunice argues even more accurately: "I don't know
whether he would or not. I don't think he would be under any
obligation to if his servant deliberately encumbered himself with
more of a family than he had brains to support" (26). The injustice
of the proposal itself becomes even clearer with the additional information that Wilson "was not thirsting for love and communion with
a kindred spirit" since his wife's death a year ago, "but for a capable
woman who would take care of his four clamorous children without
a salary" (27). In other words, he seeks an unpaid servant in a
woman who appears to be plain and aging, "without prospects."

The most startling moment in the story comes with Eunice's view
of herself in the mirror just after her assertive refusal to marry. Here
Freeman's use of the psychological double is quite powerful. Early
in the story Eunice had looked "unhappily at herself in her little
square glass," seeing within that geometrical square all the limita-

tions of her life. But now, as Eunice begins to entertain the idea of giving way to her infatuation with Burr Mason, the dashing new young man in town, the mirror image transforms in a rather curious way:

> Standing before her glass, combing out her rather scanty, lustreless hair, her fancy pictured to her, beside her own homely, sober face, another, a man's blond and handsome, with a gentle, almost womanish smile on the full red lips, and a dangerous softness in the blue eyes. Could a third person have seen the double picture she did, he would have been struck with a sense of the incongruity, almost absurdity of it. Eunice herself, with her hard uncompromising common-sense, took the attitude of a third person in regard to it, and at length blew her light out and went to bed, with a bitter amusement in her heart at her own folly. (28)

The passage is a mysterious one and can be interpreted in several ways. What does Eunice see when she looks at her own reflection? And how does this vision reveal her self-conception? On the surface, the scene merely describes Eunice's imagination at work; she pictures Burr Mason's handsome image beside her own as her lover. Yet the details of the passage, given what we learn about Burr Mason and her attraction to him, suggest something else as well. Standing back as a third person viewing this "double picture," Eunice sees a reflection of two sides of herself—two selves gaze back at her from the mirror. One is the "homely," resigned, "sober" self, while the other is a "womanish" man's face with a "dangerous softness in the blue eyes." This second self, able to indulge in male aggression, is capable of rejecting Wilson and assertively becoming the lover of Burr Mason despite his engagement to another woman. As the plot unfolds, we learn that Burr, who is "terribly vacillating," has drifted away from his fiancée, Ada Harris, to Eunice. *His* infidelity is overlooked, even accepted, but Eunice's engagement to him is seen by Ada and her parents as "immoral," "wicked," and "cruel" behavior from a minister's daughter who has the reputation of being "so good"(32). What Eunice sees in the mirror is her own duality, for one side of her submits to the values of parsonage life and to passive self-sacrifice while the other side wishes to have access to the "wide field of action" she imagines to be available to a man like Burr. Burr is later described as promiscuous and his attentions are blatantly sensual. To the "steady" Eunice he seems "as much out of her life as a lover in a book"(30). Yet certainly her rebellious rejection of Wilson and her expression of sexual attraction to Burr mirror Burr's actions.

Freeman's "mirror" dramatization of her own self-division brings to mind two poems with similar mirror visions, poems that may help explain the complexity Freeman suggests about the process of self-definition for women who choose single life. One is a poem by Mary E. Coleridge and the other is an unpublished poem by Mary Wilkins Freeman. Mary E. Coleridge's "The Other Side of the Mirror" presents a woman whose vision in the mirror, "shade of a shadow in the glass" has "not voice to speak its dread" and stares back at the speaker with "lurid eyes." Throughout the poem, the reader senses that the woman on the "other side of the mirror," full of "fire," must somehow get out from behind the mirror.[27] Freeman's poem "The Stranger" (1901) expresses the same eerie sense of duality. The poem begins with an image of a woman sitting at her spinning wheel, watching a stranger pass by her door. But as the poem progresses, the stranger becomes increasingly ambiguous and in mirrorlike form, this stranger appears to be an extension or projection of the woman's psyche. The stranger is male, like the stranger in the mirror Eunice views, and it is the stranger who "abides" in the "flesh" and "soul" of the woman who *appears* to be calmly "spinning at her wheel." The poem ends with the duality we see in Eunice and the same fate, for the woman continues to "meekly live her quiet days" while "the stranger's look was in *her* eyes" (italics mine).[28] The poem traces the woman's developing awareness of the stranger and the widening distance between her static position at the wheel and the stranger's flight as he passes her door. On the surface, the poem indicates that the woman lives on with the memory of an actual "stranger's look," a man who passed her door and caused her soul to "flash out." But the deeper implication is that both souls belong to the woman at the wheel, that her eyes, "the mirror of her soul," have in fact the "stranger's look."

It is interesting, given Eunice's vision in the mirror, to note that, when Freeman was approximately twenty-five (Eunice's age), she "craved a bit of deviltry and found it hard to come by: one night she dressed in man's clothes, gazed at her image in the mirror, and later told one of her friends it was a 'thrilling experience.' "[29] Was the "thrill" in imagining what the world might have held for her if she could have been a man? We can only speculate. Yet given what Freeman exposes in her fiction of the limited options open to unmarried women and the community's expectations of passivity, this seems to be the implication of Eunice's double vision as well as Freeman's. Michele Clark suggests that Freeman's indulgence in male attire may indicate a latent, hidden homosexuality. Clark points out that Freeman's closest relationships were with women and that there are often women characters in her work who have passionate feelings for each other.[30] In accordance with this theory, it is possible to view Eunice's vision as an indication of her desire to possess Ada through Burr; one might say that she therefore sees Ada in Burr through the mirror image. The stronger implications of the story, however, are that Eunice sees in the male mirror image the side of herself that has been long suppressed, the aggressive self capable of living as freely the unmarried life as Burr has done. Still, in the passage in which Eunice sees her double vision in the mirror, there may be subtle, unconscious suggestions of Eunice's buried homosexuality. It is strange that there is no detailed physical description of Burr other than that he is "boyish." Yet we do get a clear description of Ada Harris, Burr betrayed fiancée. She has "red lips" like the feminine-male image in the mirror, "blond hair," and "blue eyes" with a "fierce light in them" as well as "strong passions" (31–32). Later Eunice remembers how Ada had rested on her lap when she was younger; her "golden head had nestled on her bosom" and this makes her regret her own aggressions toward Burr. There are many layers of meaning to this uncanny mirror scene and the power of the passage lies in its ambiguity. The mirror image, then, may be as much Ada as it is the passionate side of Eunice or an image of Burr.

What is apparent in the story is that the freedom Burr has as a male is foreign and unattainable to the steady Eunice. In almost every respect, Burr is a double of Freeman's imagined sweetheart, her unrequited love, Hanson Tyler. In fact, it was while Hanson was off on a cruise that Mary indulged in her "thrilling experience" of dressing as a man, perhaps imagining Tyler's freedom for herself. Hanson was a "lady's man" as much as his fictional counterpart, Burr. While Mary was in her twenties and still pining after him, Hanson wrote home to his father: "I have some pretty pictures hung about my room and standing on my bureau. The latter are of young ladies with whom I have had flirtations at various times of my life."[31] Burr has the same "careless freedom." Equally important, Burr is a man of action and sensual abandon. "Boyish" like Hanson, he "took part in all the town frolics with gusto"(29). Like Hanson, Burr suggests all that is free and untouched by village boundaries. Both Hanson and Burr are creatures from far-off places. They travel. Hanson was a sailor and the fictional Burr "was reported to be running a cattle ranch in one of those distant territories which seem almost fabulous to New Englanders" before his return to his father's home(29). That Burr is a figure associated with the distant "fabulous" West is significant. To the New Englander Freeman describes, the West was that place of adventure so far away one could never get to it; traditionally it was associated with the setting sun or the pot of gold at the end of the rainbow. Freeman's attraction to such mystery and freedom reflects her own restlessness and longing. It is an attraction to the freedom of male bachelorhood, which carried neither the stigma nor the restrictions of spinsterhood.

In *Psychology of Women*(1994) Helene Deutsch comments on aggression and inhibition in words that are still pertinent today and applicable to both Freeman and her heroine Eunice. Deutsch's theory, although it goes on to conclusions that may be questionable, seems to explain Freeman's rebel well, particularly Eunice's ultimate withdrawal from that other "man's" image in the mirror: "With regard to the girl . . . the environment exerts an inhibiting influence as regards both her aggressions and her activity. The effect of this inhibition depends on the intensity of environmental influence and on the strength of the girl's active urge." According to Deutsch, while the same "aggressive tendencies" exist in the girl as in the boy, the boy develops in a world where such behavior can be expressed in acceptable patterns. In contrast the girl can find no such channel for assertive self-expression. Instead, there is a "societal prize or bribe for renouncing" her "aggressive components." [32] Through her characterization of Eunice, Freeman explores her own attraction toward the freedom she never experienced.

In order to be loved and accepted, Eunice submits and sacrifices her own needs so that she can remain "good." But she does so unwillingly and only when her won "conscience" becomes a sort of monster. At first Ada confronts her with what she considers the harshest accusation: "It is all for yourself—yourself" (33). If Eunice continues to indulge in the affair with Burr, she cannot remain "good" in the eyes of the rest of the world. Only in self-sacrifice and

the suppression of her formerly "active" impulses can Eunice rid
herself of Ada's accusations of wickedness. Still, at first Eunice continues to rebel. She answers only an abrupt and continual "no" when
Ada begs her to give Burr up. She points out that Burr has betrayed
Ada, but again Ada persists in only seeing Eunice's aggression as a
"minister's daughter" as evil.

After her confrontation with Ada, Eunice views her own rebellion
as something fearful and monstrous. In light of the twist the story
takes as Eunice begins to withdraw from her second attempt at rebellion (the first being her refusal to marry Wilson), Jean Baker Miller's
comments on women's fear of power in *Toward a New Psychology of
Women* are fascinating: "What are the reasons women fear their own
power?" Miller asks. "In the first place, women's direct use of their
own powers in their own interests frequently brings a severely negative reaction from the man. This in itself has often been enough to
dissuade a member of a dependent group from using her own power
directly." [33] Eunice has received positive reinforcement only for serving others, remaining subservient. When she does try to use "her
own power directly," by refusing to accept a marriage that would
require utter servitude, she meets with her father's "severely negative
reaction." How has she attempted to gain some sense of power? First,
she has defended her right to refuse to be Wilson's servant-wife; but
then, having been condemned by her father, she seeks power
through Burr as her identification with his image in the mirror
scene indicates. What Eunice inevitably develops is what Miller calls
women's "exaggerated inner equation: the effective use of their own
power means that they are wrong, even destructive." As Miller explains it:

> [t]his message is conveyed to girls from early childhood, even before they
> have a chance to test it in their own lives. Is it surprising, therefore, that
> women have developed an inner sense that their effective and direct use
> of themselves must be destructive of someone else? In fact the way wom-
> en's lives are arranged, and considering the things that women are sup-
> posed to be doing for others, current reality has a good chance of seeming
> to confirm this conception for them. Acting for oneself is made to seem
> like depriving others or hurting others. [34]

Eunice becomes terrified when she begins to absorb Ada's accusations that she is destructive and hurtful. It is interesting that Freeman
places Eunice in this position as a result of her choice to love Burr

and serve herself. She casts her heroine, after all, in the role of depriving another, "hurting" Ada by feeding herself. Perhaps this tells us something about the extent to which Freeman both struggled with and understood the very "inner equation" (acting for oneself means depriving someone else) that Miller describes.

Freeman skillfully returns her heroine to the confining bedroom in which she first uncovered the seeds of Eunice's dissatisfaction. The images take us back to the old Eunice who dutifully performed her task as "good girl." Once again, she wraps herself in a shawl and once again she lies down on her bed to gaze at the familiar objects in the room. With the shawl wrapped around her, *binding* her, she begins a process of withdrawals, a return to the old restrictions which both oppressed and protected her. The contrast between this scene and the earlier bedroom scene is striking. Before her rejection of Wilson and her courtship with Burr (her two acts of rebellion), the objects in her room offered her security as well as entrapment. She "had faith" in them. Now the objects had a "strange and awful" look just as we see a "strange look" of horror on Eunice's face. Hallucination in Freeman's work is unexpectedly revealing:

> She was very pale, and there was a strange look, almost of horror, on her face. She stared, as she lay there, at all the familiar objects in the room, but the most common and insignificant of them had a strange and awful look to her. Yet the change was in herself not in them. The shadow that was over her own soul overshadowed them and perverted her vision. But she felt also almost a fear of all those inanimate objects she was gazing at. They were so many reminders of a better state with her, for she had gazed at them all in her unconscious childhood. She was sickened with horror at their dumb accusations. There was the little glass she had looked in before she had stolen another woman's dearest wealth away from her, the chair she had sat in, the bed she had lain in. (34)

The room full of objects that once reflected Eunice's passive existence and her imprisonment becomes a symbol of her alienation. Her rebellion has firmly erased the dutiful Eunice and the new rebel cannot rest safely in the room that had housed her previously submissive self. In other words, Eunice is in a state of extreme self-alienation as a result of the social ostracism she has experienced because of her rebellion.[35] What she fears in the once reassuring though confining room and all its objects are the ramifications of her new assertiveness. The objects become "reminders of a better state," a state of being that was acceptable to Ada and to the parsonage on the whole, a state of passivity. Now the objects stare back at her rebel self accusingly. She faces the loss of the socially acceptable self and the discovery is so frightening that she is moved to part with Burr. When Eunice had first gazed in the "little glass" she felt only her homeliness and the sense that no "change could be made for the better." Now that she has "stolen" Burr, she misses her state of resignation, and wants to rid herself of guilt and destroy the rebel self. She responds with horror to the self who no longer fits in this tiny room shaped only for self-sacrifice.

This story does not end with the neat, sentimental conclusion so often evident in Freeman's fiction. It is true that Eunice renounces her rebellion by taking Burr Mason to Ada's house and explaining that she has broken the engagement. But "A Moral Exigency" does not leave us with the sense that Freeman has evaded the issues she has raised. Although Freeman does have her rebel seemingly submit in the end, she does not attempt to justify or rationalize the ultimate submission, nor is the submission itself unambiguous. Out of her sense of duty, Eunice suppresses heterosexual longings by parting with Burr, but her reasons remain unclear. There is certainly some emphasis given to her deep love for Ada. She remembers their friendship at school and in the end, after her sacrifice, Eunice draws the "golden head down on her bosom." Hence, the rebellion is not completely deflated or undercut (as is sometimes the case in Freeman's depiction of rebel women in other stories), for her reversal at the end is also an act of friendship. Furthermore, there is no suggestion that Eunice will renege on her decision to reject Wilson for the sake of obedience toward her father. In effect, she achieves a compromise with herself, her father, and Ada by rejecting Wilson, but also giving up Burr. And perhaps relinquishing her hold on Burr involves some unconscious understanding that he might not have been the answer to her desires for self-fulfillment.

We are left with the sense that Eunice's choice of loving self-sacrifice is not a satisfactory answer. In this story, Freeman depicts the complexities of loving and being loved, suggesting that for women to negotiate these complexities successfully, they must suppress rebellion, stifle self-interest or even self-love. This at least is what Freeman shows us in Eunice's struggle, a struggle Freeman shared. In response to Ada's gratitude in the last scene, Eunice's last words and the final words of the story capture the dilemma in painfully ambiguous terms: " 'Love me all you can Ada,' she said, 'I want— something' " (35).[36]

"Louisa"

"Louisa" provides an interesting contrast to "A Moral Exigency." With their focus on the early choice of spinsterhood, both stories capture the range of voices Freeman's spinsters reflect. Louisa's decision to remain single, unlike Eunice's, is not a consequence of her love and protection of another woman, nor an act of self-sacrifice requiring the suppression of rebellion, nor a cause of remorse and self-doubt. On the contrary, Louisa's struggle to remain single in the face of the economic and social pressures to marry is a struggle toward self-realization, a form of rebellion in fact, and ultimately a cause for celebration. Like Eunice, Louisa rejects a suitor in favor of single life; but Louisa does so without the sense of isolation we see in Eunice. Louisa's mirror image is not shaken, nor does she feel her identity threatened by this decision.[37]

In essence, the fight to remain single strengthens Louisa's self-knowledge. Feeling no love for Jonathan Nye, the only man who is both available and financially secure in the village, but facing the alternative of hunger and poverty, Louisa persists in courageously resisting marriage. Interestingly, the greatest pressure toward marriage comes from Louisa's mother. It may be that Freeman was exploring here the painful rift she must have felt in rejecting her own mother's hopes for her. The story opens with Mrs. Britton's inability to comprehend her daughter Louisa's resistance: "I don't see what kind of ideas you've got in your head, for my part." The story's power comes in its subtle way of revealing just what ideas do rest in Louisa's head and how much it takes to be heard or understood: "She had never heard of the princess who destroyed her beauty that she might not be forced to wed the man whom she did not love, but she had something of the same feeling, although she did not have it for the sake of any tangible lover." [38] Significantly, Freeman compares Louisa with the princess who dreads the forced marriage and even longs for self-destruction in its place, but not "for the sake of any tangible lover." Although she "had never seen anybody whom she would have preferred to Jonathon Nye," Louisa celebrates the dreams she holds in her interior life. And it is to preserve those dreams that she heroically resists the guilt her mother attempts to impose upon her.

As the daughter, like Louisa, of "poor hard-working people" (394), Freeman captures in this story the link between the financial decline her own family experienced and the push toward marriage. Loving her mother and grandfather, functioning as their only source of survival, and having lost her job as a teacher, Louisa works hard planting potatoes and working in the fields. She responds without ambivalence to her mother's concerns about how this labor appears to others: "If they don't like it, they needn't look," and she reminds her mother that the work she is doing is as legitimate for a woman as for a man: "Why can't I rake hay as well as a man?" (398). Louisa's struggle to resist marriage, unlike Eunice's, is an act of rebellion rather than an act of repression or self-sacrifice. In fact, if she were to submit to her mother's wish she would then be submitting to a life of self-sacrifice. When her mother asks her to flirt with Jonathon Nye to win him back after her rejection, Louisa replies "I wouldn't do such a thing as that for a man I liked . . . and I certainly sha'n't for a man I don't like" (400). The pressure mounts as her mother cries out, "then me and your grandfather'll starve." Marrying off "the only daughter I got" is placed in the context of survival. Witnessing the near starvation of her family, though, Louisa is desperate to find some better means to save them. Asking not for money, but for food, Louisa goes to the home of her rather unfriendly uncle and is told she can take as much as she can carry.

Her journey with the heavy loads is almost unbearable, but Louisa sees it as her way out of a marriage without love or the hope of autonomy:

> She took up the bag of meal and the basket of eggs and carried them out to the gate; then she returned, got the flour and ham, and went with them to a point beyond. Then she returned for the meal and eggs, and carried them past the others. In that way she traversed the seven miles home. The heat increased. She had eaten nothing since morning but the apples that her friend had given her. Her head was swimming, but she kept on. Her resolution was as immovable under the power of the sun as a rock. Once in a while she rested for a moment under a tree, but she soon arose and went on. It was like a pilgrimage, and the Mecca at the end of the burning, desert-like road was her own maiden independence. (404)

though she too would succumb. Lucy's mother, much like Freeman's mother, sees marriage for her daughter as a protection of her "little ewe lamb," a way of being "well settled in life with someone to shield her from its storms before she herself was taken from her." Urged by her mother not to let Edsel Abbot get away, Lucy's response captures Freeman's hesitation: "I don't want to marry anybody. I don't like men. I am afraid of them. I want to stay with you" (155). Marriage will require that she part with maternal protection and this is why she most wants to resist it. But, unlike Louisa Britton, Lucy gives in to her mother's wishes.

On her wedding day, she visits the arethusa in what seems to be her "last assertion of her maiden freedom." Long after she marries and has children, however, she continues to steal away to visit the arethusa alone. The visits are equivalent to Freeman's time alone with her writing, the time she would take to continue writing fiction in her new home with Charles. Lucy's husband supports her by preventing her children from joining her on these visits, considering them a harmless indulgence. What he doesn't understand is the deeper meaning of her visits, "not dreaming that it had its root in the very depths of her nature, and that she perhaps sought this fair neutral ground of the flower kingdom as a refuge from the exigency of life." As Freeman's use of myth conveys, Lucy's visits are also efforts to recall her individuality despite her husband's view of her as his possession: "In his full tide of triumphant possession he was as far from the realization of the truth as was Alpheus, the fabled river god, after he had overtaken the nymph Arethusa, whom, changed into a fountain to elude his pursuit, he had followed under the sea, and never knew that, while forever his, even in his embrace, she was forever her own" (169). Alone with the flower, Lucy was "forever maiden" despite her marriage, forever linked to this "anomalous flower," and "forever her own."[41]

"One Good Time"

Freeman named the heroine of "One Good Time" after Narcissus. Narcissa Stone, a middle-aged spinster, is determined to serve herself with "one good time" before she finally settles into marriage. She wears a "frown like a crying repetition of some old anxiety and indecision."

When her father dies, Narcissa and her mother receive insurance money. To the dismay of the villagers who now expect her to marry William Crane, Narcissa chooses to apply the money toward a wild, good time in New York City. She explains to William her determination to defy expectations and to have an experience she knows marriage will not provide.

> "I'm going," said she—"I'm going to take that money and go with mother to New York, and you mustn't try to stop me, William. I know what you've been expecting. I know, now father's gone, you think there ain't anything to hinder our getting married; you think we'll rent this house and mother and me will settle down in yours for the rest of our lives. I know you ain't counting on that insurance money; it ain't like you."[42]

Understanding that William expects Narcissa to put the money in the bank "for a rainy day, in case mother got feeble," and knowing that this would be the responsible thing to do, Narcissa nevertheless insists upon pursuing her "one good time":

> "I ain't never done anything my whole life that I thought I ought not to do, but now I'm going to. I'm going to if it's wicked. I've made up my mind. I ain't never had one good time in my whole life, and now I'm going to, even if I have to suffer for it afterwards." (210)

Describing her life to William, Narcissa reviews a career in which she has "drudged and drudged" in her father's domain. To enter marriage immediately after his death would be to continue in the same "old tracks" of patriarchy, and she is determined "to get out of them for awhile" (210).

It is interesting that Freeman does not release Narcissa beyond this single celebration in New York. She returns to William in the end. The escape to New York, however, is an essential prelude to the marriage:

> "If I had to settle down in your house, as I have done in father's, and see the years stretching ahead like a long road without any turn, and nothing but the same old dog-trot of washing and ironing and scrubbing and cooking and sewing and washing dishes till I drop into my grave, I should hate you, William Crane." (213)

Narcissa and her mother spend more than $1,500, all of the insurance money and more. Narcissa returns to tell William the story of their escapade in elaborate detail. Staying in luxurious hotels, buying each other an array of Christmas gifts, going to the theatre, wearing extravagant clothing, attending the opera, hearing splendid music, Narcissa admits that they left New York having spent every penny of their savings and owing ten dollars to the hotel. The action was, as Josephine Donovan explains, an effort to "reject the traditional female world of love and drudgery in favor of another, more exciting world, and of new knowledge."[43] Narcissa thought of nothing but the pleasure she was deriving and enjoys telling the story of her indulgence to William. In her conclusion, however, Freeman curiously chains her freed spinster, seeing Narcissa's return to the pining William as a necessary submission to responsibility. But Narcissa's confession is an important piece of that submission, alerting Freeman's readers to exactly what marriage will destroy:

> "Well," said Narcissa, "I've come back an' I've spent all that money. I've been wasteful an' extravagant an'—There was a gentleman beautifully dressed who sat at our table, an' he talked real pleasant about the weather, an' I got to thinking about him a little. Of course I didn't like him as well as you, William, for what comes first comes last with all our folks, but somehow he seemed to be kind of a part of the good time. I sha'n't never see him again, an' all there was betwixt us was his saying twice it was a pleasant day, an' once it was cold, an' me saying yes; but I'm going to tell you the whole. I've been an' wasted fifteen hundred dollars; I've let my thoughts wander from you; an' that ain't all. I've had a good time, an' I can't say I ain't. I've had one good time, an'—I ain't sorry. You can—do just what you think best, William an'—I won't blame you." (232–34)

Narcissa speaks of her "good time" without apology and seems to relive the joy of her rebellion in her description to William. Yet Freeman's conclusion is an example of that "undecidability" to which Elizabeth Meese refers. While the "one good time" was essential to Narcissa's developing understanding of her own need for self-fulfillment, a wonderful description of spinsterly rebellion at its best, her submission in the end cannot be overlooked. When William remains loyal and simply asks if she "can be contented" to remain with him, Narcissa responds, "I wouldn't go out again if the bars were down." With her arm around his neck, Narcissa binds herself to William and describes the life she will lead in images of imprisonment with bars, up or down, through which she will not pass again. In "One Good Time," Freeman manages to express both the voice that longs for sheer self-indulgent and excessive pleasure and the voice that accepts the expectations of conventional womanly submission and self-denial. Her conclusion leaves readers with almost the same ambivalence we hear when Eunice says to Ada, "I want—something."

"Christmas Jenny"

In "Christmas Jenny," Jenny Wrayne defines herself against rather than within the context of male values. As Josephine Donovan explains, much of Jenny's self-fulfillment stems from her protection and care of wild animals which have been injured by the traps men set, the "mechanized masculine operations that destroy that natural life with which . . . women identify." [44] Jenny is an autonomous aging spinster who owns a home and a few acres of land on a mountaintop overlooking the village. She is set apart from the rest of the community in many ways. When rumors spread in the village that Jenny is "love-cracked," having been in love with a man who married someone else, her only close friend replies: "I know one thin'—if she did git kind of twisted out of the reg'lar road of lovin', she's in another one, that's full of little dumbies an starvin' chippies an' lame rabbits, an' she ain't love-cracked no more'n other folks." Redefining love then, in matriarchal terms, Jenny chooses an alternative to the "reg'lar road of lovin' " by loving creatures of nature instead of a husband. Freeman's physical description of Jenny is a celebration of her unity with the natural environment: "She made one think of those sylvan faces with features composed of bark-wrinkles and knot-holes that one can fancy out of the trunks of trees. She was not an aged woman, but her hair was iron-gray, and crinkled as closely as gray moss." [45] The source of Jenny's autonomy, in fact, is nature itself. Jenny comes down from her mountain abode to sell evergreen trees and wreaths in the winter and vegetables in the summer.

> The woman looked oddly at a distance like a broad green moving bush; she was dragging something green after her, too. When she came nearer one could see long sprays of ground-pine were wound around her shoulders, she carried a basket trailing with them, and holding also many little bouquets of bright-colored everlasting flowers. She dragged a sled, with a small hemlock-tree bound upon it. She came along sturdily over the slippery road. (163)

With this first image of Jenny, Freeman conveys womanly strength all bound up in Jenny's link to nature, with "ground-pine wound around her shoulders," and the ability to walk "sturdily" on the icy road that most are unable to travel.

Freeman analyzes through Jenny, as Barbara Johns has noted, "the notion of the spinster as mystic, a person so misunderstood by her society that she is considered strange, yet so united with the universe that she is capable of profoundly influencing two of society's most unyielding institutions, marriage and the church." Jenny's influence on the married couple down the road is fascinating. The Careys "represent a nineteenth-century marriage in which the woman has internalized all the features of the 'cult of true womanhood.' "[46] Jenny helps Mrs. Carey transform her domesticity into a form of power, and her husband's tantrums subside once Jenny teaches Mrs. Carey the use of strategy. Ignoring Mr. Carey's imperiousness, Jenny has Mrs. Carey enjoy the feasts she prepares without beckoning her whining husband to the table to participate. Jenny's "sensitivity, power, and self-sufficiency" transfers to Betsey Carey, the married friend, and in this way Freeman shows that "women united can go on to resist whatever institution attempts to keep them in their place."[47]

Freeman's analysis of the effect of the eccentric Jenny on her community is superb. Blind to the meaning or beauty of Jenny's world, the villagers alert the minister and Deacon Little to the rumor that Jenny mistreats the animals she has caged in her home and a deaf boy who lives with her. Their visit to Jenny's home is reminiscent of other visits from members of the church to the homes of "odd" or unacceptable elderly spinsters in Freeman's stories. More than any other story, however, "Christmas Jenny" captures the injustice of the stigma and the possibility of surmounting community prejudice. When the minister and Deacon Little come to Jenny's home, their visit is an invasion into what Freeman calls "sacred space."

When they arrive at Jenny's "curious sylvan" abode, the men immediately upset the images of nature surrounding Jenny: "They started up a flock of sparrows that were feeding by Jenny's door; but the birds did not fly very far—they settled into a tree and watched" (169). It is as though these creatures are connected to Jenny and are there to protect her from this intrusion. When the men enter her home, they "could not see anything at first." Their inability to see has many levels. They are blinded by the contrast of moving from the "brilliant light outside" to the darkness of Jenny's "weather-beaten hut," and they are equally unable to see the principles her home represents. When their eyes fall upon the deaf boy who "looked up in their faces with an expression of delicate wonder and amusement," they notice without comprehension that "he is dressed like a girl, in a long blue gingham pinafore," and sits "in the midst of a heap of evergreens, which he had been twining into wreaths; his pretty, soft, fair hair was damp, and lay in a very flat and smooth scallop over his full white forehead" (169–70). Noting that he looks "well cared for," they still cannot, as Johns clarifies, "envision the boy as an embodiment of Jenny's values, or as a sign of the unity that makes Jenny, the forest, the house, and he himself inseparable, indivisible. The boy's 'wild and inarticulate' cry, united with the cries of the caged creatures, is 'like a soft clamor of eloquent appeal to the two visitors.' But it is futile. The men cannot understand what they see and simply stand 'solemn and perplexed.' "[48] Perhaps what is most disturbing to these representatives of the community is Jenny's satisfaction in her spinsterhood, the fact that she has defined new connections, new possibilities of self-fulfillment through her tie with nature, with a boy, with a married woman down the road, and through the economic independence she has won by selling her goods. This elderly woman living alone cares for others rather than requiring that others care for her, and her home, strange as it seems to the men, is a home that represents her strength rather than her weakness.

Betsey Carey gives voice to the story which the men are so incapable of interpreting, becoming, in essence, Jenny's tongue: She tells the men, "I ain't goin' to have you comin' up here to spy on Jenny, an' nobody to home that's got any tongue to speak for her" (171). Betsey is the translator. Standing before them "like a ruffled and defiant bird that was frighting them as well as herself with her temerity," she sums up the beauty of Jenny: "I dunno but what bein' a missionary to robins an' starvin' chippies an' little deaf-an'-dumb children is jest as good as some other kinds, an' that's what she is" (172). Freeman's reference to a "witch-hunt" in this story is significant. "It was a witch-hunt that went up the mountain road that December afternoon" (174). Determined to dispel the myths that yield "witch-hunts" and render self-sufficient single women the equivalent of witches because they have not conformed, Freeman celebrates Jenny's world through the voice of the conventional and once-passive Mrs. Carey. Together, Jenny and Betsey Carey overthrow the judgments of the church, the community, and the world in which marriage is the only acceptable path for women.

The deacon and minister "retreat" quickly and apologetically, with praise for Jenny's generous spirit. They send her a turkey for Christmas, the turkey that Betsey and Jenny eat together at the end of the story. In Johns's words, the two women have "transcended together the pettiness and the narrowness of a church which sits in judgment of women, which twists charity into abnormality or perversity; and they have transcended a culture which prescribes that there is only one 'reg'lar road of lovin.' "[49] The meal the women share at the end is a bonding of kindred spirits, and the spinster's life has played a crucial role in that of the married woman. Together, they have confronted male institutions and transcended the witch-hunt. In this way Freeman offers a subversive vision of women in nineteenth-century New England.[50]

Freeman's subversion in "Christmas Jenny" is quite remarkable. She creates, through the colossal figure of the spinster, a mythic, matriarchal power capable of radically reversing the power structure itself. The maternal values so evident in Jenny's approach to the animals, the boy, the married couple, the entire community in fact, are invested with uncanny power. In "The Great Goddess in New England: Mary Wilkins Freeman's Sister Jenny," Sarah Sherman argues convincingly that Christmas Jenny is "a Virgin Mary radically redefined." Through an analysis of the Christian and mythic imagery in the story, Sherman demonstrates that with her knowledge of the language of the animals (similar to Saint Francis's, or Adam's before the Fall), Jenny is a "prelapsarian Mother," that she is in essence a "Great Goddess" figure, the "archetypal shadow of maternity itself."[51]

Having never married or given birth, the spinster is here redefined, able to enjoy the pleasures of motherhood without the burdens of domestic entrapment and subjugation; furthermore, this new concept of maternity reverses the concept of deprivation. We do not see a spinster who is hungry for love and motherhood. It is Mrs. Carey's husband who is hungry for more than a Christmas dinner at the end of the story. He comes to the table with "sober dignity," and

Freeman has him smile at the boy who Jenny has taken into her home, the feminized male child. The story suggests that an entire community must be attentive to the wisdom of the spinster.

"Lombardy Poplar"

Extending her subversion still further, Freeman allows Sarah Dunn, her spinster heroine in "Lombardy Poplar," to assert her differentness, to distinguish herself from her community through her association with the much-criticized tree that stands majestically in front of her house. Her cousin's critique of the "old popple-tree" is similar to critiques of the aging spinster:

> "It just stays, stiff and pointed, as if it was goin' to make a hole in the sky; don't give no shade worth anything; don't seem to have much to do with the earth and folks, anyhow. I was thankful when I got mine cut down. Them three that was in front of our house were always an eyesore to me, and I talked till I got father to cut them down. I always wondered why you hung on to this one so." [52]

Sarah Dunn begins to know the meaning of her own life as a spinster in a community that requires conformity as she listens to her cousin's attack on this tree "that ain't a tree," that she calls "a stick tryin' to look like one." It is not unlike the attack on women who choose to remain single and are accused of not being women, not serving any purpose, like the shadeless poplar tree. The phallic suggestion in her cousin's description of the tree that "just stays, stiff and pointed, as if it was goin' to make a hole in the sky" is interesting when considering Sarah's ultimate identification with the tree. The sexual reference here is of the phallus, detached from association with reproduction, bare sexuality that makes "a hole in the sky" but goes nowhere, produces nothing.

> "That's why I like it," replied Sarah Dunn, with a high lift of her head. She gave a look of sharp resentment at her cousin. Then she gazed at the tree again, and her whole face changed indescribably. She seemed like another person. The tree seemed to cast a shadow of likeness over her. She appeared straighter, taller; all her lines of meek yielding, or scarcely even anything so strong as yielding, of utter passiveness, vanished. She looked stiff and uncompromising. Her mouth was firm, her chin high, her eyes steady, and, more than all, there was over her an expression of

individuality which had not been there before. "That's why I like the popple," said she, in an incisive voice. "That's just why. I'm sick of things and folks that are just like everything and everybody else. I'm sick of trees that are just trees. I like one that ain't." (149)

After their exchange, Sarah begins to recognize the beauty of being a woman who is unlike the traditional women of the village. She soon comes to church dressed unlike any other woman, particularly unlike her cousin who had taken to wearing all of her twin's clothing once the twin had died. "No Dunn had ever worn, within the memory of man, any colors save purple and black and faded green or drab, never any but purple or white or black flowers in her bonnet. No woman of half her years, and seldom a young girl, was ever seen in the village clad in red. Even the old minister hesitated a second in his discourse and recovered himself with a hem of embarrassment when Sarah entered the meeting house" (164). Sarah deliberately "sails in" after the sermon has begun, challenging all codes of acceptability in her "shimmer of red silk" and "toss of pink flowers." Like her poplar tree, dressed in the most uncharacteristic dress, Sarah celebrates difference. Dressed in the color of sexual passion, Sarah is linked again to the poplar tree, for she is an image of sexuality, acceptable for bachelors but not for spinsters, detached from associations with marriage and consequent reproduction.

Sarah's need for self-realization and individuation within a narrow community is something Freeman understood only too well. It is the need that writing filled for Freeman. She wrote about this need in the context of defying conventional dress codes with her reference to writing as an opportunity to earn "money with which to buy a French hat."[53] Jenny Wrayne and Sarah Dunn serve as examples of Freeman's fierce need for independence, although they finally do live within the codes of their community. In each story, the community response to the individuality of the spinster is an outlet for Freeman's rage at the narrowness of her own community whose vision of "unattached" women negated the possibility that these women lived rich inner and outer lives that transcended the confines of the village.

Freeman's effort to define the experience of spinsterhood in her fiction intensified and became, in some sense, more outwardly rebellious after her marriage to Charles Freeman. "The Selfishness of

Amelia Lamkin" and "Old Maid Aunt," both published in 1907, are good examples of the degree to which her unfortunate marriage seemed to give her, in retrospect, the insight necessary to more clearly define the value of spinsterhood. In these works, more so than in her earlier stories, Freeman chose to use nineteenth-century marriage and the associated context of the "cult of true womanhood" as an index for comparison, a means of better understanding the choice of spinsterhood. Both stories set the "old maid" in the family beside conventional images of wife and mother.

"The Selfishness of Amelia Lamkin"

In "The Selfishness of Amelia Lamkin," Freeman offered a painful portrait of the "true woman" as wife and mother who sacrifices self in order to serve those she loves. As Barbara Welter explains:

> The woman in the "Cult of True Womanhood" presented by the women's magazines, gift annuals and religious literature of the nineteenth century was the hostage in the home. In a society where values changed frequently, where fortunes rose and fell with frightening rapidity, where social and economic mobility provided instability as well as hope, one thing at least remained the same: a true woman was a true woman, wherever she was found. . . . the attributes of True Womanhood by which a woman judged herself and was judged by her husband, her neighbors and society could be divided into four cardinal virtues—piety, purity, submissiveness and domesticity. Put them all together and they spelled mother, daughter, sister, wife—woman.[54]

Amelia's life helps clarify the intensity of Narcissa's need for that "one good time" before marriage. The spinster in this story is immediately set in contrast to the married Amelia:

> Nobody pitied Amelia Lamkin, least of all her own family. She had always waited upon them and obliterated herself to that extent that she seemed scarcely to have a foothold at all upon the earth, but to balance timidly upon the extreme edge of existence. Now and then Amelia's unmarried sister, Jane Strong, visited the Lamkins, and always expressed her unsolicited opinion.[55]

Jane's world is entirely self-directed, while her sister focuses only on the lives of others. Unlike some of the spinsters in Freeman's earlier work, Jane fully recognizes the advantages of single life and does not long for an Amelia-like existence. At the thought of marriage, Jane expresses satisfaction in her single state rather than envy: " 'Of course you know,' said Jane, 'that I'm enough sight better off the way I am. I'm freer than any married woman in the world. Then I've kept my looks. My figure is just as good as it ever was, and my hair's just as thick and not a thread of gray' " (129–30). Jane is the first in the family to recognize Amelia's self-immolation. She observes and criticizes Amelia's patterns which include serving nutritious food to her family while starving herself. Attempting to conform to the image of the "true woman" and the associated ways of expressing love, Amelia comes close to complete self-destruction. As Lee Chambers-Schillers points out, "Amelia Lamkin's spinster sister Jane had seen and analyzed Amelia's fault but did not, as an earlier maiden aunt would have, step in to reorganize the household and reorient its values. Jane tasked herself with her own selfishness, her preference for her 'easy, unhampered life in her nice, little apartment.' " [56]

In this story, Freeman's duality again emerges; although she celebrates the superiority of Jane's choice of spinsterhood, she also has Jane guiltily express misgivings when Amelia faints away from overwork.

> "Lord!" she said, "What on earth have I been thinking about? I knew Amelia was overworked. What was to hinder my coming here at least half the year and taking some of the burden off her? I knew Addie was young, and Annie none too strong, and Josiah fussy, like all men. Why didn't I come? . . . You've made a nice mess of it, Jane Strong! Instead of snooping around to find the sins of other folks, you'd better have looked at home." (158)

Her story is essentially an attack on the concept of the "cult of true womanhood." But, paradoxically, Jane's regret and self-recrimination is also an expression of the voice of the "true woman." Freeman joins in the condemnation by giving these words of self-laceration credibility. At the same time, she renders Jane helpless to lift the family out of the crisis by having her slip and sprain her ankle in her one effort to offer physical assistance. Jane manages to remain free of the burdens of family obligation and, because of her incompetence, she is able to return to the "unhampered life." The title of the story indicates that selfless mothering such as Amelia's is, in fact, selfish for it incapacitates all other family members, determines their utter helplessness in the face of a crisis. Since so much of the story dwells on the horrors of Amelia's self-abnegation, the story becomes an indirect testimony to spinsterhood and its benefits, a context for understanding the preference for unmarried life.[57]

"Old Maid Aunt"

Freeman defined the spinster's life and its advantages still more effectively when she wrote her contribution to *The Whole Family,* an experimental collaborative novel by twelve authors. Freeman's "Old Maid Aunt" was the second chapter; it followed William Dean Howells's patriarchal opening chapter, not surprisingly entitled "The Father." Although as a whole, the project was an aesthetic failure, Freeman's rebellious portrait of spinsterhood offered one of the liveliest and most appealing chapters in the novel, and it caused quite an outrage. Like "The Selfishness of Amelia Lamkin," she wrote "Old Maid Aunt" during her marriage to Charles. It remains one of the best works of this period.

Howells's original conception of the novel was of a "realistic portrait of a typical American family" with the engagement of a young woman in the family as the unifying link among chapters. Each contributor was to write a chapter focusing on one member of the family. Following his chapter on the father, Howells had planned that the chapter that would logically follow would be "The Mother." Freeman turned things topsy turvy. Alfred Bendixen's summary in his introduction to *The Whole Family* is useful:

> And then along came Mary E. Wilkins Freeman. She clearly felt the need to start the plot moving, to give the story some momentum. She had a great deal of respect and admiration for Howells, but apparently his remarks on women in the first chapter, particularly his treatment of the old-maid aunt, irritated her. Freeman felt that Howells's conception of the aunt was based on outdated values that condemned a single woman in her thirties to an eternal and dowdy spinsterhood.[58]

Howells's brief reference to Lily Talbert in his first chapter reveals the social attitudes that may have driven Freeman to marry Charles; in the words of the neighbor-narrator, Miss Talbert "had long been a lady of that age when ladies begin to be spoken of as maidens. . . . From the general impression in Eastridge we gathered that Miss Talbert was not without the disappointment which endears maiden ladies to the imagination . . ." (19). Howells also makes reference to

Lily's frequent travels, a reference Freeman expands upon considerably in her effort to transform Lily into a boldly sensual and liberated single woman. After reading Howells's chapter, Freeman decided to revolutionize the novel by making Lily a major rather than a minor character. Freeman disrupts the conservative peace of the family by allowing Peggy's fiancé to express his passionate love for Lily, the "old maid," rather than for her young and eligible niece. She thus creates a spinster whose life is enviable rather than pitiful and who mocks the dull stability of her brother's world.

Freeman wrote "Old Maid Aunt" in the first person, and Lily Talbert's voice combines the full range of emotions Freeman associated with the experience of spinsterhood. The aunt speaks from the start with the self-awareness and authority that few of Freeman's other spinsters demonstrated. The opening paragraph immediately establishes Lily as rebel and anomaly:

> I am relegated here in Eastridge to the position in which I suppose I properly belong, and I dare say it is for my best spiritual and temporal good. Here I am the old-maid aunt. Not a day, not a minute, when I am with other people, passes that I do not see myself in their estimation playing the role as plainly as if I saw myself in a looking-glass. It is a moral lesson which I presume I need. . . . Since—well, never mind since what time—I have not cared an iota whether I was considered an old maid or not. The situation has seemed to me rather amusing, inasmuch as it has involved a secret willingness to be what everybody has considered me as very unwilling to be. I have regarded it as a sort of joke on other people. (30)

Accepting the role of the "old maid" as if performing before a distorted mirror, Lily admits to the game of playing a joke on her society. Her "secret willingness," her pleasure in the single life, is what she conceals—and yet she never conceals her sexuality, her "womanly pride," her subtle mockery of those who expect her to be "very unwilling" to remain a spinster.

Freeman's portrayal of Lily defies the stereotype that Howells's version of Lily suggests. Lily is vibrant, dynamic, attractive, energetic, witty, passionate, and wise. All the men are drawn to her and all the women come to envy her seeming indifference to masculine attention, her knowledge of her own strengths, her sophistication. Commenting on the ignorance of members of her family, Lily notes, "they do not know that today an old maid aunt is as much of an anomaly as a spinning wheel, that she has ceased to exist, that she is prehistoric. In short, they do not know that I am not an old maid aunt except under this blessed mansard roof" (33). Lily clarifies that the unhappiness, the asexuality, the lifelessness once associated with the spinster at the spinning wheel no longer applies. As so many of Freeman's portrayals of spinsters suggest, a powerful sexuality exists beneath the surface mask of delicate gentility, of lilacs and gardens and orderly bureau drawers. Lily releases the sexuality fully, enjoying her rebellion against social expectations and her pleasure in self-love.

Using dress code as another index for her rebellion, Lily recognizes that "they all unanimously consider that I should dress always in black silk, and a bonnet with a neat little tuft of middle-aged violets, and black ribbons tied under my chin." Instead, "knowing I am wicked," Lily wears a bright pink gown and hat and enjoys imagining "how they will stare when I go down!" (45). And they do stare, shocked by the sight of a spinster with a parasol lined in pink. Taking considerable delight in her rebellion, Lily confides, "if I had been Godiva, going for my sacrificial ride through the town, it could not have been much worse" (45).

Given the degree of Lily's rebellion, it is puzzling to find once again a clear expression of Freeman's duality. Despite her "secret willingness" and enjoyment of single life, Lily Talbert does betray ambivalence. She admits she is not wholly contented: "I have remained in tact—I have always grasped all the minor sweets of life, even if I could not have the really big worthwhile ones. I honestly do not think that I have had the latter. But I don't feel if I can't have what I want most, I will have nothing" (33).

Freeman's chapter conveys the idea that Lily's "minor sweets of life" have surpassed the sweets available to the married or soon-to-be married women in the novel. Nevertheless, Lily admits that she has not had what she "wants most." Whatever the "really big worthwhile" sweets are, Lily senses that they are not available to the spinster. Freeman has her heroine internalize the view that she cannot have the most important pleasures of life without marriage. Like Jane Lennox in Freeman's unfinished story, Lily seems to give space to the notion that to remain single is to miss the worthy, "decent" life.

Freeman was unable to leave Lily in a state of unambivalent gratification. Lily faces a moral dilemma when she discovers that her niece's fiancé is passionately in love with her. This situation triggers old memories. Lily recalls an earlier love that ended over a silly quarrel with the young man whom she would have been likely to marry. She also remembers a second lover, Ned Temple, who still professes his love for her even after his marriage to another woman. These memories leave Lily with the regret we have seen in other Freeman stories. Recognizing that "nothing has really mattered since I was about Peggy's age and Lyman Wilde . . . vanished into thin air," Lily expresses an awareness of what she has missed:

> I have what is left to me—the little things of life, the pretty effects which go to make me pretty (outside Eastridge); the comforts of civilization, travelling and seeing beautiful things, also seeing ugly things to enhance the beautiful. I have pleasant days in beautiful Florence. I have friends. I have everything except—well, except everything. That I must do without. I will do without it gracefully, with never a whimper, or I don't know myself. (47)

This expression of loss suggests that Freeman's spinster, even at her most rebellious, has missed the imagined "everything" that marriage would have offered. In this chapter, however, Freeman reverses this expectation even as she gives Lily these regressive thoughts. It is obvious that Lily has more of "everything" than her married counterparts. The "little things" she enjoys become larger than life when set beside the trivial world of the wives in Freeman's chapter. Lily looks at the jealousy of Mrs. Temple, for example, and celebrates her own freedom: "I was disgusted and sorry and furious at the same time. I cannot imagine myself making such a spectacle over any mortal man" (53). Lily emerges as a woman superior to the married women in the novel and capable of moral superiority as well. To protect Peggy's feelings, for example, she conceals from her the fact that her young fiancé is unimaginably in love with an "old maid."

Lily returns to a life free of the ties that bind and bars that block the "good time" that Narcissa pursues before marriage. Whatever Lily feels she has missed, it does not seem to be life bound to any man. While she feels "the best lamp of life went out" years ago, Lily does not specifically refer to marriage or even an individual man as the thing that is missing. Freeman's ambiguity here is significant. Lily plays the role of "old maid aunt" as though mocking society, as if watching herself going through ludicrous paces in a looking glass. She is aware of the misconception others have of her life and rejects it with laughter. Finally, Lily is proud of having control over her own destiny, unlike the other women in Freeman's chapter, and she recognizes her powers: "I have had much womanly pride, and that is a powerful tonic" (34).

William Dean Howells, Henry van Dyke, and other contributors wrote to the editor of the novel, Elizabeth Jordan, in shocked dismay after reading Freeman's chapter. Their responses clarify all that Freeman was up against. Although it would seem that attitudes toward unmarried women had improved by the early twentieth century, these reactions indicate otherwise. Freeman was forced to defend her portrayal of Lily Talbert, and in this sense she began to define more clearly her understanding of the unmarried life she now remembered and missed.

Transforming the passive figure of Miss Talbert in Howells's chapter into what Bendixen calls "the moving force behind the novel," Freeman enraged Howells. All that was predictable in the Howells chapter became unpredictable in Freeman's hands. Peggy's fiancé, a young man, became hopelessly infatuated with the "old maid." Even Howells's calm and stately narrator, Ned Temple, who mentions Lily Talbert with considerable pity and then dismisses her from his mind in the first chapter, now reveals his passion for Lily as the woman he wished he could have married. The editor, Elizabeth Jordan, who was forty and herself unmarried, rejoiced in Freeman's chapter, although she had to face the battle that followed. Jordan admitted that Freeman's chapter was "the explosion of a bombshell on our literary hearthstone."[59] The men's reactions to Freeman's chapter matched the very prejudices that Freeman's chapter exposed. "Heavens!" responded Henry van Dyke "what a catastrophe! Who would have thought that the maiden aunt would go mad in the second chapter? Poor lady. Red hair and a pink hat and boys in beau-knots all over the costume. What *will* Mr. Howells say?" (xxii). Bendixen explores Howells's response in some detail. Howells despised Freeman's chapter and asked that Jordan eliminate it: "Don't, *don't* let her ruin our beautiful story!" (xxii). Jordan felt that Freeman's chapter gave the novel "the push it needed for cumulative interest" and she liked Freeman's transformation of the spinster character (xxiv). She commented that Howells "took the decision like the scholar and gentleman he was; but he let me see that he thought the novel was wrecked and that he himself lay buried among the ruins" (xxiv).

As Bendixen explains, Howells's rage is at least partly directed at his loss of control over the direction of the novel which, to his mind, "had been demolished." But the rage went still deeper, to the core of prejudice Freeman was attempting to uncover. Freeman's letters to Jordan indicate how far she had come, how ready she now was to assert the value of autonomy in women's lives and the advantages she saw in the unmarried life she had left. The first letter she wrote to Jordan summing up her efforts in "Old Maid Aunt" describes the effort it took to stir things up with a portrait of Lily that would reverse the suggestions of the first chapter:

> You would have received my chapter before this but it was more work than I had anticipated. I began to realize that I must start some action or plot, or rather indicate a plot, and at the same time not diverge from Mr. Howells's character description. It was quite a task. . . . To tell the truth such an innovation in the shape of a maiden aunt rather frightened me, but the old conception of her was so hackneyed. . . . I did think some plot ought to be started—and I could see no other way.[60]

Using the need to develop a plot as her excuse, Freeman revealed that it was the "hackneyed" portrait of the maiden aunt that she felt compelled to transform. It is not surprising that she described feeling somewhat "frightened" by the transformation, since this was the first spinster she had created in direct response to the stigma that had been promoted by established writers such as Howells. It took great courage, self-possession, and determination to submit that chapter and resist the revisions suggested by Howells.

Freeman's next letter to Jordan demonstrates how far she had come in her developing understanding of the rebel spinster. Her tone is no longer apologetic and in no way suggests that the need for plot determined her creation of the transformed Lily Talbert. Instead, for the first time and in the midst of recognizing the difficulties of her marriage, she succinctly defines the modern single woman:

> Mr. Howells evidently clings to the old conception of her [the old maid]. You and I know that in these days of voluntary celibacy on the part of women an old maid only fifteen years older than a young girl is a sheer impossibility, if she is an educated woman with a fair amount of brains. Moreover, a young man is really more apt to fall in love with her. . . . At this minute I can think of a score of women who fifty years ago would have carried out Mr. Howells's idea of the old maid aunt. To-day they look

as pretty and as up-to-date as their young nieces—and no pretense about it, either. They really *are*. Their single state is deliberate choice on their own part, and men are at their feet. Single women have caught up with, and passed, old bachelors in the last half of the century.

I don't think Mr. Howells realizes this. He is thinking of the time when women of thirty put on caps, and renounced the world. That was because they married at fifteen and sixteen, and at thirty had about a dozen children. Now they simply do not do it. Peggy was twenty, and her aunt thirty-four. It is obvious nonsense to make it impossible that a man should fall in love with Elizabeth, and that she should still be beautiful. . . . Suppose Peggy was even considerably older; the possibility, even probability, remains that the aunt would still have the advantage.[61]

Freeman's defense of her chapter is an attack on the misconceptions that burdened her own "maidenhood." She celebrates not only the "new woman" as defined by her portrait of Lily, but also the aging woman whose beauty, sexuality, and desirability surpasses that of any young niece. Dismissing the outdated conception as "obvious nonsense," Freeman's tone fully shifts from her earlier apologies to aggressive confrontation; here she comes as close as she ever would to matching Susan B. Anthony's description in 1877 of the single woman as a model for all women to emulate. At the time of Anthony's statement, Freeman was twenty-five, already living with the spinster stereotype, but not yet ready to recognize the truth of Anthony's words. Although she was far too conflicted throughout her lifetime to become active in the early feminist movement, Freeman's words to Jordan in 1906 reflect her growing understanding of spinsterhood in radical terms. Dismissing the objections of her male readers, she even attributes "the whole freshness and novelty of the book to my conception of that part." [62] Her letter exposes and rejects the cultural stereotyping of the spinster or old maid and offers a feminist analysis of the importance of "the deliberate choice" women may make of "the single state."

4

SEXUAL POLITICS IN *PEMBROKE*

∞

She meekly lived her quiet days,
They knew no difference in her guise,
But while she drew her breath of life,
The stranger's look was in her eyes.

Mary Wilkins Freeman, "The Stranger"

IN MUCH OF her short fiction, Freeman wrote about the degree to which heterosexual relationships in the nineteenth century threatened the possibility of autonomy in women's lives. She turned to the genre of the novel to explore the complexity of female sexuality and the politics of patriarchy. Her novels *Pembroke* and *Madelon* portray society's restrictive attitudes toward women's efforts to express sexuality and the consequent effects of sexual repression. The intricate network of lovers in both novels and the implications of their separations and marriages suggest Freeman's perspective on issues of gender in surprisingly radical terms. Both novels have layers of unexpected meaning in subtle moments in women's kitchens, in the words or faces of lovers and friends engaged in simple activities: baking pies, picking cherries, sitting on a sofa in the parlor. As Deborah Lambert explains in her perceptive essay, "Rereading Mary Wilkins Freeman: Autonomy and Sexuality in *Pembroke*," the "quest . . . of marriage, independence, sexuality, and female power occurs within town boundaries and substitutes for a journey west or down the Mississippi." Thinking in these terms, it becomes possible to read Freeman's novels beside the novels of her male contemporaries

Mark Twain and Henry James and to evaluate them in terms of "the complex meaning of everyday things in women's quests," to "decode" by moving beyond traditional male definitions of what constitutes meaning.[1]

In these novels Freeman developed still further what she had experimented with in "A Moral Exigency." Characters look at each other in distorted mirrors, continually reflecting their opposites in haunting patterns of aggression and submission. Freeman's main characters are mirrored by polar opposites: repressed, passive, socially acceptable characters at one extreme and socially unacceptable, sexually aggressive characters at the other. In both novels, Freeman's creation of psychological doubles reflects her own conflict between feminine rebellion and passivity. Freeman's self-division about the expression of sexuality is connected to her recognition of a fundamental dilemma in the lives of women in the nineteenth century: a single woman who expressed sexual desire would become an object of censure if she remained unmarried, or she would attract a man into marriage. The latter fate inevitably required tolerating the oppressive politics of marriage which rendered women relatively powerless and men ignorant of their worth.

Freeman was forty-two and still unmarried when she wrote *Pembroke* in 1893. She had met Charles Freeman in 1892, which was the same year she learned that Hanson Tyler had gotten married in California. Up to this point, clinging to the hoped-for return of Tyler was Freeman's protection against more attainable marriage. The novel was written during her period of conscious resistance to the very real possibility that now arose, that of marrying Charles Freeman. Leading an autonomous life in her partnership with Mary Wales while recognizing the temptation of marriage to Charles Freeman, she approached the subjects of marriage and spinsterhood almost therapeutically in *Pembroke*. Freeman's conflict between unconventionality and conformity was never more intense than in this transitional period before her marriage to Dr. Freeman. Her decision to live with Wales in 1883 can be interpreted as a decision to, as Lambert speculates, find a "wife" rather than become one. Wales took care of all of the daily tasks that might have interfered with Freeman's productivity, protected her from intrusion, provided her with a work space of her own and steady emotional support. Her discomfort, however, with the label of spinster is apparent both in her letters and in her short works. Freeman frequently clarified her desire to "establish her credentials as a conventionally feminine woman."[2] There is evidence in her many letters of dismay over her appearance in photographs, her weight, her age.[3] Being cared for rather than caring for a husband and child, Freeman worked hard at presenting an acceptable public image that might conceal the fact that she was living a life "more 'masculine' than 'feminine.' "[4] Her attraction to the masculine life seemed a strong preference, but she was also acutely conscious that her failure to marry was a failure to follow the prescribed path for women. Given this tug, it is not surprising that she hesitated so long before marrying Charles Freeman—a total of nine years from the time she met him. Writing *Pembroke* seems to have been Freeman's way of voicing both the fear of and the need for a heterosexual partnership.

Freeman's "Introductory Sketch" for *Pembroke* suggests her understanding of the limitations she had observed in the New England village, limitations that shaped the experience of those who longed to love, longed for autonomy, and at the same time, needed to cling to established codes of acceptability:

> There is often to a mind from the outside world an almost repulsive narrowness and a pitiful sordidness which amounts to tragedy in the lives of such people as those portrayed in *Pembroke*, but quite generally the tragedy exists only in the comprehension of the observer and not at all in that of the observed. The pitied would meet pity with resentment; they would be full of wonder and wrath if told that their lives were narrow, since they have never seen the limit of the breadth of their current of daily life. . . . Though the standard of taste of the simple villagers, and their complete satisfaction therewith, may reasonably be lamented, as also their restricted view of life, they are not to be pitied, generally speaking, for their unhappiness in consequence. It may be that the lack of unhappiness constitutes the real tragedy.[5]

Recognizing the "tragedy in the lives of such people," Freeman was the "observer," both inside and outside the world she described. The additional layer of tragedy Freeman saw was the lack of awareness of the New Englanders she observed, their unconscious acquiescence to a "restricted view of life" which hampered their ability to express love and to be loved. She must have known that the restrictions to which she referred played a part in her own unhappiness, but she suggested that having these insights is somehow less tragic than

being unaware. In a sense, her ability to write about restricted lives
was therapeutic, her way of coming to terms with the narrowness
that shaped her own upbringing and her conception of herself as a
woman.

Pembroke is based on an actual incident in Freeman's mother's
family.[6] Because it was one of those family stories that is repeated
through the generations, Mary heard it for the first time as a child.
The house which the Wilkins family inhabited in Randolph had
been built by Mary's mother's father, Barnabas Lothrop, for his son
Barnabas Junior. Barnabas (the model for Barney Thayer in the
novel) was to marry Mary Thayer, but after a political argument with
Mary Thayer's father, Barnabas was ordered out of the house forever.
Neither man would yield and Mr. Thayer demanded that the match
be called off. Mary Thayer submitted to her father's will; Barnabas
left town and the unfinished house remained empty for ten years.
Barnabas finally gave the house to Freeman's parents, Eleanor and
Warren. Time after time, Eleanor would explain the stubbornness of
the two men to Mary as simply "their way," but this was precisely
what Freeman saw as the tragedy. Most disturbing to her was the
irreversible separation of the lovers. Gripped by the knowledge that
the home she had occupied had its origins in denial and unconsum-
mated love, Freeman was haunted as well by the reality that the
direction of a woman's life could be determined by the will of men,
by "their way." The family legend summed up the injustices of patriarchy in the silence of the daughter, Mary Thayer, whose future was
determined by her father and fiancé. With great subtlety, in the
kitchens and parlors of *Pembroke*, Freeman created an arena for the
silenced voices of women like Mary Thayer.

Revisiting her family history, Freeman brought the same basic
plot, full of the frustrations of thwarted love, to a significantly different conclusion. She refused to allow the separation of the lovers to
be final. Instead, she was determined to have them overcome the
obstacles of patriarchy. It is interesting, as Marjorie Pryse suggests,
that Freeman added a subtle twist to her own family history by changing the name of her uncle, Barnabas Lothrop to Barnabas Thayer. It
is as though "he has not only married Mary Thayer but also taken
her name as his own." Perhaps Freeman took pleasure in reconstructing her family history, much as she had reconstructed her
mother's story in "The Revolt of 'Mother.' " Here, she was able to

enjoy the power of her skill as a writer to "intervene" in the past, as Pryse argues, and "thereby change the shape of her family history."[7]

One of the questions that Freeman explored in *Pembroke* is where to channel passion and find fulfillment in an environment that essentially forbids such satisfaction, particularly for women. Set within the context of Freeman's sharp analysis of Calvinist orthodoxy, the plot of *Pembroke* centers on three love relationships. The central lovers are Charlotte and Barnabas, whose struggles indirectly trigger the struggles of two other unmarried pairs in the novel. Through the love and separation of Charlotte and Barnabas, Freeman transformed the story of Mary Thayer and Barnabas Lothrop into a story about gender and the effects of patriarchy. When Barnabas visits Charlotte's home and becomes embroiled in a political argument with Cephas, Charlotte's father, the women whisper at first, then gesture, then cry out, but their voices are ignored by Cephas and Barnabas.

Although the ostensible explanation for the denial of sexual fulfillment in the novel is New England Calvinism, on another level the novel probes into questions of gender and politics. The central problem associated with heterosexual union in *Pembroke* is the woman's inevitable loss of power and self-possession, her subjugation as lover or wife. The underpinning for almost all of the heterosexual relationships in *Pembroke* is the fundamental inequity that the fate of women's lives rests with men. While much of the novel suggests the beauty of female sexuality through omniscient narration, Freeman also reminds her readers through the male perspectives of Barnabas, Richard, William, and Cephas that the open expression of women's sexuality is threatening to men and must therefore be continually judged as inappropriate, unbecoming, or bordering on insanity. The shame the men in the novel feel is linked to the influence of orthodox Calvinism and oppresses them as well. But all decisions to indulge in or resist sexuality are in their hands and the women must simply watch and wait lest they lose their chance to experience love. With the rift between Charlotte and Barnabas at the center, two other couples circle about in similar deadlocks, unable to unite. Freeman establishes that the male determination and blindness apparent in Barnabas creates the difficulties that Richard and Sylvia and William and Rebecca will experience. The root then for all the disharmony between the sexes is the inability of the male characters to hear the voices of women and to acknowledge the worth of their values, to hear Charlotte's call for recognition that sustaining meaningful human relationships is more important than winning or losing a political argument.

In the process of delaying her own marriage, Freeman chose to prevent Charlotte and Barnabas from marrying for most of the novel. What conditions are necessary, in Freeman's terms, before marriage can be accomplished? This question is at the heart of *Pembroke*. Essentially, it is not until Barnabas begins to acknowledge and even adopt the feminine principles that he had ignored in the pivotal scene with Cephas that marriage becomes a possibility. In the critical opening scene in which Cephas and Barnabas argue, Freeman establishes her analysis of gender dynamics. All other events in the novel are connected to the separation of Charlotte and Barnabas. It is therefore crucial to study closely the implications of the argument itself, what leads to it, and what follows.

From the moment that Barnabas leaves his home to visit Charlotte, Freeman presents the contrast between the masculine and the feminine. Barnabas observes the "many apple trees behind the stone-walls that bordered the wood."[8] The "soft blooming branches" of the flowering apple trees are contained within manmade stone walls and look "strangely incongruous." Barnabas immediately translates the vision of the blooming branches into an economic construct, looking up at the apple blossoms and calculating how much money might be lost if there is a frost. His thoughts about the trees connect to his expectations in marriage, for he hopes that the trees will prove profitable so that he can buy Charlotte silk gowns and new bonnets when they marry. His vision of nature, then, immediately becomes transformed into a vision of domination, possession, and profit. Even before the scene in which the silence of women in the face of male power becomes so poignant, Freeman hints that Charlotte has no more power than the apple trees. She is subject to the reductive interpretation of the men in her life, whether father or fiancé. Just after looking at the apple trees, Barnabas remembers that when he had attempted to give Charlotte a new shawl, her father had returned it and Charlotte had explained, " 'Father don't feel as I ought to take it, and I guess you'd better keep it now, Barney,' she said with regretful tears in her eyes" (5).

Freeman positions Charlotte imagistically, from the moment she enters the novel, as a woman caught in a space between male voices. When she greets Barnabas, she stands between an "inner door" behind which her father waits and an outer door in which the figure of Barnabas appears. The sexual tension of the scene is powerful as the "all radiant" Barnabas grasps Charlotte's hand and kisses her passionately. The commanding voice of her father, Cephas, interrupts the kiss and the lovers move inside. There is in Charlotte "an involuntary impatience and longing in every nerve of her body," but her needs are deemed secondary, irrelevant. She has learned to conceal them and, as the narrator indicates, "nobody would have suspected" her longing (12). What gets vocalized are the needs of Barnabas and Cephas. Barnabas openly expresses his longing for Charlotte when he pursues her for one more kiss, and Cephas's imperious words from within express an equally powerful need for domination as he calls for an end to such "loverlike familiarity." While Barnabas listens for the "crackle of the hearth fire" in the room in which he and Charlotte hope to be alone together, Cephas asserts his will by prohibiting "any solitary communion between the lovers," insisting that "if Barnabas Thayer can't set here with the rest of us, he can go home." A contest of male will over the fate of a woman, the expression or suppression of her sexuality, is in fact the pretext for the political argument between Cephas and Barnabas. Just before the argument begins, "Charlotte unobtrusively moved her chair a little nearer her lover's; her purple delaine skirt swept his knee; both of them blushed and trembled with Cephas's black eyes upon them" (12).

The scene that follows is a superb example of Freeman's capacity to explore the gender gap and its consequences. Occurring before women had a voice or a vote in our political system, the argument is set in the context of that exclusion:

> Charlotte never knew quite how it began, but her father suddenly flung out a dangerous topic like a long-argued bone of contention, and he and Barnabas were upon it. Barnabas was a Democrat, and Cephas was a Whig, and neither ever forgot it of the other. None of the women fairly understood the point at issue; it was as if they drew back their feminine skirts and listened amazed and trembling to this male hubbub over something outside their province. Charlotte grew paler and paler. She looked piteously at her mother. (13)

Listening to the "male hubbub," the women recognize themselves as outsiders to the world of power and politics. Their voices, given expression through gesture as much as through speech, are not heard or felt by the men who are busily engaged in the struggle to dominate the argument. In essence, the male political system that denies women the right to vote is reflected in the competitive argument between Cephas and Barnabas which allows no room for the values of women. "Charlotte laid her hand on her lover's arm and kept it there, but he did not seem to heed her. 'Don't,' she said; 'don't, Barnabas. I think there's going to be a frost to-night; don't you?' But nobody heard her" (13). Charlotte's gentle gesture, her plea for peace in place of war, human connection in place of domination, love in place of power and envy, goes unrecognized. The other women in the scene share Charlotte's values and are equally powerless to intercede. Her spinster aunt, Sylvia, merely "clutched the arms of her rocking-chair with her thin hands." Charlotte's mother, Sarah, attempts to convert her husband's anger into constructive discussion with her quiet prompting, " 'Now, Father, don't,' " but "it was like a sparrow piping against the north wind" (13).

Freeman was almost as quiet as her female characters when she attempted to comment on the injustices of a political system ruled by masculine principles of domination and control. She proclaimed almost proudly in one letter that "I am not a suffragette." But in the same letter, in her usual vein of subtle subversion, she suggested her politics. The letter is worth studying for its implications in relation to her politics in *Pembroke*. Beginning with a reference to the comparative weakness and even inferiority of husbands, she moved on to comment on the political system as it is run by men:

> So your husband is off in pursuit of bugs and things again. Well mine goes up once a week to look after business, and the rest of the time, smokes, and stays here like a real nice happy boy. It pleases me to see him having such a good time. He gets nervous, and used up if he does not have good times. I imagine most men do. Women have, on the whole, . . . more back bone under difficulties.
>
> Why not? They have had harder training. They or their ancestors have borne and reared the men. Funny how men ignore their feminine sources. Also women have incidentally had fathers. Also women have not as a majority enough time to waste on such disgraceful affairs as that Chicago Convention, where all the little boys without their ma's handy to spank 'em fought and rolled in the dust of politics for office.[9]

Reducing the political battles of men to an arena for "little boys without their ma's handy to spank 'em," Freeman manages here to assert her own vision of exactly what is missing in the politics of patriarchy: an awareness in men of "their feminine sources."

In painting the pivotal scene of *Pembroke*, Freeman essentially asks her readers to study the relative "back bone" of men and women amidst the foolishness of the political realm established by men, to get beneath the surface of the argument between father and future husband, and to recognize the fundamental issues at work.

The aftermath of the scene in which Cephas and Barnabas argue is even more revealing as a statement about conflicting masculine and feminine values. By contrasting the behavior of Charlotte and Barnabas following the argument, Freeman is able to outline indirectly the obstacle to happiness in the nineteenth-century marriage. Cephas orders Barnabas to leave and Barnabas swears he will never return. Charlotte defies her father by following Barnabas and calling to him to come back, but "Barney never turned his head; the distance between them widened as Charlotte followed, calling" (14). The widening distance between the characters is Freeman's symbol for the distance between genders.

Whereas Barnabas retreats alone and seeks isolation in his misery, Charlotte turns to the companionship and protection of Sylvia. Her father bolts the door and forbids her return to the house, but Sylvia and Sarah conspire to nurture and soothe the younger woman. Charlotte's call is a cry for human communication and for love that is superior to the patriarchal trappings of the argument. Barnabas's silent retreat places patriarchal pride above the value of loving; it is an act of self-absorption, and a tribute to his own pride. It is impossible for him to emerge from the self so that he can imagine Charlotte's grief, but Charlotte expresses an intuitive understanding of what he is feeling.

Retreating to the unfinished house which he was in the process of constructing for his life with Charlotte, Barnabas poses the question, "What have I done to be treated in this way?" (18). Barnabas turns to the precepts of his Puritan ancestors and inflates the incident into an inexplicable act of the patriarchal God against him, stressing that he is a man who has "kept all thy commandments from childhood." With the repetitive use of "I" in Barnabas's outcries, "Oh, I am mocked, I am mocked," Freeman accentuates the dilemma of the male ego. Barnabas is incapable of moving beyond the inflated "I."

In contrast, the words of Charlotte and those who tend to her place an emphasis on moving beyond self-interest, on caring for other women. Recognizing that she has lost Barnabas and barred from reentering her home by the door Cephas has bolted, she hears the voices of her aunt and mother:

> A low voice, which was scarcely more than a whisper, called her, a slender figure twisted itself around the front corner of the house like a vine. "Charlotte, come; come quick." Charlotte did not stir. "Charlotte, do come. Your mother's dreadful afraid you'll catch cold. The front door is open." Charlotte sat quite still. The slender figure began moving towards her stealthily, keeping close to the house, advancing with frequent pauses like a wary bird. When she got close to Charlotte she reached down and touched her shoulder timidly. "Oh, Charlotte, don't you feel bad? He'd ought to know your father by this time; he'll get over it and come back," she whispered. (15)

In place of Barnabas's monologue, Freeman creates womanly dialogue and touch. Voices softly dwell on the needs of others rather than on concern for the self. A hand touches a shoulder, a voice murmurs the word "feel." Merging with images of nature, Sylvia's hand is the "twisting vine" that draws Charlotte back into the pain and beauty of living. Her mother's worries, her aunt's concern, their protective gestures are all acknowledgments of the feminine principles that stand in radical contrast to the patriarchy within which they are contained and subjugated. Sarah has left the front door open for Charlotte in the hope that Cephas will not notice. But Cephas takes charge, and Charlotte must go to the home of Sylvia. Both Sylvia and Sarah sacrifice their immediate happiness to aid Charlotte. Sarah evokes Cephas's wrath and Sylvia, in the time it takes to coax Charlotte to come to her home, misses the visit she has longed for from Richard. Their strategy of survival is problematic for their voices are whispers that only they can hear. Through subterfuge they gain their only access to power, and even then they are unable to succeed in changing their circumstances. Yet in these contrasting scenes, Freeman is celebrating the superiority of the peaceful network of support, which the women have established, in place of the isolation of Barnabas's religious self-obsession.

The remainder of the novel focuses on the effects of the delayed marriage of Charlotte and Barnabas. If they are to have a successful marriage, what must change? To what extent are conflicting value systems at the heart of the marriage problem as Freeman saw it? In this light, it is fascinating to study Freeman's critique of the marriage option itself through two married couples. Barnabas's parents and Charlotte's parents offer the only models of traditional marriage in *Pembroke*. The problems these marriages present for women who long for power or autonomy help explain Freeman's compulsion to delay both fictional marriages in her work and her own marriage to Charles Freeman.

In Charlotte's parents' marriage, the woman is powerless despite her moral superiority. Freeman continually demonstrates Sarah's wisdom, but it is Cephas who rules the household and Sarah who acquiesces. When questioned by her sister Hannah, Sarah replies, " 'I tell you it is his way,' . . . And she said it as if 'his way' was the way of the King" (11). Urging her daughter to "mind" her father whether he is right or wrong, Sarah shows she has been trained to submit to his power. Freeman undercuts male power within this traditional marriage, however, mocking Cephas's lack of insight, his blindness in matters of the heart. Interfering with the sympathetic conversation of the women in Sylvia's kitchen, Cephas intrudes just after Hannah sums up and deflates the workings of the patriarchal pattern in her description of the argument between the men.

> I guess they don't think much about the country; it's jest to have their own way about it. I'd like to know what mortal difference it's goin' to make to Barney Thayer or Cephas Barnard which man is President? . . . It's jest like two little boys—one wants to play marbles 'cause the other wants to play puss-in-the-corner, an' that's all the reason either one of 'em's got for standin' out. Men ain't got too much sense anyhow, when you come right down to it. They don't ever get any too much grown up, the best of 'em. (43–44)

Hannah's astute description of male competition reduces Cephas and Barney to the level of children. By following this scathing feminist analysis with Cephas's assertion that his women should return home, Freeman accentuates the oppression of women as all the more ludicrous and unjust. Hannah and Sylvia stand at the window watching Charlotte follow her mother, who in turn follows Cephas. "They went in a procession of three, with Cephas marching ahead like a general, across the yard" (46). Concluding with an acknowledgment of the advantages of spinsterhood, Hannah assures Sylvia Crane that "you ought to be mighty thankful you 'ain't got any man at all" (47).

The scene of the procession is sandwiched between Hannah's assertion in Sylvia's kitchen and another kitchen scene that also deflates Cephas's attempts to assert his superiority. This scene is a good example of Freeman's subversion. After depicting the subjugation of Sarah and Charlotte, she undermines Cephas's authority. Cephas determines that "animal food kind of quickens the animal nature in us" and attempts to dominate in the realm of Sarah's kitchen. His obvious fear of the sexuality he had witnessed in his daughter's response to Barnabas drives him to attempt further control. But here, Freeman celebrates the only arena in which Sarah can maintain some degree of power. Cephas becomes helpless in his wife's territory—her kitchen. For the first time, Sarah "pluck[s] up boldness" and vocally objects as Cephas makes a pie without flour or grease, pounds away at the useless dough, and "gallop[s] so ruthlessly over her own familiar fields." Cephas becomes impotent in Sarah's arena and Freeman concludes the scene with Sarah's bold observation: " 'To think of eatin' it!' she groaned quite openly; 'it looks like p'ison' " (56). He has failed in the sphere where women convene and communicate, the woman's sphere.

Sarah's relative powerlessness in her marriage contrasts sharply with the dynamics in the marriage of Barnabas's parents. Deborah's relentless imposition of rules exposes the destructive quality of her adherence to orthodox Calvinism. Deborah is the only strong woman in the novel, the only matriarch, and she rules the Thayer household in almost every respect. Freeman presents her as a matriarchal monster, a woman with no arena for power except within her domestic domain. Early in the novel, we learn that Deborah has long expressed her resentment of the house in which she must live, the house her husband Caleb has chosen. It is a home with "little tucked-up bedrooms instead of good chambers, because folks' fathers had been scared to death of wind" (6). Her husband and his father had a "horror and fear of wind," a fear of nature unleashed, and as a result, Deborah must live in a one-storey house, locked into these men's conception of safety. Placed in this subservient position, Deborah nevertheless finds a means toward her instinctive desire for power. Within Caleb's one-storey home, she overthrows the political structure that has placed her there. Caleb shudders in her presence, fearing and obeying her demands. Their son Ephraim dies because the illness he has worsens after a wild, forbidden ride on Barnabas's sled. The death, however, occurs just after Deborah whips him for failing to follow her instructions to tell Caleb he must pare some apples before dinner. Although Deborah has been carefully ordered by the doctor never to whip Ephraim because of his condition, she feels she must "so that he will do right." She explains that "it is better you should be sick than be well and wicked and disobedient" (239). Discovering later that her behavior may not have caused his death, that "maybe I haven't killed him, after all," her relief is at such a pitch that she has a heart attack (249).

In Deborah, Freeman presents a single alternative to female passivity within marriage, feminine power in destructive form. Deborah heads the Thayer household, but her negative influence becomes the central power in a dramatically dysfunctional family. Freeman grants Deborah power over others, has her abuse that power, and then punishes her for the abuse. As Lambert argues, having "failed to relinquish autonomy" within the boundaries of marriage, Deborah becomes "woman-turned-monster." Freeman's presentation of Deborah as a woman whose misplaced energy destroys those she loves is a comment on the limited options of women who marry. Lambert notes that Deborah's only means toward power is ironically to "enact the role prescribed for women in patriarchal law: the teachings themselves and her entrapment in orthodoxy are responsible for the ruin of the family. Since the gospel Deborah lives by is male, biblical, and patriarchal, Freeman's text implies that great destructiveness develops in a woman who carries out patriarchal injunctions, as, of course, generations of women have." [10] By creating the only authoritative woman in the novel as a woman whose power destroys, Freeman suggests that constructive female power is not possible within the restrictions of marriage as defined within patriarchy.

Having presented the limited alternatives of marriage, to become the passive Sarah or the monstrous Deborah, Freeman quickly turns her novel to the dilemma of repressed sexuality, an inevitable dimension of unmarried life. Throughout the novel she exposes male attitudes toward female sexuality and nonconformity. Charlotte's lingering longing for Barnabas works as a backdrop for the novel's fragmented characterizations and relationships. For both Charlotte

and Barnabas, Freeman creates shadow figures, doubles whose behavior becomes an index for understanding the effects of their repressed or released rebellion and sexuality. With a circle of rebellious
and submissive characters mirroring Charlotte and Barnabas, Freeman manages to satisfy both the need to rebel and the need to
conform, to expose the wrongs of patriarchy while simultaneously
keeping her characters safely within its limits.

Charlotte's cousin Rose, "a slender creature . . . overwrought with
nervous excitement," arrives to talk to Charlotte shortly after her
separation from Barnabas (63). When she speaks in response to the
incident with Barnabas, "a curious quality" is "in the girl's voice as if
some great hidden emotion in her heart tried to leap to the surface
and make a sound, although it was totally at variance with the import
of her cry" (66). Rose's words and actions reflect the unexpressed,
passionate side of Charlotte. This comes across most clearly in the
discussion concerning Barnabas's departure. Rose speaks of how she
"wouldn't bear it" if Barney had left her. Her face quivered and grew
"suddenly intense, and seemed to open out into bloom and color
like a flower. The pupils of her blue eyes dilated until they looked
black; her thin lips looked full and red; her cheeks were flaming;
her slender chest heaved" (67). The language itself carries the
throbbing rhythm of Rose's impassioned energies. The description
of Charlotte's response to Rose's ardor creates a striking link between the two characters: "Charlotte looked at her, and a quivering
flush like a reflection was left on her fair, steady face" (67). Rose's
fiery appearance mirrors what rests behind Charlotte's "fair, steady
face." Rose appears to be Charlotte's opposite, at least to the extent
Charlotte presents herself publicly. But inside Charlotte, Rose's sort
of "fierce passion" struggles to find expression. Freeman frees that
expression in the aggressive and rebellious words of Rose who says
she "wouldn't be ashamed" to pursue Barnabas "in the face and eyes
of the whole town" (69). Embodying the unconventional self, Rose
has no time for Charlotte's socially conscious "pride." Furthermore,
Rose does not attempt to hide the "longing in every nerve of her
body" which Charlotte so carefully suppresses. In addition to her
"red swelling lips," her name itself suggests her sexuality. Freeman
often uses the rose as a symbol of sublimated sexuality. In "Evelina's
Garden," for example, Evelina devotes herself to her garden as if to
a surrogate lover and when "she saw the first rose, her heart leaped

as at the face of a lover." In "A New England Nun," Louisa Ellis distills the essences from rose petals and stores them away as she stores away her own sexuality. But in *Pembroke* Rose seeks no surrogates, no substitute lovers in a garden of flowers. She will not run from a lover with the burden of a dove on her shoulder as Caroline does in "A Symphony in Lavender." On the contrary, Rose fairly dazzles with sexuality. "Rose's face between the green sides of her bonnet had in it all the quickened bloom of youth in spring; her eyes had all the blue surprise of violets; she panted softly between red swelling lips as she walked; pulses beat in her crimson cheeks. Her slender figure yielded to the wind as to a lover" (79). Whereas the violets to which Caroline is compared are "hidden somewhere under the leaves," Rose's violets are visible, full of "blue surprise." Rose merges with images of nature and fights no battle against the natural expression of sexual desire.

In the seventh chapter of *Pembroke*, the center of the novel, the main characters attend a cherry-picking party. Here Freeman expands upon and celebrates the link between feminine sexuality and nature. The narrative perspective of this chapter, as Lambert suggests, favors rather than judges the open expression of sexuality:

> Their laughter and gay cries formed charming discords; their radiant faces had the likeness of one family of flowers, through their one expression. The wind blew harder; the girls' muslin skirts clung to their limbs as they moved against it and flew out around their heels in fluttering ruffles. The cherry boughs tossed over their heads full of crisp whispers among their dark leaves and red fruit clusters. (138)

With such abounding sensuality, Freeman never inserts moral judgment or suggests that such "reckless exhilaration" ought to be brought under control. Her description builds instead to a virtual climax. In the midst of the game the young women play with the men who frolic with them in the fields, "the girls' cheeks flushed deeper, their smooth locks became roughened. The laughter waxed louder and longer; the matrons looking on doubled their broad backs with responsive merriment. It became like a little bacchanalian rout in a New England field on a summer afternoon, but they did not know it in their simple hearts" (138).

It is the judgment of men that transforms the free and natural expression of sexuality into something problematic and shameful. Observing and even participating in the celebration, Barnabas simultaneously feels threatened by the display of female sexuality, particularly that of Charlotte, the woman he was to have possessed. Standing beside her double, Rose, Charlotte appears to be "gleaming in the sun, her neck showing pink through her embroidered lace kerchief." Barnabas feels "the fierceness of the instinct of possession" when he notes that her neck is uncovered, imagining "that this was his wife's neck; no one else should see it" (131). In contrast to the lovely images of nature and yielding, Freeman incorporates an analysis of the male psyche as Barnabas "felt like tearing off his own coat and covering her with brute force" (131).

In the next scene, Rose invades Barnabas's self-protective realm, confronting him with sexual possibility. Rose appeals to the locked up sexuality in Barnabas. Just at the moment that he longs to cover up Charlotte's exposed skin, Rose appears and speaks in "adoring cadences." The description of Rose stresses the sensuality Barnabas and Charlotte both desire and fear: "Rose's crisp pink muslin gown flared scalloping around her like pink petals of a hollyhock; her slender white arms showed through the thin sleeves." Again associated with nature, Rose's teasing sensuality suggests her expression of Charlotte's sensual self. Even more to the point, while Charlotte works hard to look at Barnabas as though he were "old Squire Payne," Rose unashamedly allows her eyes to betray her longings: "Barney could not look away from her wide-open, unfaltering blue eyes, which suddenly displayed to him strange depths. Charlotte during all his courtship had never looked up in his face like that" (131). This comparison of Charlotte and Rose reinforces the link between the two characters. Trained and restricted by the same rules that have shaped Charlotte, Rose nevertheless chooses sexuality over repression: "Rose, in the heart of New England, bred after the precepts of orthodoxy, was a pagan, and she worshipped Love himself. Barney was simply the statue that represented the divinity; another might have done as well had the sculpture been as fine" (131–32). In the contrast between Charlotte's "respect" and Rose's paganism, we see the polarities of Charlotte's character, her self-division. Charlotte longs for the freedom to worship "Love," but she stays within the bounds of "the precepts of orthodoxy." Rose enjoys entertaining the sexual possibilities that Barnabas's handsome figure suggests to her. Whereas Charlotte outwardly expresses restrained submission to the "heart of New England," Rose outwardly expresses the pagan lover within. Barney has a dual response to Rose's display of sexual desire. Although he remembers "breathing in great pants" when he was the aggressor with Charlotte, he is finally repelled by sexuality when initiated and acknowledged by the woman.

If Rose suggests the sexual rebel in Charlotte, Barnabas's frail brother Ephraim suggests the libidinal energy that Barnabas stores up and denies. Described as a feminine boy whose fragility determines an excessive degree of familial protection, Ephraim acts upon the impulses that Barnabas continually hides. Ephraim emerges as a rebellious character only after Freeman establishes Barnabas's conflict between the feminine and masculine impulses he harbors.

The house Barnabas builds becomes the arena for his silent expression of self-division. Early on, Freeman had clarified that Barnabas makes a special point of having two stories rather than one when he begins to build a home for his life with Charlotte. Freeman transforms Barnabas Thayer into a man who wants to break away from the fear of winds or storms that had terrified his father and grandfather. (Incidently, Freeman's maternal grandfather, Barnabas Lothrop, had also had a strong neurotic fear of winds and in defiance of the architectural styles of the day, he had built a low, rambling, one-storey house with a windowless room in which to retreat during a storm.) Barnabas expresses a longing for space and freedom. His vision of the house, with its two stories and open spaces, encompasses the possibility of danger.

Beyond being a statement of Barnabas's defiance, the house is also a symbol of his longing for freedom from the masculine codes of behavior that foster a resistance to emotion and love. Before his dispute with Cephas and his separation from Charlotte, he looks at the fireless hearth and imagines the warmth it will give the room he will share with Charlotte:

> Her rocking chair can set there, said Barnabas aloud. The tears came into his eyes; he stepped forward, laid his smooth boyish cheek against a partition wall of this new house and kissed it. It was a fervent demonstration not towards Charlotte alone, nor the joy to come to him within those walls, but to all life and love and nature, although he did not comprehend it. He half sobbed as he turned away; his thoughts seemed to dazzle his brain and he could not feel his feet. (7)

The feminine self within Barnabas instinctively feels things, expresses emotional irrationality as he kisses the wall, sheds feminine tears of joy about "life and love and nature" instead of considering questions of income or possession. With thoughts that "dazzle his brain," Barnabas parts with the need to "feel his feet," to maintain stable control. But at this point Freeman offers a powerful reminder that Barnabas is a divided man. Shortly after his intoxicating moment of feminine self-revelation, Barnabas "suddenly started at a long black shadow on the floor. It vanished as he went on and might have been due to his excited fancy" (7). The shadow of Barnabas's other self emerges soon after this scene in his refusal to submit to his love for Charlotte. In effect, Barnabas gives way to the "black shadow" self, the life-denying self he witnessed just after his moment of ecstasy in shadow form, "inherited from generations of Puritans." It is as though Barnabas must punish the man who responds to female passion and expresses womanly emotion. A place of potential freedom, the house also becomes a symbol of his fear of the feminine. It is to this house that Barnabas will retreat for ten years in a determined attempt to resist his passion for Charlotte. Fear of the very intensity of his own capacity to love drives him to an ultimate state of hermitage.

Through his brother Ephraim, Freeman releases the side of Barnabas capable of open rebellion against the masculine dictates, the rules of decorum, that draw him away from Charlotte. Frail and sickly, Ephraim is isolated from other children and lives under the strict rules of his mother. Like Freeman, Ephraim is born after the death of a sibling and overprotected accordingly. He is rarely allowed outdoors and spends most of his time reciting his catechism. For both Freeman and Ephraim, the rigidity of the religious schedule of worship along with excessive concern about health interfered with the spontaneity of childhood.

As Barney's opposite, Ephraim has a "spirit of boyish rebellion." His "gawky figure" was "perpetually uneasy and twisting, as if to find entrance into small forbidden places" (97). Ephraim is a highly sensual boy; a boy who longs for freedom, for all that is forbidden in the Thayer household. Perhaps Freeman derived some pleasure from the plums she allowed her character, Ephraim, to steal: "he dearly loved plums, although they were especially prohibited" (97). When possible he would "roll one quietly under his tongue" and hope that his mother Deborah would not see (97). Freeman describes his enjoyment of the plums in great detail. Even though

Ephraim must suffer for his pleasure (he experiences immediate physical pain and becomes short of breath whenever he eats the fruit), he also feels a sense of triumph: "This depriving him of the little creature comforts which he loved, and of the natural enjoyments of boyhood, aroused in him a blind spirit of revolution which he felt virtuous in exercising. Ephraim was absolutely conscienceless with respect to all his stolen pleasures" (100).

In Ephraim, Freeman offers her first and perhaps only figure of "conscienceless" rebellion. Yet even Ephraim's stolen pleasures are ambiguous, for the physical suffering that results may be an expression of "conscience." Nevertheless, Freeman justifies his rebellion by emphasizing the severity of the deprivation in his life. While Ephraim longs for sweet cake, his mother sits him down firmly to the task of studying catechism. The harsh criticism Freeman offers here through the descriptions of Ephraim's monotonous recitals of the catechism demonstrates how bitterly she herself resented this approach to education. When Ephraim weakly stumbles away from the desk after his studies, he feels even weaker for having stolen forbidden hard, red apples earlier in the day. Deborah's forms of restriction, however, are depicted as far more dangerous. Freeman indicates that the harsher the deprivation, the stronger will be the longing for the forbidden.

Significantly, Ephraim's crowning act of rebellion and revolt occurs on his brother's sled. He leaves the Thayer home, "like a captive from prison," and runs to the great hill to sled. His hard-won freedom will cost him his life, but for Ephraim this is the "one unrestrained hilarity of his whole life" (229). The ultimate pleasure that caps the evening for Ephraim is a forbidden mince pie which he steals. He sneaks back to his room and "devour[s] the rich, spicy compound and the fat plums melted on his tongue, and the savor thereof delighted his very soul. . . . For the first and only occasion in his life, he had had a good time" (231).

The description of Ephraim's ride is especially revealing in light of the restraint we see in his brother's life. This complete release, the total freedom that Ephraim experiences, is something that terrifies the conscience much as it appeals to the sense of the repressed characters who surround Ephraim. Other than Rose, he is the only figure of freedom in the novel. The price he must pay for such pleasure is nothing less than death.

Freeman describes Ephraim's sledding accident on Barnabas's sled as a fight "against bondage and deprivation and death," a moment in which the boy gives "full cry to the natural voices of youth and his heart." In the "white moonlight and the keen night air," he gives way to an adventure in which "he was free" (229).[11] Ephraim dies shortly after his act of rebellion, partly because of his momentary release. Perhaps Freeman was suggesting with Ephraim's death the impossibility of such freedom within the restrictive world of nineteenth-century New England. His death does not figure into the main plot of *Pembroke* and acts instead as an index for interpreting the relative freedom or entrapment of the lovers in the novel who struggle toward and away from rebellion.

The symmetry of Freeman's mirroring characterizations is quite remarkable. Her descriptions of Rose's sexuality and Ephraim's rebellion celebrate the freedom that Charlotte and Barnabas do not have. The behavior of Rose and Ephraim becomes a projection of what lies beneath Charlotte's composure and Barney's self-imprisonment. Freeman creates as well two couples who mirror Charlotte and Barnabas in their struggle toward marriage. Just as Sarah's and Deborah's marriages suggest the limited options for women who choose to marry, the struggles of Sylvia and Barnabas's sister, Rebecca, suggest the limiting alternatives (particularly in the context of sexual self-expression) of unmarried life. The male response to each woman's sexuality and potential assertiveness leads to despair and isolation. As Freeman was coming to terms with the possibility of marriage, her portrayals of Rebecca and William (Charlotte's cousin) and Sylvia and Richard reveal her understanding of the complexity of communication between men and women, the difficulties of gender difference and male power in heterosexual relationships.

Freeman links the troubles both couples experience to the rift between Charlotte and Barnabas whose separation is due to Barnabas's inability to acknowledge the significance of love and nurturance. The impediment to his marriage to Charlotte is Barnabas's blindness to the beauty of the feminine principles implicit in Charlotte's plea for reconciliation. What follows is virtually an avalanche of thwarted marriages. Sylvia's efforts to comfort Charlotte delay her return home and she therefore misses a long-awaited proposal from Richard. Barney's behavior also causes a feud between his family and

Charlotte's, determining that Deborah initially forbids Rebecca from courting or marrying Charlotte's cousin William.

While Rose mirrors the impulse toward rebellious self-expression in Charlotte, the marvelous portrait of Charlotte's aunt Sylvia mirrors her self-restriction. Freeman offers her most definitive exploration of the psychology of spinsterhood with Sylvia. She appears to be about the age of Freeman at the time Freeman wrote *Pembroke*, and so it is interesting to note the connections between this "spinster" figure and Mary Wilkins Freeman. Like Freeman, Sylvia worships a man who shows no signs of ever proposing to her. Their thwarted romance becomes a grotesque mirror for the future of young Charlotte and Barney. Sylvia loves Richard Alger passionately and dreams about him daily; but for eighteen years, she meets with him in her home every Sunday only to sit stiffly in her living room and long for him. Sylvia is a woman of "long fostered maiden reserve" who harbors "sundry dreams which had never been realized, of herself and Richard sitting side by side and hand in hand, as confessed lovers on that sofa" (26). Instead, "in all those eighteen years," Richard "had never made love to Sylvia, unless his constant attendance upon Sabbath evenings could be so construed" (26).

Through Sylvia and Richard, Freeman emphasizes the social expectation of female passivity and the consequent dilemma for women. Fully uncovering the interior life of Sylvia, Freeman devotes a chapter to Sylvia's intricate thoughts about Richard's eighteen-year courtship. During those years, Richard would visit Sylvia every Sunday night and sit in "the great best rocking chair" which Freeman refers to as his "throne of state," while Sylvia would sit "waiting and trembling," wishing that he might move beside her on the sofa (29–30). Mirroring Charlotte's wait for Barnabas's self-recognition and return, the imagery of this courtship immediately suggests that all the power rests with Richard. Sylvia must simply wait for his expression of love, attending to the requirements of "decorum and long-fostered maiden reserve." Sylvia's sexuality seethes beneath the surface: "her thoughts seemed shivering with rainbows that constantly dazzled her with sweet shocks when her eyes met them." When Richard finally moves beside her on the sofa, on the Sunday before the mishap of her delayed return from Charlotte's home, Sylvia must still wait for Richard's touch and for his proposal of marriage. On the verge of words of love, seeing her "inarticulate assent," Richard leaves. On the next Sunday, fully anticipating the consummation of their love after so many years of waiting, Sylvia comes to church with a new appearance; people whisper about the change, seeing that she seems to be exposing the sexual creature within. She looks "as if all her youthful beauty had suddenly come up, like a withered rose which is dipped in a vase." That night, however, Sylvia misses the critical visit. But Freeman suggests that Sylvia's display of physical longing in church, her subtle indication through gesture and facial expression of her need for sexual fulfillment, may also account for Richard's still stronger resistance. As he sings in the church choir, wanting to look away, Richard finds that "her face held him. A color slowly flamed out on his pale brown cheeks; his eyes became intense and abstracted" (33).

Despite her anticipation that they will finally have their passionate embrace on the sofa, Sunday after Sunday, Richard does not return and Sylvia is placed in the position of endless and disappointing expectation. Perhaps still more damaging than this frustration, Sylvia has already internalized male judgment of her sexuality, viewing her "dreams of endearments" with "shame" (26). Offering a magnification of Charlotte's dilemma, Freeman explains that Sylvia "had been trained to regard love as one of the most secret of the laws of nature, to be concealed with shamefaced air, even from herself" (27).

While pagan Rose views nature openly, and love as something to be celebrated and revealed to all, Sylvia represses the secret and locks away her passion. Yet Sylvia feels the same stirrings Charlotte and Rose experience. Although she would "spring away" from Richard should he act out her dreams, she nevertheless dreams on. Even her physical appearance stresses a contrast between outer control or shame and inner desire. Her face has the "slim angularity and primness in elderly women who are not matrons" but it also has a "delicate bloom" and "a wistful wonder of expression which belonged to youth" (24). Sylvia resembles another aging spinster, Fidelia Almy, in Freeman's short story, "A Patient Waiter." In this story, for forty years, Fidelia walks to and from the post office in the hope of receiving the letter she had been promised by the man she had expected to marry. With no other channel for their passion, Sylvia and Fidelia present similar cases of unfulfilled longing.

Sylvia is often associated with nature: "her face in her white cap

had the shadowy delicacy of one of the flowering apple sprays outside." The "flowering apple sprays" suggest a blossoming fertility
Sylvia will never realize. Like Charlotte, Sylvia goes about with her
face "irresponsibly calm" so that "nobody dreamed of the turmoil in
her heart" (29). This well-developed mask of propriety was an implicit requirement for nineteenth-century women. As Lillian Faderman explains, "female chastity which was held to be vital in earlier
centuries took on even greater importance in nineteenth-century
America, since an unchaste woman could distract a man from his
larger purpose." Faderman cites a writer in 1808 who suggests that
young men "test the virtue of a woman whom they wish to marry by
making sexual advances to her. If she does not respond with 'becoming abhorrence,' she is not a proper girl and would not make a
good wife. In this way, women were taught to deny any heterosexual
urge." [12] The scene on the evening in which Richard moves to the
sofa captures the painful consequence of such denial. In dramatizing
the tension that accompanies the urge for sexual union, Freeman
captures the weight of Sylvia's dilemma. Sylvia moves to light a can-
dle, but Richard stops her, almost as though he is following the
advice of the writer that Faderman cites:

> They had sat in the twilight and young moonlight all the evening. . . .
> That had somehow made the evening seem strange and freighted with
> consequences; and beside the white light of the moon, full of mystic
> influence, there was something subtler and more magnetic, which would
> sway more than the tides, even the passions of the human heart, present,
> and they both felt it. (29–30)

The magnetism between the two lovers, the "passions of the human
heart" evident in this scene, are powerful expressions of sensuality.
Richard moves "curiously, rather as if he was drawn than walked
of his own volition over to the sofa" (30). At first, Sylvia moves
away out of "pure maidenliness." But she tremblingly glances "side-
wise, timidly and adoringly, at Richard's smoothly shaven face,
pale as marble in the moonlight, and waited her heart throbbing"
(30). The tension of desire in this scene is followed by Richard's
abrupt departure, but the narrator reminds readers of long suppressed needs: "they both felt it." Richard then hurries out the door
leaving Sylvia's "heart in a great tumult of expectation and joyful
fear" (30–31).

Richard never returns to visit and Sylvia reacts to his abandonment of her with new and unexpected rage. The misplaced energies of sexuality in Freeman's work are continually channeled into outlets of rage.[13] Alice Glarden Brand claims that Freeman "condemns women who exhibit open hostility," but Sylvia's defiance is presented in what Susan Allen Toth terms "a positive light."[14] Although Sylvia cannot define her anger, and this is problematic, Freeman seems to condone rather than condemn Sylvia's capacity to express rage at the agony and waste of waiting Sunday after Sunday for Richard to arrive. What Freeman condemns, as her "Introductory Sketch" for *Pembroke* indicates, is Sylvia's inability to understand the target of her anger or the complex fears underlying it.[15] On the morning after the missed meeting with Richard she felt "disposed to go out of her way to sting and as if some primal and evil instinct had taken possession of her. She felt shocked at herself but the more defiant and disposed to keep on" (38).

The thwarted romance between Charlotte and Barnabas is mirrored in the long-term frustration of Richard and Sylvia. Perhaps the scene that most explicitly presents Richard and Sylvia as counterparts to Barney and Charlotte is the one in which Sylvia hears footsteps and pathetically mistakes Barnabas for Richard. Here Freeman analyzes the effects of prolonged repression on the psyche. She creates an eerie sense of double vision as readers begin to make the same mistake Sylvia has made. Furthermore, we find ourselves mistaking Sylvia for Charlotte. Barnabas has chosen to lead the "life of a hermit," although he has continued to long for Charlotte (166). He wanders out in the evening, his mind "engrossed with his own misery." When he reaches Sylvia Crane's house and sees her in the doorway, "he started for he thought it might be Charlotte" (168). Freeman has deliberately attempted to clarify the connection between Charlotte and her older self, Sylvia. Sylvia calls to him, "You ain't goin' past, Richard?" and wails the phrase again and again, "clinging to the old gatepost" (168). Despite Barnabas's repeated words "I guess you've made a mistake," Sylvia persists in seeing him as Richard in a scene powerful for its psychological implications. Sylvia sits down on the sofa and clings to Barnabas's arm "and it seemed to him that he was forced to sit down beside her or be rough with her" (169). Sylvia's hallucination is haunting and compelling:

She looked straight in his face with a strange boldness, her body inclined toward him, her head thrown back. Her thin, faded cheeks were burning, her blue eyes eager, her lips twitching with pitiful smiles. The room was dim, with candlelight, but everything in it was distinct, and Sylvia Crane, looking straight at Barney Thayer's face, saw the face of Richard Alger. (170)

The language here is almost frenetic in its insistence upon doubling: each noun in the description of Sylvia is modified by an adjective, and the paired phrases prepare us for Sylvia's double vision of Barney as Richard. Her desperate expression of crushed needs comes to us in the image of "pitiful smiles," "faded cheeks . . . burning" and "lips twitching." In this scene, Sylvia acts out dreams that both Sylvia and Charlotte share—dreams of unacceptable female aggression and sexual fulfillment.

Unashamedly, Sylvia complains, " 'I've had this—sofa ten years . . . ten years, Richard—an' you never set with me on it before, an' —you'd been comin'—here a long while before that came betwixt us last spring, Richard" (170). For Barnabas the whole incident is terrifying. Suddenly he feels and believes he is Richard Alger, the timid and unyielding lover of Sylvia: "Suddenly Barney himself had a curious impression. The features of Richard Alger instead of his own seemed to look back at him from his own thoughts. He dashed his hand across his face with an impatient, bewildered motion, as if he brushed away unseen cobwebs and stood up" (170). In nightmarish, magnified form, Barnabas sees the horror of his own resistance to Charlotte's sexuality through the image of Richard Alger.

Again, in an act of female aggression which until then Sylvia had kept under tight control, she pulls Barnabas down beside her and "before he knew what she was doing, had shrunk close to him and laid her head on his shoulder" (170). Without her old fear of aggression, she goes on to demand a show of affection: " 'Can't you put your arm around me jest once, Richard?' she went on. 'You ain't never, an' you've been comin' here a long while. I've had this sofa ten years' " (171). Charlotte and Sylvia have resembled each other in their passivity. In this scene, Sylvia actively demands affection for the first time in her life in a way that Charlotte never had. The scene, however, has the same dream texture as Wheatcroft's "hall-bedroom" excursions or Caroline's lavender dream.[16] It takes place as "it grew dusky"; she stands in the "dim shaft of candlelight which streamed from the room beyond" (168). Furthermore, Freeman allows Sylvia to express her ardent needs only in the circumstances of her hallucination. When she later realizes that she has mistaken Barney for Richard Alger, she sinks back into her old passivity and never confronts Richard openly.

An important comment on women emerges. Through Charlotte's and Sylvia's acceptance of the world as shaped by the actions of Cephas, Barnabas, and Richard, we see the consequences of female subservience. Earlier in the novel, Sarah Barnard says to Sylvia, "Women don't worry much on their own accounts, but they've got accounts," and Sylvia responds with a "quick shrinking, as if from a blow" (27). In essence, both Charlotte and Sylvia live by denying and suppressing their "accounts." Only in this scene are women's "accounts" forcefully and painfully voiced. Sylvia's open statement of need shocks Barnabas into a recognition of his own needs. He cannot escape the link between the two sets of lovers, for even the mention of ten years matches his ten-year separation from Charlotte. Hence Barnabas, "with no volition of his own," does put his arm around Sylvia, and he "trembled with Sylvia's sobs" (171). In the most telling passage, Barnabas sees the ghost of his double—the man who is responsible for Sylvia's sobs—in his own patterns of behavior.

> He sat with a serious shamefacedness, his arm around the poor bony waist, staring over the faded fair head, which had never lain on any lover's breast except in dreams. For the moment he could not stir; he had a feeling of horror, as if he saw his own double. There was a subtle resemblance which lay deeper than the features between him and Richard Alger. Sylvia saw it, and he saw his own self reflected as Richard Alger in that straining mental vision of hers which exceeded the spiritual one. (171)

Like Richard, Barnabas helped create the situation in which female sexuality can only find expression "in dreams." The doubling is even further intensified after Barnabas forces Sylvia to see that he is not Richard. Sylvia insists that he not tell a soul, "when you're doin' jest the same as Richard Alger yourself, an' you're makin' Charlotte sit an' watch an' suffer for nothin' at all, jest as he makes me" (173). Of course, although Sylvia is completely correct in her summing up of the situation, she persists in her own form of denial by forbidding Barnabas to ever speak of her desperation.

When Barnabas leaves, he seems to have embraced the feminine side of himself. Much like Sylvia, he "was all trembling and un- nerved." He tries to convince himself that Sylvia is mentally dis- turbed, "laboring under some sudden aberration of mind." But he cannot escape the truth she has forced him to see:

> Was he not like Richard Alger in his own desertion of Charlotte Barnard? and had not Sylvia been as little at fault in taking one for the other as if they had been twin brothers? Might there not be a closer likeness between characters than features—Perhaps by a repetition of sins and deformities? and might not one now and then be able to see it? (174–75)

Through the confrontation with his double, Barnabas is forced to see what he has done. He also sees the double figures of Charlotte and Sylvia: ". . . was Charlotte like Sylvia? Was Charlotte even now sitting watching for him with that awful eagerness which comes from a hunger of the heart?" (175). Both Charlotte and Sylvia have spent their lives submitting, obeying, accepting life as defined by men, only to be left with a "hunger of the heart." Richard and Sylvia represent the repressed sides of Barnabas and Charlotte. All four characters suffer from a "hunger of the heart."

Freeman explores still more fully, through her depiction of Barna- bas's sister, Rebecca, the complexities of heterosexual desire in unmarried life. Focusing on the way women internalize male inter- pretations of their sexuality as shameful, Freeman offers Rebecca's "transgression" as the only alternative to Sylvia's repression. Rebec- ca's experience conveys the consequences for women of sexual activ- ity outside marriage. At first Rebecca disguises her sexual needs when she is with William. When Rose implies that Rebecca deliber- ately visits their shop in order to see her brother, William, "there was no falsehood that she would not have sworn to to shield her modesty from such a thought on his part." As soon as Deborah forbids her to see William, however, Rebecca rebels more openly. Driven by the desire to comfort William after a dispute he has had with his father, Rebecca visits him and initiates their first sexual encounter. Her action is an expression of love, an effort to soothe William as though he were a "hurt child," an action, then, which is based on the very principles of femininity that the men in the novel shun.

> She looked up in his face; her mouth was quivering with a kind of helpless shame, but her eyes were full of womanly courage and steadfastness. "Wil-

liam," said she, "I ran away in the face and eyes of them all to comfort you. They saw me, and they can see me now, but I don't care. And I don't care if you see me; I always have cared, but I don't now. I have always been terribly afraid lest you should think I was running after you, but I ain't afraid now. Don't you feel bad, William. That's all I care about.... Suddenly Rebecca raised both her arms and put them around his neck; he leaned his cheek against her soft hair. (142)

Freeman immediately reveals the impact of Rebecca's assertiveness. Young girls "blush hotly" as they walk by, whispering "did you see? his head? her arms?" (143). When Deborah discovers that Rebecca is pregnant, she "pushes the girl violently from her" and casts her out with disdain. Revealing her pregnancy "was like uncovering a disfigurement or a sore" (192). This imagery suggests that female sexuality without the sanction of marriage is associated with disease. Despite Freeman's earlier depiction at the cherry-picking party of the natural beauty of sexuality, the consequence of Rebecca's aggression is "disfigurement." She must flee her home in shame. Eventually, William marries her, but his view of Rebecca perpetuates her ostracism despite the marriage. Once responding to her kisses with warmth, he now responds with "very little love for her . . . he felt nothing but a kind of horror" (206). Rebecca comes to view herself in the same way and internalizes the patriarchal judgment that the association of sexuality and disfigurement implies. For most of the novel, she keeps herself "well-hidden," lives "with curtains down and doors bolted . . . she would not go to the door if anybody knocked." Self-imposed isolation in a marriage built on shame becomes her only option.

After depicting Rebecca as a social outcast, Freeman creates yet another double. Fleeing from Deborah just after the discovery of her pregnancy, Rebecca takes refuge in the home of Mrs. Sloan who, as Lambert indicates, "has been judged guilty of unspecified sexual misdeeds." The whole community thinks of Mrs. Sloan as "a byword and a mocking to all the people." Wearing Mrs. Sloan's shawl, Rebecca's "very identity seemed to be lost" (210). This is the shawl she wears when she marries William. The attitudes of Barnabas and William toward female sexuality are most pronounced in their reaction to Mrs. Sloan. Barney has "always felt a loathing for the woman" (202), and William looks at her house as an image of "the shame and squalor of the soul itself" and feels "transplanted into a veritable hell" (205). Rebecca's efforts to find fulfillment in love are thwarted by attitudes like these. It is only when she shows herself to be a loving mother that she is redeemed and somewhat forgiven for her earlier rebellion.

The conclusion to *Pembroke* seems on the surface to be merely a sentimental threading together of all the loose ends, with conjugal bliss as the final goal. Charlotte does not marry the conventional Thomas Payne as her family has hoped. Instead, Barnabas and Cephas are reconciled and Charlotte and Barnabas are reunited. Richard saves Sylvia from life in the poorhouse and finally proposes. The seeming simplicity of these solutions, however, is part of Freeman's strategy. Appearing to offer the acceptable message that marriage is the happiest of all conclusions for her characters, Freeman incorporates a subversive message as well. One possible interpretation of the message, as Lambert proposes, is that "marriages occur when women become vulnerable, not when they remain strong."[17] Lambert argues that Barnabas and Richard are finally willing to marry Charlotte and Sylvia "once their circumstances are diminished." On the surface, this seems to be the case since Charlotte suffers from her community's judgment when she goes to care for Barnabas in his home during a six-week illness. Lambert interprets the marriage as a means for Barnabas to save the weakened Charlotte. In turn, Richard saves Sylvia when she is "penniless and half-starved," humiliated by her own helplessness.

The more radical statement Freeman makes, however, has more to do with the power of women's values and the necessity of recognizing them as a precondition of marriage. She only allows Sylvia and Charlotte to marry when the men begin to acknowledge and adopt the feminine principles they had so violently denied throughout the novel. Richard only marries Sylvia once he can acknowledge that he was mistaken in his resistance to her love. In his reunion with her, he becomes maternal and comforting. He sits in the rocking chair, now a symbol of maternal caring, and reaches out to Sylvia. He moves his chair close to hers and tells her to put her head down on his shoulder in a gesture of nurturing love.

Before Freeman can allow Barnabas to marry Charlotte, he must recognize the values which his actions on that fateful Sunday night attempted to negate. Barnabas has become a physically weakened character, whose curved spine is a symbol of his diseased soul. When

asked about his injured back, Barnabas responds, " I've hurt my soul.
. . . It happened that Sunday night years ago." His illness progresses
to the point that he "lay there all that time, and his soul became
fairly bound into passiveness with awful fetters of fiery bone and
muscle; sometimes he groaned but nobody heard him" (315–16).
Calling out for comforting now, and for all the love that he had
rejected, Barnabas longs for "the maternal and protecting element
in [Charlotte's] love, and all that he missed or wanted" (316). This
recognition is a critical statement about Freeman's understanding of
what rarely informs heterosexual relationships, the celebration and
acknowledgment of feminine values. Having spent a lifetime denying
emotion, Barnabas sobs in Charlotte's presence. Freeman describes
his "helpless clinging to Charlotte." Barnabas now articulates vulner-
ability and need by telling Charlotte his fear that she will leave if he
recovers from his illness. Freeman also transforms Charlotte, for now
she must have the courage to defy her society. Despite the growing
rumors and the community's disapproval of her for living with
Barnabas out of wedlock, she persists.

The feminized Barnabas, in the conclusion of the novel, has
adopted a new lens. Unlike his earlier vision of nature as a source of
utility and profit, he now observes nature and parts with his earlier
impulse toward domination and control. With no mention of walls
around the trees, he sees that they "were full of that green nebula of
life which comes before the blossom. Little wings, bearing birds and
songs, cut the air" (329). Barnabas now celebrates the beauty of
nature, yielding in fact to images of sensuality as he smells "the
strange fragrance which is more than fragrance, . . . being the very
odor thrown off by the growing motion of life and the resurrection."
What is resurrected through the reunion of Charlotte and Barnabas
is the capacity for love detached from social trappings and judgments
of patriarchy. In the concluding scene Barnabas comes to Cephas in
a state of "humility." Although Charlotte takes the first step forward
in the scene, the values she represents are no longer threatening.
Reunion and marriage, in Freeman's terms, are therefore possible.
With Freeman's reversal of sexual politics, Charlotte has gained a
subtle form of power. As she looked toward her own marriage, this
was a power Freeman hoped she herself would not lose.

5

"SAVAGE SQUAW" AND "FAIR ANGEL"
IN *MADELON*

∞

ONE YEAR AFTER the publication of *Pembroke*, Freeman began to work on a still more graphic study of sexuality and repression. Published by Harper in 1896, *Madelon* is the first work in which Freeman explored the connections between violence, sexuality, and the oppression of women. In this novel, Freeman's interest in character doubles as a literary device went beyond her use of the technique in *Pembroke*. The motion of *Madelon* is dizzying as a series of character pairs propels readers from scenes of rebellion to submission, unconventionality to conventionality, passionate release to painful constraint.

The twisted intricacies of the plot of *Madelon*, particularly in its second half, account for Edward Foster's complaint that it is "obviously and disturbingly uneven";[1] but it is in some sense more interesting for its unevenness. Even when writing *Pembroke*, her most self-contained novel, Freeman worried about the longer form, and expressed doubt in her letters about "her frantic attempt" to complete the work.[2] In *Madelon*, Freeman knew that she was experimenting still further. She thought of the short story as a "simple little melody" and the novel as a "grand opera."[3] Perhaps it was this assumption that drove her to write portions of the novel with an effort toward grandeur, losing the refreshing simplicity, directness, and credibility of her short fiction.

Her own doubts as she worked on *Madelon* were explicit. To one friend, she wrote: "I hope you may like my new novel. I am rather

nervous about it myself, it is so much more romantic than anything
I have ever done. I did not really plan to write it. It commenced as a
short story, then could not seem to keep within short story space."[4]
As she describes it here, it is as though the novel has a force of its
own, beyond her control, an energy that grows beyond the short
form. In another letter, Freeman responded to praise of *Madelon*
with equal uncertainty:

> It was odd, but the very morning of the day, on which I received your
> letter, I had been in a very discouraged frame of mind, and had written
> to a friend, that I wished I could have some praise, quarts, and gallons of
> it, to hearten me up. Therefore you can readily understand, that your
> letter, was very acceptable. I am truly glad, that you like *Madelon,* and I
> appreciate most gratefully, your kindness in telling me so. I have felt
> especially sensitive about this book, it is such a deviation from my usual
> line of work.[5]

Her discomfort with the structural demands of the longer form is
apparent and understandable. Her critics, as Brent Kendrick indicates, complained when they read her novels, of their "excessive
realism, monotony of incidents, and improbable and strange manipulation of situations." These works were seen as "bad novels by a
good short story writer."[6]

The plot of *Madelon* does serve as an example of Freeman's leaning in her longer prose toward improbability. Many of the complica-
tions and incidents seem unnecessary and cumbersome. Yet the veil
of surface entanglements in the plot serves Freeman's purpose in
some sense; they disguise the forbidden subject at the center of the
text: Madelon's aggressive sexuality and potential for violence. The
question underlying all of the twists and turns of the novel is what
women are to do with their most forbidden impulses and desires in
this "little Vermont village."

Madelon's multiple subplots make any attempt to summarize it a
challenge. The central dilemma in the novel is the result of a collective understanding that Madelon Hautville, a dark-haired, passionate
heroine, part French Canadian, part Native American, is not considered a "fair match" for Burr, a man of pure Anglo-Saxon blood. Burr
is torn between the sensual Madelon and the acceptable Dorothy
Fair, the daughter of the orthodox village parson. On the night of
the pivotal incident in the novel, Burr indicates his preference for
Dorothy. That evening the enraged and passionate Madelon returns

home through the forest with a knife under her cloak. Infatuated with Madelon, Burr's cousin, Lot Gordon, approaches her in the woods and attempts to kiss her. Mistaking Lot for Burr, Madelon stabs him.

The second half of the novel becomes, as Foster suggests, a "confusion of cross purposes."[7] Burr suddenly arrives to protect Madelon from the consequences of her crime by sending her home and going to prison in her place, claiming that he is the culprit; Madelon then battles heroically to be recognized as the assailant in order to spare Burr; and finally Lot, who miraculously survives the stabbing until the very end of the novel, swears his injury is a result of a suicide attempt. In return for lying to save Burr, Lot requests that Madelon marry him, and she agrees; but when Lot sees that she cannot love him, he releases her from the promise and kills himself. The scenario includes what Perry Westbrook calls a ludicrous "chain of self-sacrifice."[8] But if we ride on only the surface of this tiresome plot, we lose the very real power and value of the novel.

What becomes most interesting in an analysis of *Madelon* is Freeman's "strange manipulation of situations." She could not, as she herself admitted, "keep within short story space" because of the weight of what she was attempting to sort out—nothing short of the status of women in her society and her own buried needs and conflicts at the critical stage before she decided to leave Mary Wales for Charles Freeman.

Susan Harris, in her intriguing article "But Is It Any Good? Evaluating Nineteenth-Century American Women's Fiction," discusses the difficulty of constructing a method to evaluate the quality of nineteenth-century American women's novels:

> One avenue is to learn how to describe noncanonical American women's literature in terms of process—that is, to see it within the shifting currents of nineteenth-century American ideologies. Acknowledging that imaginative literature is both reactive and creative, we can examine the ways that it springs from, reacts against, or responds to the plots, themes, languages in the discursive arena that engendered it at the same time that it creates new possibilities for that arena by reshaping old words into new ones.[9]

In terms of Harris's redefined criteria for evaluation, Freeman's novel takes on new dimensions and possibilities. Rather than offering the traditional embodiment of "timeless truths," *Madelon* is a superb example of what Harris describes as "reactive and creative," and it therefore has significant political meaning for readers today. What Harris calls "process analysis" offers a way into Freeman's novel, a way of thinking about its implications, however twisted its plot.

Freeman's decision to pursue longer fiction was at least partially a result of her desire to increase her market. Despite the limitations of her novels, the longer works did have wider appeal. They were financial successes. Except for *Madelon,* her novels were serialized before being published as books. She received ample serial payments and royalties. She earned $2,500 in serial payment for *Pembroke* and $3,000 for *Jerome.* Kendrick indicates that for both books, and most likely for *Madelon* too, she received a 15 percent royalty rather than the 10 percent she had received for her first novel, *Jane Field.* The money she earned from her novels allowed her to have, by 1895, "cash assets exceeding $10,000." She became financially "secure and independent." [10] Harris suggests that in order to win such financial success, nineteenth-century women writers such as Freeman had to "conform to the strictures" that encouraged female conformity and passivity; at the same time, to get across their more subversive message about the oppression of women and its effects, they had to "find a form that would embody these dual, and often contradictory ideas." [11] This is precisely what Freeman does in *Madelon.*

Freeman gives her heroine more leeway to rebel in *Madelon* than she did in *Pembroke.* In the later novel she does not shy away from violence and passion, nor does she completely succeed in thwarting her heroine's aggression. It is not surprising that Freeman admitted her doubts and insecurities in her letters. *Madelon* was Freeman's boldest and most flawed attempt at fictive rebellion. The flaws, however, seem to follow the pattern in all of her work on rebels in love; to varying degrees, she worked to tame her boldest women lovers who engage and then withdraw after unleashing their passion.

Perhaps the amount of rebellion she did manage to incorporate in this novel accounts for the contemporary critical reception of *Madelon,* which is best summarized by an article written by George Preston in 1896. Preston was offended by the "many unrefined references to the promiscuous kissing that sounds throughout the book like the popping of fire-crackers." [12] Scene after scene of the novel defies the prudish attitude suggested by Preston's response. The very intensity of its defiance of such attitudes may indeed explain the aesthetic shortcomings of the novel.[13] Charles M. Thompson complained of the absence of "charming people charmingly drawn" in Freeman's work.[14] Freeman did not attempt to appease these distorted reactions to *Madelon*.

It is interesting that Freeman had read *Crime and Punishment* shortly before writing *Madelon*. Madelon's crime, as Westbrook notes, is quite different from Raskolnikov's for it is committed without premeditation, a crime of passion.[15] And yet, the effect *Crime and Punishment* had upon Freeman is important. She said to J. Edgar Chamberlain after reading the novel, "I am at odds with the whole thing, but it is a wonderful book. He writes with more concentrated force than Tolstoi. This book seems to be like one of my own nightmares, and told on my nerves."[16] Certainly the texture of nightmare is apparent in Madelon's fury and in the series of consequent entanglements indeed the entire twisted and frenetic movement of the plot itself suggests that the writer's "nerves" are struggling to ward off some frightening dream throughout the novel.

Freeman seems to have been influenced as well by the work of Emily Brontë. In 1901 she wrote an essay on *Wuthering Heights* which is worth examining for what it suggests about Freeman and her creation of *Madelon*.

> All that Emily Brontë is intent upon is the truth, the exactness of the equations of her characters, not the impression which they make upon her readers or herself. She handles brutality and coarseness as another woman would handle a painted fan. It is enough for her that the thing is so. . . . How she ever came to comprehend the primitive brutalities and passions, and the great truth of life which sanctifies them, is a mystery. . . . She had given to her a light for the hidden darkness of human nature, irrespective of her own emotions. . . . It [the love of Heathcliff and Catherine] is made evident as one of the great forces of life; . . . it does not deal with the social problem; it is beyond it. . . . *Wuthering Heights* from first to last is an unflinching masterpiece. Here is evident no quiver of feminine nerves in the mind or hand.[17]

Athough she did not seem to recognize her link to Brontë, her comments apply to her own life and work as much as they do to Brontë's. At some level, Freeman longed to achieve in *Madelon* the same freedom and passion that she admired in *Wuthering Heights*.

In writing *Madelon*, Freeman worked hard to keep the "quiver of feminine nerves" out of her novel. She attempted to give way to the

paganism which her own New England could never embrace. As
the epigraph to her novel indicates, Freeman hoped to celebrate a
passionate love similar to the love of Heathcliff and Catherine: "Love
is the crown, and the crucifixion, of life, and proves thereby its own
divinity."[18] She admired Brontë's ability to handle "brutality and
coarseness," and she attempted to invest her heroine with all the
forbidden energies she never expressed in her lifetime. One can
almost apply Freeman's comments on Brontë to herself: "How she
ever came to comprehend the primitive brutalities and passions, and
the great truth of life which sanctifies them, is a mystery."

In a rare acknowledgment of their similarities, F. O. Matthiessen
commented that Freeman's statements about Emily Brontë's uncanny capacity to depict passion could be applied to her: "How did
a girl [Freeman] in her twenties who had little experience that could
be measured in external events and who had been shut in upon
herself by delicate health, how did she contrive to know so much
about life, to understand so accurately love and hate, to have pene-
trated souls that were consumed with cruelty and festering mean-
ness, to have guessed the secrets of others that confronted the world
with grim humor and silent courage?"[19] But given the circumstances
of Freeman's own life, she really could not, much as she wanted to,
capture the "primitive brutalities" without expressing a simultaneous
ambivalence and a leaning toward Puritan conscience; nor could she
fully believe in "the great truth of life which sanctifies" such passions. Freeman seems, at times, uncomfortable with her own sympathy for Madelon because this heroine contradicts all that she had
been taught. In subtle ways and at unexpected moments in her
novel, Freeman does give way to what she felt Brontë was able to
ignore: "the impression which they [her characters] make upon her
readers."

One might almost imagine Freeman's consciousness divided between Charlotte and Emily Brontë, a division that is central to her
novel *Madelon*. Like Emily Brontë, Freeman lived an isolated existence, but her imagination was burdened by restrictions that Emily
Brontë more successfully escaped through her fictive lovers. Emily
Brontë may have wavered between the liberty of Wuthering Heights
and the limitations and safety of Thrushcross Grange, but the tug of
the conventionality of New England was something more powerful

and harder for Freeman to resist. In this sense, it becomes much easier to link Freeman to the far more socially concious Charlotte Brontë than to Emily. Yet her attraction to what she called the "hidden darkness of human nature" in *Wuthering Heights* and her sensitivity to the "great forces of life" expressed in that novel may account for the grating inconsistencies of *Madelon*. More rooted in the world of morality than Emily Brontë, Freeman both gave wings to her heroine and grounded her because of her own conflict between her passion and her fear of the penalties.

Charlotte Brontë's sense of restrictions in the parsonage dramatically invaded her work, much like Freeman's Calvinist strain did hers, but there is a difference between Charlotte Brontë's comments on *Wuthering Heights* and Freeman's reaction. Freeman read the love between Heathcliff and Catherine as "one of the great forces of life"; Charlotte Brontë called Heathcliff's love "a sentiment fierce and inhuman." Charlotte Brontë's criticism of her sister's novel had none of the openness to passion that was evident in Freeman's response. Freeman spoke of her admiration for the fiery love of Heathcliff and Catherine, but Charlotte Brontë was careful to direct readers away from the lovers' "perverted passion and passionate perversity" and particularly from Heathcliff who "stands unredeemed" in his "infernal world." She asked readers to note instead the "true benevolence" of the conventional and moral Nelly Dean or the "constancy" of Edgar Linton.[20]

The heroine of *Madelon* differs from women characters in Freeman's earlier works. As she described her in one of her letters, "I have a New England woman, with a strain of Indian blood, for a heroine."[21] Unlike heroines such as Eunice and Charlotte, Madelon suggests wild abandon and heightened sexuality. The character of Rose in *Pembroke* seems to have been a working sketch for Freeman's fuller development of female sexuality through her characterization of Madelon.[22]

From the very start, Freeman's imagery suggests the extent to which Madelon stands outside of village boundaries, just as the approach to her house requires a departure from Ware Center. Burr Gordon, the man with whom Madelon is desperately in love, walks along an isolated pathway which will bring him to Madelon Hautville's house.

There was a new snow over the village. Indeed, it had ceased to fall only at sunset, and it was now eight o-clock. It was heaped apparently with the lightness of foam on the windward sides of the roads, over the fences and the stone walls, and on the village roofs. Its weight was evident only on the branches of the evergreen-trees, which were bent low in their white shagginess, and lost their upward spring. (1)

As in so many of Freeman's regional descriptions, the images here establish an important backdrop for later events in the novel. Nature indifferently blankets all of the sheltering surfaces and borders of a civilized New England village: fences, stone walls, and village roofs. Only Madelon's actions, based upon her instinctive passions, can bring fire into the icy village scene described in the opening paragraph.

As Burr makes his way through the forest toward Madelon's house, parting with the "fences," "stone walls," and soundlessness of the village, Freeman's images become increasingly dreamlike:

In places the branches of the opposite pines stretched to each other like white-draped arms across the road, and slender, snowladen saplings stood out in young crowds well in advance of the old trees. At times the road was no more than a cart-path through the forest, but it was a short-cut to the Hautville place, and that was why Burr Gordon went that way. (2)

Unlike those old branches bending under the snow in the village, the branches here take on the characteristics of lovers as they stretch toward each other. The image of "slender, snowladen saplings" in "young crowds" suggests sensuality and fertility even in seemingly sterile whiteness. Village sounds of civilization fade so that Burr hears "no roll of wheels, or shout, or peal of bell" (2).

What he does hear marks the ultimate shift from village to forest, from the civilized to the primitive, from sterility to passion, from cold light to warm darkness. Madelon's rich soprano voice reaches him from the Hautville house: "When he came close to the house the low structure itself, overlaid with snow, and with snow clinging to its gray-shingled sides like shreds of wool, seemed to vibrate and pulse and shake, and wax fairly sonorous with music, like an organ"(2). The image of snow upon Madelon's house differs from the lifeless snow in the village. In an uncanny sense, the snow becomes full of warmth as it clings to the sides of the house like "shreds of wool." Even more surprisingly, the house "seemed to vibrate and pulse and shake." Already the vibrant sexuality which Madelon offers invests images of frozen lifelessness with the pulse of passion.

Madelon is practicing a fugue with her family and the words of the song, as well as the power of her voice, beckon Burr even as he resists them "with his head bent." She sings and Burr pauses to listen:

> Come, my beloved, haste away,
> Cut short the hours of thy delay,
> Fly like a youthful hart or roe,
> Over the hills where the spices grow. (3)

The song calls for an impulsive flight, a return to animal instincts. The reader learns that "the very breath of the spices of Arabia seemed borne into the young man's senses by that voice. He saw in vision the blue tops of those delectable hills where the myrtle and the cassia grew; he felt within his limbs the ardent impulse of the hart or roe" (3). After listening intently to Madelon's voice, however, Burr resists its pull and returns to the village. This time he travels the main road with a steady view of the "village lights."

After Madelon's actions have upset the peace within the village itself, bringing the primitive into the civilized world, the setting is no longer clearly divided between forest and village. In fact, there is a mounting sense of the inadequacy of all of those roofs, fences, and walls to keep out what Madelon comes to symbolize. Much later in the novel, Freeman describes the village again.

> In this little Vermont village, lying among peacefully sloping hills, away from boisterous river-courses, there was small chance of those physical convulsions which sometimes disturb the quiet of generations. The roar of a spring freshet never smote the ears of the dwellers therein, and the winters passed with no danger of avalanches. From its sheltered situation, destructive storms seldom launched themselves upon it; the oldest inhabitant could remember little injury from lightning or hail or wind. (315)

Every image now contributes to the sense of protected isolation. But, Freeman warns, "physical convulsions" will disturb the quiet of the village when passions "lash themselves . . . into the fury of storm," for "it was here in this little village of Ware Center, which could never know flood or volcanic fire, as if a sort of spiritual whirlpool had appeared suddenly in its midst" (315). Freeman was determined to go a step further than she had allowed herself to do with her characterization of Rose in *Pembroke* by introducing "volcanic fire," and yet she was unequipped to do so effectively without threatening the credibility of her portrait of this "little village."

Madelon and Dorothy exemplify the conflicting images of womanhood at the heart of Freeman's self-division. As Sandra M. Gilbert and Susan Gubar suggest, "even the most apparently conservative and decorous women writers obsessively create fiercely independent characters who seek to destroy all the patriarchal structures which both their authors and their authors' submissive heroines seem to accept as inevitable."[23] Freeman does this with her character Madelon in her mad, spontaneous stabbing. Madelon's behavior is then pitted against the passive Dorothy Fair and in a strangely powerful way, Madelon becomes Dorothy's double, acting upon passions that remained locked inside Dorothy. In turn, Madelon seems to express Freeman's anxiety and rage. Perhaps her characterizations of Dorothy and Madelon provided a way for Freeman to "come to terms with uniquely female feelings of fragmentation."[24] In her own life, Freeman had been expected to play the role of a Dorothy, but Madelon's rebellious impulses hovered beneath the surface and emerged in her writing; inevitably she grew to fear both selves.

It is useful here to remember Freeman's mysterious, unfinished story in which she created the angry narrator, Jane Lennox, rebel spinster: "Here am I, a woman, rather delicately built of rather delicate tastes, perfectly able to break those commandments, to convert into dust every one of those Divine laws. I shudder before my own power, yet I glory because of it."[25] A "rather delicately built" woman fits the descriptions we have of Mary Wilkins Freeman and of her character Dorothy. But the power to break commandments and to "convert into dust" the Divine laws of a patriarchal world remained buried inside Freeman and only found full expression in Madelon's actions. Her persona, Jane Lennox, both shudders and glories in this power, just as Freeman both fears and takes flight with it in her creation of Madelon.

Yet another point made by Gilbert and Gubar is crucial in connection to Freeman's creation of Dorothy and Madelon. However indirectly, Freeman does punish Madelon for her rebellion by the end of the novel. Although our sympathies lean toward Madelon in the beginning, by the middle of the story she is both tyrannical and ludicrous. Gilbert and Gubar explain the impact of this process of punishment: "By projecting their rebellious impulses . . . into mad or monstrous women (who are suitably punished in the course of the novel or poem), female authors dramatize their own self-division, their desire both to accept the strictures of patriarchal society and to reject them."[26] As the novel progresses, Madelon enacts much of the rebellion that the conventional Dorothy suppresses. By the end of the novel, the passive Dorothy and the active Madelon seem to change roles so that each takes on the characteristics of the other, expressing Freeman's conflicting needs. Just as Charlotte and Rose become doubles in *Pembroke,* the acceptable and unacceptable lovers of Barnabas, Madelon and Dorothy are presented throughout the novel as two images in a distorted mirror. The difference, however, shows something new in Freeman's development, for in her earlier novel, the heroine is the good and moral Charlotte and Rose is a minor character. When she wrote *Madelon,* Freeman dared to focus upon and enlarge the figure of Rose into an explosive heroine who upsets the rigid balance of male and female roles in her village. Here it is the more passive woman Dorothy who is the minor character.

A comparison of the physical appearance of each character further dramatizes this sense of shadow selves, dark and sexual, fair and angelic. The initial description of Madelon's appearance instantly captures movement, activity, sensuality. She stands beside her brothers and sings. It is Lot who gazes on longingly although Madelon had hoped Burr would come:

> Madelon, her brown throat swelling above her lace tucker, like a bird's, stood in the midst of the men, and sang and sang, and her wonderful soprano flowed through the harmony like a river of honey; and yet now and then it came with a sudden fierce impetus, as if she would force some enemy to bay with music. Madelon was slender, but full of curves which were like the soft breast of a bird before an enemy. Sometimes as she sang she flung out her slender hands with a nervous gesture which had hostility in it. (13)

The duality of Madelon's personality is apparent. Her voice offers harmony along with "sudden" ferocity. Her body is gentle, soft, bird-like, even vulnerable, but her gesture has "hostility in it." Freeman implies that Madelon's mixed heritage almost predetermines the split in her character, which becomes increasingly dramatic as the novel progresses. She is rebel and saint, monster and angel, "savage squaw" (as she calls herself when she sees fair Dorothy) and selfless lover of Burr (32). Yet Freeman magnifies the savage side of Madelon, and she does so with an odd mixture of admiration and condemnation.

Unlike Madelon, Dorothy Fair "came of a gentle and self-controlled race of New England ministers" (8). With her "fair curls," her "face pink and smiling openly like a child's" and her "utter daintiness" she provides a radical contrast to the dark Madelon whose "lips were fuller of warm red life than the roses" (27) and whose "black eyes" gaze longingly at Burr.[27] For Burr, Dorothy's "softly affectionate kisses were to Madelon Hautville's as the fall of snowflakes to drops of warm honey" (10). Furthermore, Dorothy is accepted by the village community while Madelon represents an "alien race" and is "looked upon with a mixture of fear and aversion in this village of people whose blood had flowed in one course for generations" (10–11).

Madelon's consequent self-conception is twofold. She both prides herself in her aggressiveness and internalizes the village view of her inferior status. When Burr convinces her to come to sing and play the fiddle at the dance, Madelon, who has prepared to attend the dance in the hopes of being with Burr, agrees to do the job. Having decorated her old black dress with vibrant red roses, she appears as a figure of dazzling sexuality. When she sees the delicate Dorothy enter the ballroom, however, she is confronted with an angel of acceptability.

Every detail of Dorothy's appearance contrasts radically with the earthy images associated with Madelon; the difference between the two women dramatizes Freeman's fragmented conception of womanhood:

> Dorothy Fair, waving a great painted fan with the tremulous motion of a butterfly's wing, with her blue brocade petticoat tilting airily as she moved, like an inverted bell-flower, with a locket set in brilliants flashing on her white neck, with her pink and white face smiling out with gentle gaiety from her fair curls, stepped delicately, pointing out her blue satin toes, around the ball-room, with one little white hand on Burr Gordon's arm. (31)

The airy motions, the unearthly delicacy, the fair curls, and the "little white hand" all contribute to the effect of Dorothy's ethereal unreality; with the "tremulous motion of a butterfly's wing," she is angelic, transient, ephemeral. In essence, she is otherworldly, "tilting airily," performing a predetermined role she can neither control nor comprehend.

In the contrast between Madelon and Dorothy, and in Madelon's consequent self-image, Freeman offers an analysis of the destructive effects of society's standards of beauty for women. Madelon's reaction to this vision of womanhood to which she can never conform foreshadows the self-punishment to come; she internalizes the social disdain for her own contrasting sexuality and feels shame for her vibrant cheeks and lips. Her transformed self-conception is interesting: "Suddenly all Madelon's beauty was cheapened in her own eyes. She saw herself swart and harsh-faced as some old savage squaw beside this fair angel. She turned on herself as well as on her recreant lover with rage and disdain—and all the time she lilted without one break" (32). This vision of herself accompanies Madelon as she walks through the forest to return home on the night she stabs Lot.

By attending the dance, Dorothy has also broken a rule and rebelled in the eyes of her father, Parson Fair, since she "had been brought up to believe in the sinful and hellward tendencies of the dance" (32). Already Dorothy's and Madelon's identities begin to cross as each harbors what the other suppresses. Dorothy's small act of rebellion becomes a shadow for Madelon's forthcoming crime. Later Dorothy's angelic morality will color Madelon's behavior.

Given her self-condemnation in the face of Dorothy's angelic pose at the dance, it would seem that Madelon attempts to kill not only Burr but that side of herself, rooted in her "squaw" sexuality, which invites Lot's or Burr's sexual advances. Like Raskolnikov in *Crime and Punishment*, Madelon is both the "tormenter and the tormented," victimizer and victim.[28] Her attempt to destroy Burr when she walks home with a knife is an attempt to destroy the passion Burr evokes inside the "savage" self, the self that interferes with acceptability and refuses to submit to the "fair angel" image. It becomes increasingly apparent that Madelon's hostility is directed inward and that it is the passionate side of herself that she wishes to punish. Thus after trying to hurt Burr, she attempts to punish herself for the remainder of the novel as she offers her continual plea to be recognized and penalized for the crime.[29]

The reactions of the fathers of each heroine suggest Freeman's rage at the patriarchal conception of women which so complicates self-definition. In this sense, both men represent the male voices that most likely influenced Freeman's conception of herself as a woman. David Hautville and Parson Fair offer perspectives on women that must have been shared by Freeman's father when he became dismayed at Mary's unmarried status. Freeman employs what Susan Harris calls "a linguistic debate" in which "discursive world views are brought into conjunction or confrontation." Her analysis of the paternal response to Madelon's and even Dorothy's ultimate rebellion, in keeping with Harris's approach to evaluation, anticipates "later ideological or political debate" on gender.[30]

When Madelon continues to insist that she stabbed Lot, her father refuses to believe her and attempts to lock her in her room for her own safety. No matter how violent Madelon can become, she has a history of subsiding into docility with her father. In this case, however, she raises her hand to demonstrate to her father how she had struck the man she thought was Burr. Her father's response is significant:

> Her father looked at her gloomily, then strode on with his eyes on the snowy ground. He was still in doubt. David Hautville had that primitive order of mind which distrusts and holds in contempt that which it cannot clearly comprehend, and he could not comprehend womankind. His sons were to him as words of one syllable in straight lines; his daughter was written in compound and involved sentences, as her mother had been before her. Fond and proud of Madelon as he was, and in spite of his stern anxiety, her word had not the weight with him that one of his son's would have had. It was as if he had visions of endless twistings and complexities which might give it the lie, and rob it, at all events of its direct force. (55)

Because of what her father sees as "twistings and complexities," Madelon can never be taken seriously; she is ranked beneath her brothers in power. George Eliot explores this same dilemma in her depiction of Maggie and Tom Tulliver in *The Mill on the Floss*.[31] When Madelon begs her father to believe her and not to allow Burr to be wrongly hanged, David simply smiles at her and thinks to himself: "She's nothing but a woman" (56). He hastens her along and asks for "no more fooling." His attempt to explain away Madelon's passion with the phrase "she's nothing but a woman" is at the core of Madelon's actions, perhaps the motivation for her violence. With that phrase in mind, Freeman invests her heroine with the power to counteract such a reduction. Indeed the male voice chanting such a phrase seems to be the motivation for the entire novel, and perhaps the cause for its "unevenness."

So much does Freeman long to overthrow such a deflation of female power that she creates, in the end, a monster figure at the center of the novel. When Madelon rides a dangerous, wild mare to reach Burr in his prison, her brother asks David Hautville if Madelon has lost her sanity. Again, David's reply is curious: " 'No, she's a woman,' returned his father with a strange accent of contempt and toleration" (70). As the only daughter, Madelon has been raised with her father's "contempt" beneath a surface "toleration." Finally, Madelon must defy her father's notions of being "just a woman." He orders her to her room and she temporarily submits to his will, but her face "was deathly white and full of rebellion," and ultimately "there was no yielding in her." As she continually and almost irritatingly insists upon her guilt for the remainder of the novel, claiming that she is demanding recognition for her crime for Burr's sake, it becomes clear that her motives run deeper than a desire to save Burr. The rebellious Madelon seems to be demanding recognition for her masculine virility and power. She fights to defy the collective "town" response: "Likely story a gal did it" (53).

Parson Fair seems to be an extension of the father figure we see in "A Moral Exigency," and in some sense a double for Madelon's father. When Madelon goes to see Dorothy to demand her aid in rescuing Burr from prison, she must first face the stern, Puritan figure of Parson Fair at the door. As Madelon defeats all of his hesitations to let her enter his house, the parson is "shocked and half alarmed. He had not had to do with women like this, who spoke with such fervor of passion. His womankind had swathed all their fiercer human emotions with shy decorum and stern modesty, as Turkish women swathe their faces with veils" (83). Indeed his "womankind" were models of subservience, like Freeman's mother, so that a forceful figure like Madelon becomes a monster in his eyes. Unlike David, who dismisses Madelon's behavior, Parson Fair is terrified and sees Madelon as a great threat. The patriarchal responses to Madelon's rebellion are either the Parson's fear or David's dismissal; she is either enlarged to the size of a monster or reduced to the size of an insignificant child throwing a tantrum. In either case, she is marginalized and seen as unacceptable.

Later in the novel, a scene very like the confrontation between

Madelon and David occurs between Parson Fair and Dorothy. Parson Fair insists that Dorothy marry Burr as planned; Dorothy rebels and turns into the Madelon-like figure he fears so much, for she has fallen in love with Madelon's brother, Eugene. Although her father commands her with "a great authority of fatherhood and priesthood in his voice" (299), Dorothy will not yield. In this sense, Freeman seems to achieve an indirect revenge against her own father's will, as she has the transformed monster-daughter never yield to the authority the father exerts. Although she both yielded to and resisted her father's influence, Freeman's resistance was never open, never angry enough to release the kinds of words she feeds to Madelon and ultimately to Dorothy.

Freeman accepted and rejected her society's definition of women as subservient figures. In both cases, she faced the problem of self-definition which her novel demonstrates. Violent madwoman or agreeable angel, Madelon or Dorothy, the women characters in *Madelon* struggle against constructions of self that are not their own. Gilbert and Gubar's comments are relevant in this regard: "The woman writer acknowledges with pain, confusion and anger that what she sees in the mirror is usually a male construct, the 'pure gold baby' of male brains, a glittering and wholly artificial child."[32]

Hence Madelon gazes at her mirror opposite when she confronts the "pure gold baby" in the form of Dorothy at the beginning of the novel and sees what she must be if she is to win the prize of New England acceptability. Again and again, Dorothy appears childlike —Parson Fair's obedient shadow. But, as Dorothy transforms, she confronts her mirror opposite in Madelon and sees the figure of evil she has been warned against in her father's stern preaching. This dichotomy shaped Freeman's life. As Gilbert and Gubar put it, "whether she is a passive angel or an active monster, . . . the woman writer feels herself to be literally or figuratively crippled by the debilitating alternatives her culture offers her."[33] The consequent self-alienation is evident in a scene following Madelon's crime. She braids her black hair and gazes at the mirror:

> but the face therein did not look like her own to her, and she felt all the time as if she were braiding and wreathing the hair around another's head. One of those deeds had she committed which lead a man to see suddenly the stranger that abides always in his flesh and in his own soul,

and makes him realize that of all the millions on earth there is not one
that he knows not better than his own self, nor whose face can look so
strange to him in the light of his own actions. (58–59)

As Madelon views her reflection, the split self is strikingly apparent.
This mirror scene directly follows Madelon's conventionally dutiful
behavior toward her father and brothers. She has just "attended the
needs of the males of her family with . . . stern faithfulness," only to
confront that other self when she is alone with her hidden mirror
reflection (44). Here she sees her mirror image as that of a stranger
(and Freeman abruptly shifts to the male pronoun) whose face "can
look so strange to *him* in the light of *his* own actions." The scene
echoes the scene in "A Moral Exigency" where Eunice's image appears in double form. It captures as well the same eerie sensation of
her unpublished poem, "The Stranger." [34]

Directly after stabbing Lot, Madelon is metaphorically identified
with the masculine as she "stood for a second looking at the dark,
prostrate form as one of her Iroquois ancestors might have looked
at a fallen foe before he drew his scalping knife." A moment later
"the surging of the savage blood in her ears grew faint" and she falls
to her knees beside her victim. But in the first section of the novel
"savage blood" wins out in the battle between Madelon's antithetical
selves, and the sober New England figure takes shape in the form of
Burr's fiancée, Dorothy Fair. Similarly, in the initial confrontations
between Dorothy and Madelon, Dorothy's hidden rebel self remains
completely suppressed and only her self-restrained characteristics
are visible.

Freeman establishes striking polarities as she develops her opposing heroines: Madelon's activity, Dorothy's inactivity; Madelon's virility, Dorothy's femininity; Madelon's passion, Dorothy's restraint;
Madelon's physical strength, Dorothy's frailty; Madelon's extreme
and spontaneous outbursts, Dorothy's quiet steadiness and modera-
tion. In sum, we see the foreign, savage figure of the dark "squaw"
and the sweet, weak image of the Puritan-bred, "white and fair
angel." While Madelon acts upon her own definition of justice without concern for morality, Dorothy Fair (as her surname suggests) is
morally scrupulous—fair—according to her society's definition of
"fairness."

The first most apparent contrast between Dorothy and Madelon following Madelon's crime is in how they respond to the dilemma Burr faces. Dorothy becomes frail and ill: she takes to bed almost immediately and is utterly paralyzed with despair. Madelon, in contrast, leaps on the back of a wild mare despite the objections of all the males surrounding her. "Not another woman in the village, and scarcely a man except the Hautville sons [who Madelon now begins to resemble], would have dared to ride this roan with the backward roll of her vicious eyes and her wicked, flat-laid ears; but Madelon Hautville could not be thrown" (59). Ironically, the horse is female and becomes just one more double in the novel, like the image Madelon sees in the mirror. Madelon appears mad to all who observe her action in this scene, and the mention of the "vicious" eyes of the "wicked" roan suggests Freeman's magnification of Madelon's defiance in bestial terms.

The male response to Madelon at this point reveals the social resistance to her actions: one of the men at the stable responds, "I wouldn't tech a gal that could git the upperhand of a horse like that roan mare with a ten foot pole" (102). Indeed the guard at Burr's prison, "a great man, with an arm like a crow bar," cannot block Madelon's attempt to enter Burr's cell because she scares him so: "all his great system of bone and muscle seemed to back out of the room before her" (60–61). Here, the suggestion is of supernatural, even demonic power. Certainly Freeman's pleasure in offering her heroine such strength is apparent, for in scene after scene, authoritative males become miraculously and suddenly weak in Madelon's presence.

When Madelon confronts Dorothy, the dichotomy Freeman sees, the two sides of her own personality, appears in the contrasts she stresses. Dorothy gives way to the acceptable response of her village. She submits to the village view that Burr stabbed Lot. To Madelon's angry response, "Are you a woman, Dorothy Fair?" Dorothy shrinks away with "frightened blue eyes" (90–91). Madelon's words are fascinating for she reveals another interesting facet of Freeman's use of doubles—her link to Burr: "My God, don't you know the man you love is yourself? . . . when you believe in his guilt you believe in your own" (91). The "white and trembling" Dorothy Fair can only sob in response. Madelon swears on the "Holy Book" that her hand, not Burr's, stabbed Lot Gordon. She shows Dorothy that her hands "are strong as a man's." Dorothy meekly follows Madelon, but she does so with a mixture of "bewildered terror" and pale passivity, asking only "how?" and complaining that she is ill and must stay in bed to tend to her headache and fever. To each of Dorothy's pleas, Madelon responds violently and scoffs, "I tell you, if my two feet were cut off, I would walk to him on the stumps to set him free." The violent imagery implies the self-destruction implicit in Madelon's heroism. Dorothy, the sheltered New Englander, melts under Madelon's "fiery zeal." With her "innocent, frightened eyes" on her double's "passionate face," she allows herself to be led out of the protection of Parson Fair's home, but always with an inner resistance to Madelon's passion: "She could not withstand this fierce and ardent girl who upbraided her with the cowardice and distrust of her love" (97).

Madelon rejects Parson Fair's lame and feeble horse and heads for the nearest stable where she again insists upon driving the fastest, most dangerous horse. When the owner asks, "don't ye want a man to hitch the horse" (101), Madelon overthrows convention and is off in the open sleigh on the wintry evening before she can receive aid from any males. Madelon's goal in this journey is to have Burr confess his innocence to Dorothy, thinking he will do so for the woman he loves. Dorothy would then aid Madelon in freeing him. But Burr continues to sacrifice for Madelon, and Dorothy emerges believing in his guilt. Once again Madelon's passion is pitted against Dorothy's pallor. She insists that if Dorothy loved Burr, she would have flung her arms around him and made him tell the truth, and Dorothy responds with "cold dignity," that "I throw my arms around no man unbidden!" (113). Dorothy "drew herself up with gentle stiffness"; in contrast, Madelon "flung out the reins over the horse's back" (113).

As the contrasts heighten, Dorothy appears largely in a negative light while Freeman seems to celebrate Madelon's bravery. In a sense, Freeman gives a harsh, even bitter description of the "white flower" Dorothy has become because of her training; she expresses a kind of wish-fulfillment through the woman who openly shows her passion, the heroine who is capable of acting as a man would. But later in the novel, Freeman's approval shifts away from the active figure and in favor of passivity.

Elvira Gordon, Burr's mother, presents another example of Freeman's fragmentation, her conflict between womanly propriety and passion. Mrs. Gordon becomes a magnified extension of the Puritan conscience within Madelon, a reflection of "the self-restraint of [Madelon's] New England mother" which is periodically "upon her" (204) and which Madelon buries beneath all her outward aggression. Mrs. Gordon is, in one sense, a grown-up version of Dorothy Fair and a reflection of Freeman's carefully controlled mask of gentility. Her appearance might be a description of Freeman at a similar age: she is a "slender woman with the face of a saint, long and pale and full of gentle melancholy with large, meek-lidded blue eyes and patiently compressed lips" (148). A glance at Freeman's portrait reveals a similar image of saintly reserve, particularly in the "patiently compressed lips." Like Freeman, Mrs. Gordon married late in life. Mrs. Gordon was previously a preceptress in a "young ladies' school" (149), the locale for many of Freeman's self-restrictive characters and the place where Freeman struggled for a year as a student. Madelon's confrontation with Mrs. Gordon seems to offer Freeman an opportunity for self-laceration.

As soon as Madelon enters Mrs. Gordon's sitting room, with snow still clinging to her from her long hike, she brings with her all the passion that Mrs. Gordon has managed to repress. Beside Madelon's spirited gestures and words, Mrs. Gordon appears a pathetically pale figure. Freeman warns us, however, that "she was still the example of her own precepts—all outward decorum if not inward composure" (149). The phrase already indicates Mrs. Gordon's duality and hints at a possible "Madelon" locked inside this "punctiliously polite" woman. With the "extremist manners of the old New England gentlewoman," the reserved Mrs. Gordon leads Madelon into the sitting room where she must face her mirror opposite and counterpart in the form of the wildly raging Madelon:

> Madelon Hautville, opposite her, in her snow-powdered cloak, with her face like a flash of white fire in her snow-powdered silk hood, seemed in comparison a female of another and an older race. She might well, from the look of her, have come a nearer and straighter road from the inmost heart of things, from the unpruned tangle of woods and undammed course of streams, from all primitive and untempered love and passion and religion, than this gentlewoman formed upon the model of creeds and scholars. (150)

Freeman's imagery associates Madelon with "unpruned," untamed nature. We see Madelon's face "like a flash of white fire" and then the passage focuses on Mrs. Gordon's hands, which she kept folded "whether she walked or sat" (148). The folded hands indicate her self-control as she rests in a position of acceptance, unable to comprehend Madelon's open expression of emotion. Again, it is easy to associate Mrs. Gordon with the facade Freeman presented to her New England village, a "gentlewoman formed upon the models of creeds and scholars" (150). Unlike the theology that shaped Mrs. Gordon's and Freeman's upbringing, Madelon's active, "untempered" religion has primitive passion and feeling.

Face to face, Mrs. Gordon and Madelon act out the conflict at the center of Freeman's existence. Mrs. Gordon quietly directs Madelon to maintain her self-control. With "her folded hands in her lap" she remains motionless, "never stirring" (150). Against her immobility, Freeman presents Madelon's explosive movements: "Madelon bent towards her with a sudden motion, as if she would seize her by the shoulders." To the passionate Madelon, Mrs. Gordon's control is unbearable. She cries out, "How can you be seated, how can you rest a moment. . . . Why do you not move?" (150). Mrs. Gordon offers the standard New England response to disaster; she informs Madelon that she has prayed. Again, Madelon is a volcano beside Elvira's calm and demands that she "act to save him [Burr]" (150). The following passage is an indication of Freeman's inner battle.

> Her eyes blazed; she clinched her hands. She felt as if she could spring at this other woman with her gentle murmurings and soft foldings, and shake her into her own meaning of life. If her impulse had had the power of deed, Elvira Gordon's little cap of fine needlework would have been a fiercely crumpled rag upon her decorous head, her sober bands of gray hair would have streamed like the locks of a fury, the quiet clasp of her long fingers would have been stirred with some response of indignant defense if nothing else. Madelon, with her, realized the worst balk in the world—the balk of a passive nature in the path of an active one—and all her fiery zeal seemed to flow back into herself and fairly madden her. (151)

In this passage, Madelon's animalistic impulse to "spring at" Mrs. Gordon seems to be shared by the author. Yet, the violent imagery also transforms Madelon into somewhat of a monster with whom it is difficult to sympathize. The implications of the passage are fascinating, for as Madelon's eyes "blaze," she longs to "shake" her opposite into a monster equal in size and strength to her own "savage" self. Freeman's anger at Mrs. Gordon's passivity seems to be an anger directed at herself—given her resemblance to the character—and comes across in the eruptive images channeled through Madelon's consciousness. She achieves an imaginary attack on Elvira Gordon and in so doing, releases her rage at a lifetime of self-restraint. To undo Mrs. Gordon's well-developed New England facade seems very dangerous indeed. Elvira's little cap, the traditional cap Freeman's women often wear, becomes a "fiercely crumpled rag upon her decorous head." The edge and bite to each image builds in violence as Madelon next imagines "her sober bands of gray hair" transformed into the streaming "locks of a fury." To undo Mrs. Gordon's surface mask by removing the cap would be to uncover the rage of a hidden monster. If the passage gives us what Freeman sees as a passive nature in the path of an active one, it also signifies the dangers Freeman perceives in the active nature. If a passive woman gives way to release, she becomes, in her society's mind and in Freeman's as well, a threatening and fearful figure. Yet the urge remains to create just that, an embodiment of her revenge against society.

In the scene that follows Madelon's departure from her house, Elvira feels "shocked in all her delicate decorum by such unmaidenly violence and self-betrayal" and thinks of Madelon with astonishment and terror (153). Yet the visit has upset her carefully controlled world. When she is alone in her room, she begins to unlock a door which releases, at least partially, the Madelon she harbors within:

> Mrs. Gordon stood at one of the narrow lights beside her front door and watched until Madelon entered the opposite house; then she went hastily through her fine sitting-room to her own bedroom, and there went down on her knees, and all her icy constraint melted into a very passion of weeping and prayer. Those placidly folded hands of hers clutched at the poor mother-bosom in the fury of her grief; those placid-lidded eyes welled over with scalding tears; that calmly set mouth was convulsed like a wailing child's and all the rigorous lines of her whole body were relaxed into overborne curves of agony. (153)

Beneath the distracting sentimentality of phrases like "poor mother-bosom," the series of contrasts developed in the confrontation between Madelon and Mrs. Gordon are amplified, so that Madelon exists in the private chambers of Mrs. Gordon's consciousness. As Mrs. Gordon rushes from the outer sitting room to her own bedroom, a metaphor for the narrator's movement into Elvira's consciousness, the reader sees a hidden, passionate Elvira. Her religion is no longer a passive theology, but is instead, like Madelon's, so powerful that it causes her to "melt into a very passion of weeping and prayer." Each passive aspect of Mrs. Gordon's appearance when she met with Madelon is here turned into the very volcano Madelon longed for. The straight, rigorous lines of her body become curved, her reserve and icy constraint melt, and the images of heat in her scalding tears remind us again of Madelon. The folded hands now clutch, and her poised position on the sofa is transformed as she falls to her knees. In each case, passivity becomes activity—even if it is only the activity of grieving alone in her room. Hence Madelon's role, in one sense, is to express outwardly those energies that Mrs. Gordon (and Freeman as well) could only unleash in the privacy of a bedroom.

The male characters in *Madelon* are more difficult to interpret than the fragmented women in the novel. This can be partially attributed to the weakness of Freeman's characterizations of men and to Freeman's own ambivalence concerning their roles in relation to the heroine's aggression. Burr, for example, is never fully developed or even described and this contributes to the aesthetic problems of the novel. The reader is driven to question the heroism of Madelon when it is all for the purpose of saving a character who is more shadow than reality. The use of the psychological double, so effective in her portrayals of Dorothy, Madelon, and Mrs. Gordon, becomes awkward and redundant when she turns to the male characters of Burr, Lot, and Madelon's brother Eugene.

The men in the novel seem to be modeled after the few men Freeman knew. Hanson Tyler and, to a greater extent, Charles Freeman, certainly appear in fictive form in her novel. Around the time of Hanson Tyler's marriage in California, Mary met Charles, a man of similar temperament. Foster describes Charles Freeman as follows:

> His head was finely moulded, his eyes clear and friendly; he moved with casual grace. Though he talked well of men and women and books, something of a boyish quality lingered in his manner. Kate Upson Clark, who had arranged the introduction, said that Dr. Charles Manning Freeman refused to grow up; he drank too much, drove fast horses, courted all the girls, skillfully eluded marriage. Though a graduate of Columbia's College

of Physicians and Surgeons, he did not practice medicine and was bored
by the coal and wood business which he had managed since his father's
death.[35]

The legend of Charles Freeman's irresponsibility and of his daring
nature appealed to Mary Wilkins. Foster explains it this way: "herself
a rebel, however timid and conventional in manner, she admired the
rebellious streak in Charles Freeman."[36] Clark expands on this in
her afterword to *The Revolt of "Mother" and Other Stores:* "Charles
Freeman was a later incarnation of Tyler. Probably his lusty manner
drew her to him. She herself was so thoroughly a reserved New
Englander that it must have been a relief to meet a man who relished
the world of the senses."[37] It is Madelon, however, and not Burr
whom Freeman invests with some of the characteristics which drew
her to Charles Freeman. Indeed, Madelon becomes a female incarnation of Charles, the author's opportunity to adopt the rebellious
characteristics of her fiancé (and the "world of the senses" he represents to her) as her own through her heroine. Madelon carries herself with that same "casual grace" when she is at the height of her
sensuality at the dance, and she also drives the fastest horses. Aspects
of Charles and Hanson also seem to appear in the figures of Burr
(though the echoes are faint) and to a greater extent in Madelon's
brother Eugene. Both are boyish, impulsive, passionate, sensual. Lot
Gordon, literary, imaginative, frail, and full of unfulfilled desires,
seems to reflect the creative but reserved self in Freeman, the artist
and observer.

Early in the novel, it becomes clear that the male characters function merely as shadows for the development of the women in the
novel. Burr's character is divided between his passionate longing for
Madelon and his need for the conventional acceptance Dorothy
represents. Lot sums it up well when he tells Burr, "You're going to
see Dorothy Fair when you want to see Madelon Hautville, because
you don't want to do what you want to" (5). As the two men face
each other, looking almost exactly alike in the darkness of the forest
where they meet, Lot claims that he has "given up trying to work
against my own motions" (6). In fact, Lot pursues Madelon without
any of Burr's ambivalence. Yet Lot is paradoxically the man of intel-
lect and word. He recites melodramatic, sentimental poetry and
seems far less likely than Burr to be capable of forceful action. The

two cousins function as doubles, but they are not as interesting as Madelon and Dorothy.

Burr and Lot change identities just as Madelon and Dorothy eventually do; in the beginning of the novel, Lot does not try to "work against [his] own motions" in order to satisfy village standards of behavior, while Burr busily courts Dorothy in the hopes of attaining an acceptable position in his community. As the novel progresses, however, Burr renounces his love for Dorothy despite the knowledge that he may have more in common with her since they have both been influenced by breathing "the same noxious air as did the persecuted Quakers and witches of bygone times" (334). He finally parts with any hope of respectability and gives way to his "motions" or impulses. At the same time, Lot begins to adopt Burr's early concerns as he finds a way to clear Madelon and worries about the village view of the entire incident. By the end of the novel, Burr is capable of facing, without fear, the whispered rejection of his community, "that black atmosphere of suspicion and hatred which gathers nowhere more easily than in a New England town" (334).

Aside from the description of the initial conflict between his passion for Madelon and his engagement to Dorothy, Burr receives very little direct attention from the author. He exists as an extension of Madelon, as her purpose and identity, as the spark that ignites her fiery, almost frenetic actions. As a dark shadow in the forest, he is an image of the deeper self. When Madelon attempts to stab him, and mistakenly stabs Lot, she stabs at the passion that Burr excites in her more than she does at any external figure; she stabs at the values of a community that rejects her sort of beauty.

In her creation of Madelon's brother Eugene, Freeman attempts to merge in one character Lot's poetry and Burr's masculinity. Eugene's love for Dorothy fills him with a "sense of earthquake and revolution" (273). Yet like Burr, Eugene worries about respectability. He is shocked by Dorothy's rebellion against marriage to Burr and at first he resists her transformation. Finally, it is precisely her change in character that increases his attraction to her. Again, we receive very little information about Eugene aside from his physical similarities to Madelon. When Dorothy begins to show her attraction to Eugene, he immediately sets out for a walk in the forest with the "strain of wild nomadic blood" in his veins (192). He is in touch with nature, much as Lot is, but he does not intellectualize it. Eugene sees "the empty nests revealed on the naked trees, the scattered berries on leafless bushes, the winter larders of birds, the tiny track of a wild hare or a partridge in the snow" without attributing deeper symbolic meanings to the sights. He is simply more at home in these "surroundings" than he is within "four domestic walls" (192). Like Madelon, he is a figure of freedom, at home in nature. However, Eugene also maintains that odd mixture of freedom and self-restriction. Beyond this general sense of Eugene's duality, Freeman gives her reader very little to go on. Eugene exists as the inspiration for Dorothy's transition from passive to active loving.

Lot's description of women in love may capture Freeman's predicament as she attempted, in vain, to create vivid male characters. When Burr expresses his fear that Madelon loves Lot and not him, Lot responds with a statement that seems to sum up the dilemma for nineteenth-century women trapped within male constructs: "it is neither you nor me, nor any other man that she will ever love as he is. Woman reverses creation. She is a sublimated particle of a man, and she builds a god from her own superstructure, and clothes him with any image whom she chooses. She chose yours. Live up to her thought of you, if you can" (285). In this novel, male characters become shadows for women whose voices were rarely heard in Freeman's village. Burr and Eugene appear to be vague figures echoing the emotion and confusion of the female characters, Madelon and Dorothy, who dominate the novel. The men circle around the women as though they are merely apparitions reflecting Madelon's self-division. Clark explains, "most young men in Wilkinston make brief appearances in a world where the decisive relationships are those that women have with each other. Typically, a young man's physical appearance and economic status are briefly delineated. He comes courting, stands at the door, sits in the parlor on a haircloth sofa, or is seen working his fields. But it is as if we see him always in half-light, shadowed. Men may cause the commotion, but they never get the center of the stage."[38]

Once Lot has claimed that the stabbing was a suicide attempt and Burr has been released from prison, the focus of the novel quickly shifts back to Madelon's rebellion, which now begins to take a ludicrous turn. She devotes herself to the mission of uniting Burr and Dorothy, because, as she explains to Eugene, "I've gone past myself.

All I think of now is what he wants" (187). In essence, her identity is shaped by Burr and her rebellion is directed toward self-denial. Mistakenly assuming she acts in Burr's interest, she works with the fierce energies of self-sacrifice. Finally, when it becomes apparent that Burr and Dorothy cannot marry, Madelon attempts to keep her pledge to marry Lot in order to save Burr again from the courts of law. Seeing that she cannot love him, however, Lot releases Madelon from the pledge. Madelon's resistance to Lot is itself a form of rebellion for she openly expresses her revulsion in spite of the fact that, unlike marriage to his cousin Burr, marriage to Lot would bring security and financial benefits. The more Lot attempts to buy her love, the more she resists. Yet once released from the bond, Madelon becomes full of submissive fidelity to her lover, Burr. With no longer any cause for rebellion, she completes the journey toward utter selflessness.

Eugene sees the transition and describes the change in Madelon accurately:

> He would as soon have thought of a wild-cat which he had trailed in the woods, which knew him as his mortal enemy, whose eyes had followed him with stealthy fury out of a way-side bush, to unbend from the crouch of its spring and walk purring tamely into his house at call, and fall to lapping milk out of a saucer on the hearth. But no man can estimate the possibilities of character under the lever of circumstances, and there is power enough abroad to tame the savage in all nature. (188)

Madelon, once a "wild-cat" ready to spring at Mrs. Gordon, becomes a tamed savage, a domestic cat curled up at home on the hearth instead of attacking her enemies.

Although Freeman tames her dark heroine, she strategically manages to shift rebellious energies over to Dorothy Fair; in this way, there is still room for the expression of that desire to rebel. For Madelon, love requires self-sacrifice. Unlike Madelon's rebellion, however, Dorothy's defiance, at least initially, aims at self-gratification rather than self-sacrifice. Despite enormous pressure from her father and the community, Dorothy refuses to marry Burr because she knows he cannot meet her needs as Eugene can. On the day of her wedding to Burr, Dorothy has her moment of overt defiance. She flares at her father's command "with a convulsive flutter of her white plumage like a bird" and cries out "I will not" (299). Her earlier reserve transforms into Madelon's sort of passion as she calls to

Eugene with "no word; but her heart gave that ancient cry for its lover which was before all speech" (325). New England decorum is overtaken by the involuntary impulses she finally acts upon.

When Eugene attempts to seek safety in conventionality and directs her to marry Burr as planned, Dorothy assertively pursues him. The fair flower who would sit and wait to be called upon by Burr now becomes primitive lover and cares little for the outraged response of the villagers. Finally, Dorothy's character releases a hidden Madelon: "Dorothy . . . soft-plumaged though she was, had flown in the faces of all her decorous feminine antecedents and her goodly teaching —confronted her father with her new lover at her side" (329). Still, even with this new rebel, Freeman expressed ambivalence. The primary reason Dorothy provides for her rejection of Burr seems almost cowardly and foolish; she says she is afraid that he did indeed stab Lot. And when she marries Eugene, "with her feminine desire for all minor details of happiness," she "was aggrieved that she could never now appear before the public gaze in all the splendor of her wedding-gear" (331).

Freeman's rebels in love rebel in order to indulge in their love, but their rebellion most often involves self-sacrifice and selfless loving. When Madelon bravely rides the wild mare or walks ten miles on an icy, winter evening to appeal for help for Burr, "all thought of her own self, save as an instrument to save the life of the man she loved, was gone out of the girl" (121). Freeman's rebel lovers rarely establish any identity of their own. In "A Moral Exigency," Eunice seeks Burr Mason for some sense of herself as something other than a minister's daughter; Madelon's identity only takes full shape when she seeks to act on Burr Gordon's behalf, and Dorothy's outburst only brings her a new level of comfortable passivity with Eugene. Yet the lovers do all have a desperate need to defy codes of behavior imposed upon them. Although the defiance is sometimes misdirected, it is always a reaction against society's denial of the importance of the woman's right to choose a lover independently, to pursue that love actively, and to express sexuality openly.

The most interesting scene in *Madelon* as it relates to the dilemma shared by most of Freeman's rebellious women lovers depicts Madelon at work in the kitchen. Freeman's details highlight the disparity between the "woman's treadmill" of chores and her buried longings for freedom:

She scoured faithfully the pewter dishes and iron pots. She swept the hearth clean and baked and brewed and spun and sewed. Her lot would have been easier had her woe befallen her generations before, and she could, instead, have backed her heavy load of tenting through the snow on wild hunting parties, and broken the ice on the river for fish, and perchance taken a hand at the defense when the males of her tribe were hard pressed. Civilization bowed cruelly this girl who felt in greater measure than the gently staid female descendants of the Puritan stock around her the fire of savage or primitive passions; but she now submitted to it with the taciturnity of one of her ancestresses to the torture. (171–72)

In the painful monotone of the first two sentences of this passage, Freeman portrays the mechanics of her heroine's daily life and the expectations of the "Puritan stock around her." The paralyzing sameness of Madelon's tasks contrasts radically with her desire for activity, aggressive self-expression, and essentially acceptable male behavior. In her role on the prescribed "tread-mill" of domesticity, her passionate heritage must remain untapped. Although she strives for independent action, Madelon's sense of mission, of her own purpose in life and even of her own identity, is determined by the men in her life. The only outlet for Madelon's buried dreams of heroism comes in the form of active, passionate self-sacrifice. In the end, we leave the rebel lovers in Freeman's world submitting "to the torture" of the prevalent standards of "Puritan stock" and to their own misdirected heroism.

In 1897, just after she wrote *Madelon,* Mary Wilkins finally agreed to marry Charles Freeman. Perhaps having written a novel in which she released so much hostility and rebellion, she was able to take this step. It would be a mistake to suggest, however, that writing *Madelon* provided sufficient therapy. In 1897, her engagement confirmed, she developed nervous symptoms which affected her health. To some extent, *Madelon* provides a glimpse of the process of compromise which she must have found necessary in her own choice to become engaged after so many years of freedom. For both Madelon and Dorothy, free and rebellious behavior carries its price. Freeman therefore placed their rebellion into an acceptable framework so that they could be loved. Conjugal bliss, paradoxical and unconvincing as it may seem to readers of *Madelon,* was her final resolution for the plight of both the "savage squaw" and the "fair angel."

6

"THE TENDERNESS OF ONE WOMAN
FOR ANOTHER"

∞

The tenderness of one woman for another is farther reaching in detail than that of a man, because it is given with a fuller understanding of needs.

Mary E. Wilkins Freeman, "The Tree of Knowledge," 1900.

FREEMAN RECOGNIZED THAT marriage could not readily provide the pleasure she found in her "farther reaching" relationships with women: the open expression of emotion, the enjoyment of receiving maternal love and protection, the ability to preserve autonomy, the "understanding of needs." As is evident in *Madelon,* her attempts to depict heterosexual relationships consistently fell short of her ability to convey intimacy between women. Recognizing the repression of sexuality so prevalent in the lives of single women of her time, she channeled the expression of female sexuality into her many portrayals of women's friendships.[1] Once married, she continued and even intensified her descriptions of the sensual quality of women's relationships.

Freeman's novels and stories suggest that she preferred the "tenderness" of communication with women to interaction with men. The pattern in so much of her fiction of abrupt shifts from potentially homosexual to heterosexual ties implies, however, that Freeman could not rest easy within the homosocial network, and certainly could not accept such connections as conclusive. Instead, her resolutions almost always involve the reuniting of heterosexual partners in marriage, her acquiescence to acceptable standards of behavior for women.

Carroll Smith-Rosenberg's summary of the range of relationships between women in the eighteenth and nineteenth centuries accurately describes the contributions of women in Freeman's life and in her fiction, "from the supportive love of sisters, through the enthusiasms of adolescent girls, to sensual avowals of love by mature women. It was a world in which men made but a shadowy appearance."[2] The forms of love Smith-Rosenberg refers to were characteristic of Freeman's friendships. The supportive networks formed by nineteenth-century women allowed for a natural intimacy and had "emotional richness and complexity." Given the "severe social restrictions on intimacy between young men and women," such easy expressions of affection were virtually impossible in heterosexual communication.[3]

The primary relationship for Freeman, of course, was the one she had with Mary Wales, whose support was maternal as much as it was sisterly. When she moved in with Mary Wales in 1883, the relationship continued the pattern that had developed in childhood. As children, Mary Wales had stepped in to protect her when she was frightened by other youngsters. Now they were constant companions from 1883 until her marriage in 1902. Mary Wales took care of the daily tasks, and then was there at night when Freeman would, as Edward Foster states, awaken from her nightmares and talk with Mary "until the terror passed."[4] The only chronicle we have of Freeman's feelings about Wales is in her letters to women friends where there are scattered references to Wales. In her letters, Freeman refers vaguely but poignantly to her love for Wales. Her references indicate that the two were virtually inseparable during their years together. In any of her letters which refer to a trip, she mentions Mary Wales's companionship. When Wales went away for any reason, Freeman's letters reflect the intensity of their attachment, but do so carefully, almost passively. "My friend Mary Wales who has been away is home again, and I am very glad. I was lonely"[5] or "My friend Mary Wales goes to Portland tomorrow for a week's visit with a friend. I expect to be lonely."[6] There is little information, however, to document clearly the nature of Freeman's relationship with Wales. It is unclear if the two women were lesbians. Freeman's descriptions of sexuality in her own fiction were deliberately vague. Many of her fictive lovers separate at the moment that physical intimacy becomes a reality or a possibility. Yet these separations are most often between men and women. Sensual descriptions of women's embraces and expressions of love are always contained within the acceptable framework of one woman or another's ultimate marriage. What we do know is that Freeman's relationship with Wales was intense and primary, and most likely engendered the intimacy she channeled into her descriptions of women's friendships in her fiction.

It is useful to consider Freeman's relationship with Mary Wales in the context of friendships other women artists formed in her time. As Lillian Faderman suggests in her discussion of women artists in *Surpassing the Love of Men,* "their pioneer experiences of 'living by their brains' could be lonely and frightening in the extreme. They learned, again from Victorian society whose dogma idealized marriage, that one's spouse helped combat loneliness and fear. The individual solution of monogamy was the only conceivable one for most of them—except of course, that they altered the rules by making the two principals female." The Irish writer, Edith Somerville summarized in 1917 the choice women made to share their intellectual lives with other women, and her description suggests the nature of Freeman's relationship with Wales. "The outstanding fact as it seems to me, among women who live by their brains, is friendship. A profound friendship that extends through every phase and aspect of life, intellectual, social, pecuniary. Anyone who has experience of the life of independent and artistic women knows this."[7] The concept of a single, all-consuming friendship was vital to women artists of Freeman's time.

It was with Wales that Freeman began to understand her power as a writer. In the protected seclusion of her room on the second floor of the Wales homestead, she was aware of Wales's presence as she tended to domestic tasks on the floor below. Wales did play the part, essentially, of conventional wife to Freeman. But she went beyond that role as well. Wales was Freeman's primary audience, listening to and reading her drafts. One letter specifically refers to Wales's influence. "I have just finished a story which I do not dare send as yet . . . it is so very tragic. Mary Wales who always giggles at my pathetic points, has just burst into a flood of tears much to my alarm. I thought she was laughing, and there she was crying."[8] She was quoted by Hamlin Garland as having jokingly referred to Mary Wales's involvement in her work day when she explained that Mary

Wales "shuts me in my study each morning and won't let me out till I have written at least fifteen hundred words." [9] Foster states in his biography that Mary Wales became both "mother and sister, who misunderstood her at times but always accepted her moods of petulance and rebellion." [10]

Given the comforts of her life with Mary Wales, Freeman's decision to marry Charles Freeman was understandably difficult. He satisfied both her rebel and her conventional selves. She was introduced to him around 1892 or 1893 by her friend Kate Upson Clark in the home of a mutual friend, Henry Mills Alden. She was aware of his questionable reputation. In 1887, he had been asked to resign from his position as medical examiner for the Bureau of Pensions in Washington, D.C. He was charged with negligence on the job, smoking, showing disrespect, using profanity, arriving at work intoxicated, and "boasting of 'vicious habits and practices.' " [11] Charles objected, but was forced to resign in 1889. Although he had graduated from Columbia's College of Physicians and Surgeons, he never practiced medicine. He inherited a coal and wood business which was said to have bored him. Freeman was clearly attracted to these rebellious images of Charles, his daring, his capacity to take continual risks. Her motive for marrying him, however, seems to reflect the very duality so evident in her fiction. Along with her attraction to the male rebellion she could never act on, she was attracted to the status of marriage itself, the relief that she imagined would come when she could part with the spinster label, a desire for the "decent life" which so many of her fictional spinsters associate with marriage. Despite his reputation as a man who spent much time in Lawless's Saloon in Metuchen, Charles was considered "the town's most eligible and dashing bachelor." Mary knew that Dr. Freeman was an established businessman and that his family was "more prominent than her own and just as firmly anchored to Colonial America." As Brent Kendrick speculates, "perhaps she felt that if she were to marry at all she could hardly do better." [12]

The degree of her ambivalence is quite evident. It took over four years for Charles and Mary to become engaged. In 1897 Mary Wales's father died and Mary Wilkins Freeman supported her financially. According to Foster, Mary Wilkins gave Wales all of the royalties from one of her novels. In this same year, Mary became engaged to Charles Freeman. Having just lost her father, Mary Wales moved from her room across the hall from Mary Wilkins to the first floor in order to be near her mother. The move may have also been Wales's form of self-protection, a defense against the anticipated loss of her housemate. Foster notes that because Wales was no longer available to comfort her when she would awaken from nightmares, Freeman now obtained a powerful sedative which she came to depend on. In the period just before the marriage finally took place, Freeman's dependence on these sleeping sedatives had reached its peak.[13]

Freeman's greatest fear just before the marriage was one Charles understood and articulated when he observed that Mary's delay was in part due to her desire to keep up the momentum of her writing. One newspaper article quoted Dr. Freeman's explanation of her delay in these terms: "You see, a woman who has all her life been devoted to her literary work; who has been free to manage her own affairs; who has not been accustomed to a man taking charge of her business; a woman of that sort is naturally anxious to get her business affairs settled first."[14] Before the marriage, Mary Wales took care of Freeman's needs, but she never "took charge of her business" as she anticipated Charles would. After their secret engagement in 1897, the two had a quarrel that was serious enough to separate them until the summer of 1898. Newspaper announcements offer a record of the frequent postponements of the marriage. On 19 October 1899, the *Boston Herald* printed the announcement, "Miss Wilkins to be a Bride. Famous Author is Soon to Marry Dr. Charles Freeman." But no wedding took place. The following October, the *New York Tribune* repeated the announcement: "Miss Wilkins to Marry a Physician." Still Freeman remained single. Kendrick indicates the irritation of reporters with the frequent postponements, the most interesting of which reflects the pressure she must have felt to satisfy the expectation of her society: The *New York Telegraph* recorded that "the public is really tired of the love affairs of the literary old maid, and the sooner she marries the doctor and takes him out of the public view the more highly will the action be appreciated." The *New Brunswick Home News* (near Metuchen) published a brief prompting in 1901, "Please, Miss Wilkins, Marry Dr. Freeman." When the renovations for the house they were to live in were near completion in 1901, plans for the wedding actually began. Mary Wales participated in efforts to ward off public announcement. When Mary Wilkins visited Metuchen in November 1901 to check on the arrival of furniture, the *New York Tribune* promptly announced the marriage once again and Mary Wales mysteriously responded: "If some one says it is to be in a month he has made a good guess—or a bad one." [15]

Mary's marriage to Charles was delayed for five years from the time of their first engagement announcement, and when it finally occurred, on 1 January 1902, Wales was the witness. After her marriage, Mary began to write still more intensively, even nostalgically, about the bonds women form with each other. Having delayed as long as she did, the adjustment to marriage must have been enormous. Aside from the change in location, she had lost the daily communication with Mary Wales. The fears she had expressed in 1900 in letters leading up to her marriage—fears of losing the "old self," of being "swallowed up"—proved well founded. [16] She had wondered "if I will make a good wife and my husband will be happy," and she asserted that although she would try to "make a good wife," she was concerned about "dealing with unknown quantities," and added, "sometimes I feel afraid." [17] Although she continued to write, she no longer had Mary Wales beside her after she had completed a draft, and she missed her emotional support and protection.

Mary Wales never married, and her relationship with Freeman remained the central one in her lifetime. Freeman's letters make frequent reference to visiting Mary Wales during her marriage. She spoke of these visits as her refuge in Randolph, "here in the haunt of my spinsterhood." [18] In a sense, we learn more about the Wales-Freeman friendship through what is left unsaid in Kendrick's letter collection, when she wrote and when she did not. Writing of one of her visits with Wales "in my old haunts" on 21 November 1908, she mentions she would be returning to Metuchen in a week, and that Wales would join her. [19] Her next letter does not appear until 23 December 1908, when Freeman mentions that "Mary Wales has been visiting me, went home yesterday." [20] Indirectly, then, her letter points to more than a month of visiting. Still the long visit seemed insufficient, as she wrote bitterly of life in Metuchen just after Mary Wales returned to Randolph, complaining that "I have not a blessed thing to write about. Live in Metuchen, N.J. and see if you would have. I read a crazy diary in a paper last night which just about fits a Metuchenite. It was something like this. Jan. 8. Shook my head 17 times. Jan. 9. shook my head twenty times. Jan. 19. shook my head eight times." [21] The letter is both humorous and sad. It reflects the emptiness she felt when Wales departed. It captures the sense of aimlessness she felt in Metuchen, the place of her marriage, as much as her earlier letter from Randolph captured her sense of connection in Randolph, where she was "having a lovely time" (1908). It is not difficult to imagine that these contrasting associations were at least partly a response to the differences between her relationships with Mary Wales in Randolph and with Charles Freeman in Metuchen. The inadequacy of her marriage when compared to her life with Wales quickly became apparent.

Freeman also maintained significant friendships with women other than Wales. These friendships eventually became her refuge during the painful dissolution of her marriage. For Freeman as for most women of her time, communication with women was intimate, familiar, and comforting in a way that it could never be with men. Brent Kendrick notes in his introduction to *Infant Sphinx* "the effusions of love and friendship which [Freeman] lavishes upon acquaintances of the same sex."[22] The tone of Freeman's letters to women friends and editors contrasts with the cordial but distanced tone she adopts in the few letters she wrote to men. Her letters to close women friends were signed "Dolly," or "Pussy Willow," and reflected a consistent pattern of affectionate flirtation. In her letter to Harriet Randolph Hyatt Mayor, for example, she wrote "Do take care of yourself, you beautiful leapordess sort of creature, and let the rest of the world go hang."[23] Her letter to a literary friend, Carolyn Wells, has a similar quality of intimacy: "I have always been your unconfessed, but none the less true lover and friend, since I looked across the table at you during that Publisher's breakfast in Boston when we were in pinafores."[24]

One of Freeman's earliest and longest relationships was with Evelyn Sawyer, whom she met in 1870 in Brattleboro. Sawyer later described their attraction to each other in terms of the similarities of their personalities. "I was shy and standoffish," Evelyn stated. "Mary shy and shrinking so we seemed to come together. . . ." She spoke of Freeman's "audacity and timidity," a combination that characterized the duality in Freeman's work.[25] Their friendship was intellectual as much as it was playful. They were both avid readers. Foster records that "they talked about their discoveries as they read Auerbach, Dickens, Emerson, Greek mythology and philosophy, Hawthorne, Sarah [Orne] Jewett, Poe, Mrs. Stowe, Thackeray, Taylor's translation of Faust,

Thoreau." According to Foster, the two would stroll along Walnut Street in Brattleboro to a bench along the river. "There they talked quietly of great vague questions raised by their masters." In 1875, Sawyer married Dr. Charles Earl Severance and moved from Brattleboro to Shelburne Falls, Massachusetts. Foster suggests that this was a "severe blow" to Mary as "there was no one to take the place of the adored Evie."[26] Freeman's letters to her after Sawyer's marriage offered ongoing support and affection. In 1893, she began her letter to "Evie" with a poem suggesting, however playfully, her attachment:

> If thou were vanished far away,
> To regions hot and fiery,
> I'd be contented there to stay,
> If thou wert there, (Elviry).[27]

Her letters reflected her understanding of Evelyn's character, and revealed something of herself, a rarity in Freeman's correspondence. Attempting to comfort Evelyn, she wrote "My dear, I wish you could go to Chicago. I wish you could do something and see some people who would entertain you. You see, you are bored by people, and I never have been. I am bored by circumstances. I have a constant longing to go to a land where there are no circumstances. . . . If we could scrap susceptibilities, we could give each other a visit." Freeman's "land where there are no circumstances" would have been a place where such a visit could exist without "susceptibilities" and most likely, without Evelyn's husband, Dr. Severance. Summing up Evelyn's character, Freeman continued, "You may think this is flattery, but it is simply what I have always thought. You have certainly uncommon fervor, which never had full swing. Their checking is bad for you, but they may soar some day. I somehow believe in that sort of thing that persons do get full swing finally, in spite of everything. You've got your own true individual shine. That you needn't lose, dear."[28] The recognition Evelyn and Mary had of their respective "individual shine" is what kept this relationship alive. Writing to Evelyn just before her marriage to Charles, Freeman described her home in Metuchen as having "twenty-eight doors and five pairs of stairs" and anticipated spending "most of my time . . . trying to decide which door to go in or out of, and what stairs to descend." Although stated in jest, Freeman's letter hints at her anxiety about the marriage and her move to Metuchen, and gives a sense of her confusion and hesitation. It is interesting that in this letter she recalls with great nostalgia Evelyn's appearance and her love for her: "I don't forget you, old friend, even if I don't ever see you. How I used to trot up to see you, and we used to pop corn and discuss life. How little we knew, even you, knew none too much, and how much (or is it how little?) we have learned. Somehow, just now, those old days seem very near and I can see you, you tall, beautiful, golden-crowned thing getting around, and me tagging you." [29]

Approximately four months into her marriage to Charles, Freeman confided in another letter to Evelyn the difficulties of taking care of a house while attempting to write: "there are times when I really wonder how I can do as much as I ought to do. It is actually doing a man's work and a woman's work at once." While she describes the grounds of her new home as a "sort of Eden," she also remembers and longs for "the dear old days" which are "always deep down in my heart and a part of me." [30]

One of the strongest intellectual friendships she formed was with Mary Louise Booth, her editor at *Harper's Bazaar*, and it spanned all her adult life. As early as 1885, Freeman noted the value of the friendships she made through her work: "I begin to see that there is one beautiful thing which comes from this kind of work, and the thing I have the most need of, I think. One is going to find friends because of it." [31] Still in its early phase, the intimacy of the friendship in 1886 is reflected by the change in Freeman's signature, from "M.E. Wilkins" to "Lovingly yours, Pussy Willow." She referred to her wish to be able to "do something for you, beside love you." [32] Freeman's letters to Booth generally combined reference to her work with expressions of love. These assurances are a general theme: "I want to see you very much indeed, and I do love you" (after 17 March 1886); "I do think about you a great deal. You do know that I do don't you? And I love you truly" (31 March 1886); "I love you in the midst of the rain, and I want to see you" (28 April 1886); "I love you dearly" (before 15 November 1886); "I do love you dearly" (26 November 1886); "with much love and a kiss" (27 January 1888). When Booth was ill, Freeman wrote that Booth had entered her dreams: "I dreamed about you night before last. I thought I was in your drawing-room standing beside you, and you put your arm around me. I do hope you are better, dear Miss Booth. I wish I could do something to help you" (28 April 1886). [33]

1. Mary E. Wilkins Freeman's birthplace, 68 South Main Street, Randolph, Massachusetts. Freeman lived here until she was fifteen, when she moved with her family to Brattleboro, Vermont. Used with permission of Brent L. Kendrick, *The Infant Sphinx,* copyright 1985.

2. Warren Edwards Wilkins, Mary E. Wilkins Freeman's father. Daguerreotype, used with permission of Brent L. Kendrick, *The Infant Sphinx*, copyright 1985.

3. Mary E. Wilkins Freeman, at the age of sixteen. Used with permission of Brent L. Kendrick, *The Infant Sphinx*, copyright 1985.

4. Lieutenant Hanson Tyler, Mary E. Wilkins Freeman's "first love." Used with permission of Brent L. Kendrick, *The Infant Sphinx*, copyright 1985.

5. 3 Chase Street, Brattleboro, Vermont. Freeman moved with her family to this house in 1867. Used with permission of Brent L. Kendrick, *The Infant Sphinx,* copyright 1985.

6. Mary Wilkins Freeman Collection (#7407), Clifton Waller Barrett Library, Special Collections Department, University of Virginia Library.

This portrait of Freeman was reproduced by Hayden Carruth, editor of *Woman's Home Companion,* in "Postscript," *Woman's Home Companion* 43 (February 1916), 76. Freeman sent the portrait to Carruth on 24 November 1915 with the following letter: "I am enclosing you the *oddest* picture, in my estimation, which I have ever seen of myself. It was drawn by an English artist at the time of my winning the Long Arm Prize. The artist had never seen me nor a photograph of me. He seems to have been sort of second sight man and drew me as I looked to his imagination. While the picture undoubtedly flattered, there was and perhaps is, a curious suggestion of me. It is really much better than some of my portraits and photographs. It strikes me that it may be rather interesting to reproduce as being what I ought to have looked like, according to the fancy of an artist reader of my stories" (#416, Kendrick, 346). The portrait is a good example of the attempts to shape Freeman's image to the standards of nineteenth-century feminine beauty. On 27 November 1915, Freeman again wrote Carruth: "Of course that imaginative English Artist made me a lot better looking than I am but he thought I ought to look that way in order to be able to write stories and it seems a pity almost to interfere with such faith" (#417, Kendrick, 347).

7. Mary Wilkins Freeman Collection
(#7407), Clifton Waller Barrett Library,
Special Collections Department,
University of Virginia Library.

Freeman worried considerably about
her physical appearance, particularly
when she was asked for photographs,
and she commented on her concern in a
letter to Hayden Carruth on 27
November 1915: "I have never had a
photograph which did not misrepresent
me morally as well as physically. And—
no two look alike. I sometimes wonder if
I am really in any sense a fixed quantity,
rather a sort of transparency. There has
always been something a little uncanny
about it. . . . I have a frightful conviction
that I look capable of nothing except
afternoon teas or breaking all the
Commandments and sulking because
there are no more. My photographs have
always looked to me as representing me
in one or the other phase. I own I would
like just once to look real smart and
handsome and intelligent the way the
Artist [see fig. #6] thought I ought to
look. You cannot blame me" (#417,
Kendrick, 347).

8. Mary Wilkins Freeman Collection
(#7407), Clifton Waller Barrett Library,
Special Collections Department,
University of Virginia Library.

9. The home of Mary
Wales, Randolph,
Massachusetts, where
Freeman lived for almost
twenty years (1883–1902).
Used with permission of
Brent L. Kendrick, *The
Infant Sphinx*, copyright
1985.

10. Charles Manning
Freeman as a young man.
Used with permission of
Brent L. Kendrick, *The
Infant Sphinx*, copyright
1985.

11. Charles Manning Freeman. Used with permission of Brent L. Kendrick, *The Infant Sphinx*, copyright 1985.

12. The home of Charles and Mary E. Wilkins Freeman in Metuchen, New Jersey. The name of the house, "Freewarren," incorporates Freeman's father's name. It is just the sort of house Warren Wilkins wished he could have built for his family when they moved to Brattleboro. Used with permission of Brent L. Kendrick, *The Infant Sphinx*, copyright 1985.

13. Freeman receiving the first Howells Gold Medal for Distinguished Work in Fiction from Hamlin Garland. Used with permission of Brent L. Kendrick, *The Infant Sphinx*, copyright 1985.

Text within the image:
DEDICATED TO THE MEMORY OF MARY E WILKINS FREEMAN
AND THE WOMEN WRITERS OF AMERICA

UNFETTERED AS AN EAGLES FLIGHT
IMAGINATIONS MIGHTY SWEEP
TRANSCENDS ALL EARTHLY BOUNDS

DEEP IN THE SOUL OF MAN FLOWS
THE WELL OF THOUGHT ITS POWER
INEXHAUSTIBLE OUTLASTING TIME

14. Bronze doors, American Academy and Institute of Arts and Letters, New York:
"Dedicated to the Memory of Mary E. Wilkins Freeman and the Women Writers of
America." Used with permission of Brent L. Kendrick, *The Infant Sphinx*, copyright 1985.

Brent Kendrick and Mary Reichardt suggest that the early years of Freeman's marriage were probably happy, but there is no evidence to support this assumption. According to Reichardt, Charles Freeman was an "ideal partner" in the beginning because he supported and encouraged her in her work.[34] Yet the details from Foster's biography indicate that his support actually constituted a gradual stripping away of the autonomy she had treasured in her unmarried life. Dr. Freeman "directed her reading," dictating that Mary read only light fiction, mysteries, and the newspaper so that she could keep her focus on her work. Foster notes also that Charles "limited her social engagements that she might conserve energy for her writing." Freeman had once described the pleasure she took in baking cakes with Mary Wales.[35] But when Charles saw Mary baking a cake in the kitchen, he was quick to object: "Making a cake when the same time would produce a story worth five hundred!"[36] In equating her art with merely the income it would produce, Charles's statement must have created friction between them. Although these gestures from Charles have been interpreted as indications of support, they hint strongly at an effort to manipulate and control Mary's attempts to take charge of her pleasures in daily life. Kendrick cites the comments of an acquaintance of the Freemans as further evidence of the success of the early years: "he shielded and spoiled her because of his natural attitude toward women and because he believed it would keep her genius undisturbed." While such "shielding" might indeed seem positive, it also indicates that his "natural attitude toward women" included an assumption of their inability to manage multiple tasks.[37]

Freeman refers only briefly and evasively to her marriage in the letters she wrote during its early stages. Both Kendrick and Reichardt mention several letters to friends during this period in which they see signs of her contentment. A close look at the letters, however, indicates that her contentment did not focus on her relationship with Charles but on her new status as wife with all its accompanying satisfactions in house, garden, servants, parties, and the like. In a letter to Kate Upson Clark four months after her wedding, Freeman exclaimed "I have almost forgotten that I ever was an old maid, I am getting so used to 'Mrs.' It is queer how soon the new seems old!"[38] Although Kendrick reads this as a sign of her easy adjustment to life with Charles, it is more clearly an adjustment to the comfort of her new title. Her early insistence that her married name now be used in all her publications despite her public reputation as Mary Wilkins seems to bear out her pride in her married status. In 1904, Freeman asked *Harper's* to put her work in her married name, which Kendrick interprets as a sign of her happiness at this time: "One suspects that if the marriage had a less than firm footing, she would have continued to write under her well-known maiden name."[39] It seems more likely, however, that this request had to do with her desire to alert her public to her new position as a married woman, to rid herself of the label of spinster. In essence, the gesture is just an extension of her original motivation for marriage, an assurance of conventional acceptability.

Other references to Freeman's early happiness in the first years seem equally dubious. Kendrick finds evidence of success in the obvious interest Mary took in her new home with Charles. The couple had restored their first house just before their marriage. Freeman's letter to Evie shortly after the wedding describes her lovely grounds. "I always wanted evergreen trees, and now I have them, such beauties, with their branches resting on the ground, and there are lots of flowering shrubs . . . and there is the loveliest birch tree that I ever saw right opposite my window." Although she writes of her new surroundings as a sort of Eden, Mary makes no reference to her relationship with Charles.[40] Furthermore, she was worried about her household responsibilities, particularly as they imposed on her time for writing: "We enjoy our new house very much. I wish I were Siamese twins though to run it and yet wield the pen."[41] Her emphasis is on the house and grounds, which does not necessarily indicate the solidity of the marriage. In fact almost all her references to her marriage in these early years focus on its outward appearance, the superficial, overt signs of its existence with frequent mentions of the first and second home and the need to get each one in order, the grounds, the meals, the parties and the entertainment. It is very likely that after years of spinsterhood, Mary was determined to present an image of marital contentment through this outward display of domesticity.

The Freemans worked at conveying an image of a happy marriage. By 1906, they built a new house on five acres of land. The home would be paid for with the money Mary was to earn from *The Shoulders of Atlas* (1908). Kendrick sees the groundbreaking ceremony as

another positive indication of the state of the marriage. Mary wrote
a poem in honor of the occasion in which she expressed the hope
that they would be protected "'gainst storm and stress." It is likely
that she had already become aware of "storm and stress" in her first
home, and that this prayer was an effort to ward it off. A handwritten
house prayer composed by both Mary and Charles asks that God
"grant us some years of love, health and peace in this House." [42]
Almost prophetically, the Freemans limited their prayer to "some
years" rather than a lifetime of peace.

Kendrick sees "the final indicator that the marriage was successful
during these years" in the fact that Mary became quite close with
Charles's family. Through Charles, Mary had gained four sisters-in-
law and a mother-in-law. Mary took frequent drives with her mother-
in-law and found her sisters-in-law to be "charming" and "a great
resource." [43] More than likely, Mary took refuge in this new network
of feminine support. The need must have grown as she observed
Charles's increasingly disturbing habits. The more unavailable he
became, the more she sought the company of his mother and sisters.

Describing their individual activities in this period, Kendrick notes
that Charles began to frequent the saloon more regularly. He became notorious for his pranks, particularly for slipping purgatives
into his friends' beers. He also spent time gambling.

While Mary wrote prolifically in this period, publishing *By the Light
of the Soul* and *The Fair Lavinia and Others* in 1907, and one of her
most popular novels, *The Shoulders of Atlas* in 1908, Charles entered
the political arena. Mary's success, however, was matched by
Charles's failure. In 1905 he had become president of the financially
successful Manning, Freeman & Son corporation, but by 1907, when
he ran for mayor, Charles began to witness his own defeat. The most
obvious reason for his downfall was his excessive drinking. His defeat
was publicly humiliating. The campaign of his opponent, Jesse T.
Jackson, rested on evidence of Dr. Freeman's irresponsibility and
indecency. Jackson supporters argued that "Jackson favored decency
while Freeman did not" and that "Jackson could be looked upon
and respected while Dr. Freeman could not be." [44] Freeman lost with
197 votes to Jackson's 224, which was hardly a landslide for Jackson.
Yet to add to Charles's sense of humiliation, when Jackson died
suddenly soon after the election, a councilman, A. L. Ellis, was ap-
pointed mayor instead of Charles Freeman. Shortly after this news,

Mary was invited to Mark Twain's seventieth birthday celebration. One of nearly 200 guests, she sat beside Twain at the table. In 1908, she won *New York Herald's* "Anglo-American Competition" for her novel *The Shoulders of Atlas*.[45] Charles had taken pride in his wife's fame during their engagement period, but it is likely that her popularity and achievement now became a reminder of his own failures. In 1909, Charles's alcoholism had progressed so significantly that he had to be hospitalized in the Oppenheimer Institute, a New York sanatorium.

Although it is true that Mary did not specifically mention Charles's alcoholism in any letter or refer to consequent marital difficulties, it is hard to imagine that this was the period of contentment that both Kendrick and Reichardt indicate. Kendrick put the beginning of the decline of their marriage as late as 1918 by which time Dr. Freeman, a drug addict and serious alcoholic, had a complete breakdown. The evidence suggests, however, that years of difficulty preceded the ultimate dissolution of the marriage and of Dr. Freeman's physical and mental health.

At the time that her marriage was undergoing these strains, Freeman realized that she was about to lose Mary Wales forever. Freeman wrote in 1915 to one of her literary friends that Wales was "desperately ill." She expressed her anticipation of loss in her characteristically covert way:

> Miss Wales the friend with whom I lived before my marriage has been desperately ill. She is recuperating but when I tell you that the trouble was a growth in her breast and there has been a dreadful operation you can understand that recuperation does not mean as much as it might to a pessimistic soul. On general principles this particular brain worker has worked with her feet all the time kicking violently against the pricks. I have heard of brain workers being kept in glass cases and cotton wool but there has been little of that for me and maybe that state of shelterdom is mythical anyway.
>
> I reckon I am as well off as the rest and all the kick I make is the one against the pricks necessary to keep going at all.[46]

Recognizing by June 1916 that Wales was suffering from terminal cancer, Freeman wrote "although I try to make the best of it, my strength is affected."[47] This last reference to Wales appears shortly before Wales's death and it is the last letter Freeman wrote until September of that year.

Mary Wales died on 4 August 1916, bequeathing to Charles Freeman all her papers and books. Kendrick suggests that the collection surely included letters Freeman wrote her during their separation after Freeman's marriage.[48] We can only speculate about what happened to the collection, or about how Charles responded. There is every indication that Freeman sorely missed Wales after her marriage. It is likely that the letters Charles discovered in the collection captured the strong love the two women shared, a love that clearly surpassed her feelings for Charles. By the time the Wales collection reached Charles, the Freemans' marriage had suffered the blow of Charles's alcoholism and hospitalization.

There is only indirect reference to the depth of Freeman's grief at the loss of Wales. In December, Freeman described to Edith Tolman the illness she suffered shortly after the death:

> I have been in bed twelve days and now can sit only a little while. . . . I have had a close call from bronchial pneumonia. . . . Then back of the whole nervous exhaustion which fondly lingers on. I have really not been well for a long time. I am writing things twice over. I look like a freak, have lost so much flesh . . . I shall bob up all at once, must. Charles is so worried about me I can't do anything else. . . . I hope I shall be able to go to New York New Year's, our fifteenth anniversary. Pollyannna is not in it with me. In bed Christmas day, so glad to have a bed. I must stop, am tuckered out. So glad to be able to write till I am tuckered out. . . .[49]

Along with her recognition of "the whole nervous exhaustion," the letter also makes reference to "the prospect of not being able to work for some time." Always a fighter and a survivor, Freeman soon began to write again, but her prose after 1916 never matched the power of what she had written before Mary Wales's death.

"The Love of Parson Lord" and "The Tree of Knowledge"

Freeman's attraction to the subject of love between women most noticeably informed the fiction she wrote after she had met Charles. Two of Freeman's shorter works published in her collection entitled *The Love of Parson Lord* in 1900, two years before her marriage to Charles, treat mother-daughter love with great ambiguity. On some level, Freeman had never fully accepted the loss of her mother, Eleanor, with whom she had been so close. In a period when Freeman may have been evaluating the choice she had made to live with the maternal Mary Wales for so many years, Freeman set her descriptions of women's passion for each other beside descriptions of heterosexual love. It is as though she were weighing an eventual move away from Mary Wales. The girl named Love in the title story "The Love of Parson Lord" sees a motherly woman, the squire's wife, and feels "a sort of ecstasy, as of first love." [50] Eventually, through an elaborate and confused series of events, Love marries Richard, the grandson of the woman she has worshipped, but the most powerfully romantic imagery is associated with the mother figure of the squire's wife. Love's mother has died, and she remains in the stern and uncompromising care of her father, a Calvinist minister. In an early scene, she attends her father's sermon, and sees both Richard and his grandmother. She first gazes at Richard "with an utter calmness and unconsciousness of scrutiny, as if he were something inanimate." It is his grandmother who evokes in her an overwhelmingly passionate response:

> then Love turned her eyes from him towards his grandmother. They were suddenly alert, full of the most timid yet ardent admiration. The one love with which the child had any acquaintance, and for which she had as yet any yearning, was in the face of that elderly dame. . . . Love cast down her eyes before the sweet mother-look of the squire's lady, her heart leaped, her mouth quivered as if she would weep. She thought that never, never since her own mother, whose caresses she remembered better than her face, had there been any one as beautiful as this woman. (13–14)

Turning her eyes from Richard, Love falls in love with the woman she sees in her father's church. The awe she experiences on seeing this woman is equivalent to her father's passionate belief in a male god.

> That morning Love heard no more of her father's discourse. She was conscious of nothing except that mother-presence, which seemed to pervade the whole church. The inexorable fatherhood of God, as set forth in the parson's sermon, was not as evident to the hungry little heart in His sanctuary as the motherhood of the squire's lady. (14)

Martha Satz interprets this scene as a substitution of a mother god for a father god. "The girl's vision in one moment of love metaphorically inverts patriarchal values. Love's harsh minister father and Christianity's judgmental cosmic Father are subordinated to benignant motherhood." [51] Freeman goes still further than this inversion of religious values. She eroticizes Love's response to the mother figure:

> She continued to gaze at her at intervals, with softly furtive eyes of adoration, . . . and when she sometimes received a tenderly benignant glance in return, she scarcely knew where her body was, such was the elation of her spirit. When, after meeting, she was going down the aisle, and came abreast of the wonderful lady, and the soft sweep of her velvet cloak brushed her face like a wing, she could not help an involuntary nestle against her side, as if she were a baby. Then the squire's lady bent down, . . . and smiled, and lifted her hand, and patted Love gently on the smooth curve of her cheek. Love could have gone down at her feet. Nobody since her mother's death had ever caressed her to that extent. (14–15)

In this odd moment when Love first sees the young man she will eventually marry, the sensuality of the description is all channeled toward grandmother rather than the soon-to-be spouse, her grandson. It is her touch rather than Richard's that Love longs for, and it is her face that remains vividly in her memory. When she watches the lady leave with the squire and Richard, she sees only the woman's departure, and is noticeably unaware of the two men. The conclusion of the story establishes a pattern Freeman followed in almost all her fiction about female infatuation. Love's desire is transformed by the end of the story and directed toward the acceptable male figure.

"The Tree of Knowledge," the second story in the collection, offers what Josephine Donovan calls a "paradigmatic mother-daughter script" in a story of the obsessive love and protection of one half-sister for another.[52] This form of love is set beside heterosexual love in comparative terms, with the concession that the "tenderness" of a woman's love for another woman is always "farther reaching" than a man's love. Cornelia, the older sister, works hard to protect her younger sister, Annie, from heterosexual love. Her method of expressing her love for the young woman is not unlike Cyrano de Bergerac's. Cornelia's feelings for her sister come across visually when she looks at her with "a mild gravity of expression, which concealed a quick warmth of fire" (91). She writes love letters, signs them with a fictitious male name, David Amicus, and has them delivered to the tree where apparently all mail in this rural village is brought. Cornelia's intention, though I think there is considerable ambiguity here, is to create an ideal man, a fictive male whose love would be so pure that, because no real male could match it, Annie would remain single and continue to live with Cornelia. The love letters are also Cornelia's means for expressing and disguising her own passionate love. Annie imagines that Harry Carew, a stranger who appears one night at the tree and plans to rob the sisters' home, is the man who has written the idyllic letters. Touched by the innocence of Annie and by Cornelia's scheme, Harry Carew vows to fulfill the ideals of the letters and, despite Cornelia's despair, marries Annie. Much as Freeman wished Charles could have done, Harry transforms from gambler and thief into a respectable city official. In the end, Cornelia recognizes that she has attempted to guard the "gates of a Lost Paradise," and wonders if it might have been better to "guard the Tree of Knowledge with a flaming sword." The "lost paradise" of the mother-daughter relationship is what Freeman wrote about most effectively just when she was on the verge of parting with it by leaving Wales for Charles Freeman.

Although each story ends with a marriage, the most poignant moments are descriptions of the female paradise the women have created for themselves without men. Furthermore, the single state is presented as a viable option to marriage. Before she meets Harry, Annie asks if Cornelia is contented with their lives. Cornelia responds, "I am contented and happy since I have you. I ask for nothing more" (92). She instructs Annie to recognize that if she is not meant to marry, she must find contentment in the single life: "Every state has its compensations and nothing is as unequal as it appears" (93). In a letter written long after her separation from Charles, Freeman wrote that she could never say that her husband had been her "unshattered ideal," for there had never been an ideal man in her mind.[53] Through Cornelia's fictive male, Freeman attempted to create the image of a man worthy of a woman's affection, redefining man in a woman's terms. Cornelia explains to Harry that through her letters she "wanted to fill her [Annie's] mind with such a pure ideal that there could be no danger" (136).

While much has been said about Freeman's depiction of women in her short fiction, particularly by Mary Reichardt, Freeman's novels reveal far more about her perspective on the "web of relationships" women create. In *The Portion of Labor, By the Light of the Soul,* and *The Shoulders of Atlas,* Freeman's depictions of women's relationships may reflect Freeman's feelings for Wales and the value she placed on "the tenderness of one woman for another." These novels were written at different points in her relationship with Charles, and each one offers an intriguing gender comparison. Women form close ties with each other, but inevitably move away from those powerful and fundamental bonds and toward marriage. Freeman wrote *The Portion of Labor* in 1901, during the year before her wedding; she wrote *By the Light of the Soul* in 1906, four years into the marriage. *The Shoulders of Atlas*, written in 1908, came after six years of marriage to Charles (and six years into her separation from Mary Wales) and the year before Charles required his first hospitalization for alcoholism.

The Portion of Labor

Set within the context of Freeman's critique on the American labor system, using examples of the hardships of workers in a New England shoe factory, *The Portion of Labor* (1901) offers one of Freeman's most extended analyses of love between women. Although the novel's resolution predictably unites the heroine, Ellen, with the hero, Robert, the body of the novel explores women's lives in terms that have little to do with traditional heterosexual romance. Martha Satz suggests that this novel succeeded in capturing Freeman's capacity as "a visionary architect of women's lives . . . portraying as it does the fulfilled life of a strong woman and a web of intense, essential relationships among women . . ."[54]

One of Freeman's most modern and aggressive heroines, Ellen Brewster, leads a strike that aims to change the conditions for workers in the shoe factory in which she and her father work. Robert Lloyd, her potential lover and the owner of the factory, must recognize the worth of Ellen's arguments for social justice and equality before they can marry. Mrs. Lloyd, the wife of the original and more exploitative factory owner, (Robert's uncle), believes that "the world couldn't be regulated by women's hearts, pleasant as it would be for the world and the women, since the final outcome would doubtless be destruction."[55] *The Portion of Labor* is Freeman's attempt to expose and refute this popular position, to remake the world in women's terms without the destruction Mrs. Lloyd fears.

The implausible plot becomes the broad backdrop for a detailed portrayal of "women's hearts." The conventional sentimentality of Ellen's relationship with Robert provides a comfortable framework within which Freeman could uncover the range and beauty of women's relationships with each other. The forms these relationships take include, as Satz summarizes, "maternity, sisterhood, passionate friendship, the infatuation of the schoolgirl crush, romantic love between women."[56] Early in her childhood, Ellen witnesses the value system that places love between women above heterosexual romance when she observes her mother's relationship with her sister. Fanny, Ellen's mother, argues continually with Andrew, Ellen's father. She argues as well with her sister Eva, but Fanny makes it clear to Andrew that her tie to her sister will always be the stronger one:

> It was an odd thing that, however the sisters quarreled, the minute Andrew tried to take sides with his wife and assail Eva in his turn, Fanny turned and defended her. "I am not going to desert all the sister I have got in the world," she said. "If you want me to leave, say so, and I will go, but I shall never turn Eva out of doors. I would rather go with her and work in the shop." (9)

When Ellen runs away from her arguing parents, Eva assures Fanny that nothing is more important to her than Fanny's love and that she would take care of Fanny rather than marry.

Passionate maternal love shapes Ellen's upbringing and is echoed in almost every relationship she forms. Fanny's love for Ellen takes precedence over her commitment to her husband, which is what precipitates Ellen's attempt to run away from home. Fanny tells her that if it weren't for her love for her, she would leave Andrew and the hardships of their lives together. When she discovers that Ellen is missing, Fanny becomes wild with grief. Recognizing that Ellen feared and was defending herself against her mother's possible departure, Fanny says, "I wouldn't go away from hell if she was there. I would burn; I would hear the clankin' of chains, and groans, and screeches and devils whisperin' in my ears . . . before I'd go where they were playin' harps in heaven, if she was there. I'd like it better, I would" (34).

Cynthia Lennox, the wealthy woman who discovers Ellen when she has run away, is one of Freeman's most enigmatic characters. Like Fanny, Cynthia favors maternal love over heterosexual love. As Satz notes, it is only after Lyman Risley, who has loved Cynthia for years, becomes an invalid that Cynthia marries him. At this point, romantic love can be translated into nurturing maternal love. Cynthia's love for Ellen is passionately and obsessively maternal from the instant she finds her roaming the streets and decides to hide her from her searching family. Bringing Ellen to her lavish home and ignoring her cries for her mother, Cynthia nurtures Ellen with an intensity that betrays her own need for reciprocated nurturance in daughterly love: "Cynthia's arms were embracing all her delicate little body with tenderest violence, and kissing her little, blushing cheeks with the lightest and carefulest kisses, as though she were a butterfly which she feared to harm with her adoring touch" (42).

Ellen is only initially resistant. Quickly she "felt herself overborne and conquered by this tide of love which compelled like her mother's, though this woman was not her mother" (42). Allowing herself to be lifted out of her bed "as if she were a baby," Ellen's attachment to Cynthia becomes a secret bond. She never reveals to her family the name of the woman who had essentially kidnapped her as a child.

Cynthia gives Ellen a doll to care for, imparting the values of maternity which Ellen will carry into adulthood. When Cynthia had cared for her nephew Robert as a child, before he had left to live with his father, she had given him the same doll. Cynthia describes Robert to Ellen as having been "as pretty as a little girl and he loved to play with dolls like a little girl" (46). In essence, Cynthia had converted Robert into a girl-child, explaining to Ellen that he "had curls, and he wore dresses like a little girl" (46). With such an upbringing, Robert is the perfect suitor for Ellen. The doll becomes their source of commonality. Freeman is careful, however, to maintain the gender distinction even as she establishes the capacity for maternal love as the most important dimension of their relationship. As a child, Robert had attempted to burn the doll, hoping to wake it up. In contrast, Ellen had kissed the doll on its scar, protected and cared for it, and expected nothing in return. Nevertheless, it is Robert's appreciation of the doll as a girllike boy that attracts Ellen and makes heterosexual romance possible.

Freeman virtually celebrates maternal love in the scene that follows Ellen's stay with Cynthia as a child. When the girl returns to her family, she awakens into a utopian world of nurturance in her mother's room where the care she receives offsets the harsh realities of the factory life she will soon enter:

> When Ellen came to herself she was on the bed in her mother's room, and her aunt Eva was putting some of her beautiful cologne on her head, and her mother was trying to make her drink water, and her grandmother had a glass of her currant wine, and they were calling to her with voices of far-off love, as if from another world. (69)

Each woman seeks to ease Ellen into consciousness through the act of maternal giving.

Ellen's early training in what Sara Ruddick has termed "maternal thinking" informs her adult philosophy as a political activist.[57] She rejects Cynthia's offer to send her to Vassar in order to help support her family by working in the factory. Ellen ultimately leads a major strike that aims to better the conditions of laborers and to enlighten management about the needs of its workers. She aims to invest the factory with maternal values, to demand that the needs of her co-workers be acknowledged.

Years later, Ellen's love for Cynthia grows. She develops a crush that is more intense than any feelings she develops for Robert. When Cynthia apologizes for having kept Ellen from her mother for any time, Ellen feels a powerful "impulse of affection." The passion of Ellen's response is Freeman's tribute to the impact of love between women. Ellen feels "boundless attraction" for Cynthia, and knows that she is "under the magic of a look and a tone shook her from head to foot. She went close to Cynthia, and leaned over her, putting her round, young face down to the elder woman's. 'Oh I love you, I love you,' whispered Ellen, with a fervor which was strange to her" (252). Ellen's passion for Cynthia is unsurpassed in the novel. She dreams of Cynthia and recognizes that she is "more in love than she had ever been in her life, and with another woman" (253).

Many of Freeman's descriptions of Ellen's love for Cynthia suggest a romantic love. She rushes to bring a bouquet of delicate flowers to Cynthia, "in delight and trepidation," and she feels "as guiltily conscious as a lover that she was making an excuse to see Miss Lennox" (260). Lyman Risley, Cynthia's suitor, notices that Ellen "worships" Cynthia, and calls it "one of those aberrations common to her youth and her sex. She is repeating a madness of old Greece, and following you as a nymph might a goddess" (270). Although Cynthia attempts to define this love as merely an indication of Ellen's gratitude for the gesture she has made to send Ellen to Vassar, Risley clarifies that gratitude cannot account for the degree of Ellen's passion. Seeing her love as "one of the spring madnesses of life," Risley assures Cynthia that she needn't feel concerned because "it will be temporary in the case of a girl like that" (271).

The girlhood crush will, as Risley predicts, be converted into the "natural track of love" (271). It is as though Freeman found it necessary to force this conversion on her character. The passion for Cynthia awkwardly fades and is replaced by love for Robert. Yet even in the midst of this transition, Ellen is disappointed when she goes to visit Cynthia and finds that Robert is there as well:

> She had so hoped that she might find Cynthia alone. She had dreamed, as a lover might have done, of a tête-à-tête with her, what she would say, what Cynthia would say. She had thought, and trembled at the thought, that possibly Cynthia might kiss her when she came or went. She had felt, with a thrill of spirit, the touch of Cynthia's soft lips on hers, she had smelt the violets about her clothes. Now it was all spoiled. (268)

Ellen resents Robert's presence in this scene, wanting to enjoy Cynthia's company without male competition. She also instantly dislikes Mr. Risley when she remembers that he "had danced attendance upon her [Cynthia] for half a lifetime." While Donovan suggests that the above passage is a clear indication of the "lesbian nature of the relationship," Satz argues that to label the relationship as lesbian is to become reductive and to ignore the "intricate network of life-supporting connections" which Freeman portrays throughout the novel.[58] Although there are limits to the explicit sexuality in scenes of intimacy between women, it is clear that Freeman felt women played a more powerful role in each other's lives than men. Ellen experiences the imagined kiss from Cynthia's soft lips in highly charged terms, "with a thrill of spirit," and her dream is equated with that of a lover. Perhaps the charge was too much for Freeman to acknowledge in herself, certainly too difficult to make explicit in her fiction. As Donovan notes, Freeman abruptly drops her references to Ellen's love for Cynthia once she sets Ellen on the pathway toward marriage to Robert.

Although the central journey Ellen takes is a journey toward marriage, Freeman shapes Ellen's relationships with men to match the model of her communication with women. Even Robert essentially becomes womanlike before the romance is in full swing, remembering the doll and his "girlhood," learning to recognize the needs of the poor and to love Ellen's mind more or at least as much as her body. Ellen converts him from dominant male factory owner to caring individual and lover. During their political disputes, Robert wishes that he could "force her to a view of his own horizon," but it is Robert who must adapt to Ellen's view. Robert's "masculine insistence," his efforts to bring about "the subjugation of the feminine into harmony" fail (388). The only other man who has attempted to court Ellen is Granville, a coworker with a face "as gentle as a girl's" (178).

Women in Ellen's life are both physically and spiritually more important than any of the men. Similar to her crush on Cynthia, Ellen's love for her teacher, Miss Mitchell, is passionate. Her friendships are sensual and all-encompassing, and they carry the highest priority. When Robert offers her a ride through a snowstorm, she rejects him in favor of walking home with Maria and Abby, factory friends. The mutual commitment and love between Ellen and Abby is very similar to what Freeman experienced with Wales. Abby warns Ellen not to marry a man who is beneath her intellectually and reminds her of her own superior ability to appreciate Ellen's worth: "I think more of you than any man ever will. I don't care who he is" (228). The scene in which they discuss marriage reflects the tug Freeman must have felt in this year before her marriage to Charles. Abby grips Ellen's arm and attempts to define the nature of her love for her:

> Then she caught hold of Ellen's arm and pressed her own thin one in its dark blue cotton sleeve lovingly against it. "You ain't mad with me, are you, Ellen?" she said, with that indescribable gentleness tempering her fierceness of nature which gave her caresses the fascination of some little, untamed animal. Ellen pressed her round young arm tenderly against the other. "I think more of you than any man I know," said she. (229)

As they walk on together, "arms locked," Freeman intercepts with a narrative explanation that aims to appease the assumptions her audience may have made: "each was possessed with that wholly artless and ignorant passion often seen between two young girls" (229–30). Yet the scene that follows still more powerfully suggests the sensual nature of women's interactions and the possibility of lesbian love:

> Abby felt Ellen's warm round arm against hers with a throbbing of rapture, and glanced at her fair face with adoration. She held her in a sort of

worship, she loved her so that she was fairly afraid of her. As for Ellen, Abby's little, leather-stained, leather-scented figure, strung with passion like a bundle of electric wire, pressing against her, seemed to inform her farthest thoughts. "If I live longer than my father and mother, we'll live together, Abby," said she. (230)

Essentially, Ellen's vow to live with Abby after her parents' death is equivalent to the promise Freeman kept after the death of Warren and Eleanor when she moved back to Randolph to live with Mary Wales. As she wrote this nostalgic scene, Freeman was on the verge of breaking the pledge she may have made to Wales to continue to live with her. Ironically, it is Abby who abandons Ellen first. She decides to marry Wily Jones because "he wants me pretty bad," and Abby wants the comforts of marriage. Abby's final comment captures what Freeman must have been feeling about her pending marriage to Charles: " 'I don't love him a mite better than I do you,' she whispered, 'so there! You needn't think you're left out, Ellen Brewster.' " We are told that Ellen's lingering feeling of "desolation" has to do with her longing for Robert and her envy of Abby's success, a feeling that was "somewhat like that of a child who sees another with all the cake." The odd absence of any expression of pain for losing Abby in this scene is similar to the odd silence about losing Wales in the letters she wrote after her marriage to Charles. In some sense, the silence is more powerful than words might have been.

Extending the network of women's relationships still further, Freeman incorporates yet another intense connection. Abby's sister Maria fascinates Ellen. Frail and struggling in poverty, Maria has none of Ellen's "fire" to fight her circumstances. Furthermore, she has never been loved by a man, nor has she yearned for such love. She wishes only "that I was either an angel or a man" (309). This revealing comment captures Maria's dilemma. Unable to conform to the "angel" stereotype of appropriate womanhood, Maria "chides herself for her wickedness" (310). She channels her capacity to love toward a devotion to God. At the same time, Freeman subtly implies that Maria loves women. Unlike Abby and Ellen, who we learn "almost never kissed each other," Maria "was more profuse with her caresses." In their adolescence, Ellen had often confided in Maria, telling her that she loved a boy and had kissed him once: "the two girls lay in each other's arms, looking at the moonlight which streamed in through the window." Freeman places this scene of potential lesbianism into the more acceptable context of girlhood, and Ellen is, after all, confiding to Maria that she loves a boy. Yet in one of the most subtle moments in the novel, the women part one evening. "Maria went close to Ellen and put up her face. 'Goodnight,' said she. 'Then she withdrew her lips suddenly, before Ellen could touch them.'" Basing the withdrawal on fear of infecting Ellen with her cough, Maria resists her own longing. Ellen, however, holds Maria firmly, kissing her "full on her lips" (362).

In *The Portion of Labor*, Freeman celebrated the support women find in their love for each other through times of hardship and oppression. She presented these bonds as the emotional core of each woman's life. Through most of the novel, Ellen's voice emerges as a powerful reminder that women can bring about change and can invest the male world with female values if given an arena to voice their views. At the same time, Freeman tames Ellen in the conclusion, perhaps aiming to appeal to a wider audience of men and women. Although Robert's approach to the workers will change, Ellen will marry Robert and come around to share some of his perspective when she considers the hardships the strike has caused.

By the Light of the Soul

However awkward the mechanics of the plot of *By the Light of the Soul* (1907), this novel offers an intriguing exploration of female liaisons. The early section of the novel is one of Freeman's most autobiographical accounts of childhood. Maria Edgham, the heroine, resembles most descriptions that are available of Mary as a child. Emerging from a similarly religious background, Maria develops her own sense of the value and limits of worship. She is intelligent, imaginative, attractive, overprotected, and sensitive. Given this identification of the author with the heroine, it is fascinating to trace Maria's development into womanhood, caught as she ultimately is between her love for women and her attraction to marriage.

As does "The Tree of Knowledge," this story focuses on the love between half-sisters. Maria, the older sister, and Evelyn are almost obsessively attached to each other. When they see each other after a brief separation, their reunion captures the bond. In Evelyn's eyes, "there was a strange passion" when she looks at Maria.[59] She tells Maria, "I love you so, Maria, that I don't feel well." Maria compares her love for Evelyn to her love for a man, reflecting "how much more she loved Evelyn than she had loved George Ramsey, how much more precious a little, innocent, beautiful girl was than a man" (352–53).

Four years into her marriage to Charles at the time she wrote this novel, Freeman seems to have been attempting to come to terms with her own separation from Mary Wales. Of the three novels written during this decade, this is the only one in which her heroine does *not* end up in a comfortable and appropriate marriage. In fact, her autobiographical heroine chooses instead to live with a woman. Writing such a conclusion may have been an act of wish fulfillment for Freeman. Having been forced into a marriage by a parson in one of the more awkward moments in the plot, Maria gradually begins to love the man she has married. She discovers, however, that Evelyn is in love with the same man. Maria runs away and in the process meets Rosa Blair on the train. Rosa becomes an odd substitute for Evelyn. Maria changes her name and releases a report that she is dead. In this way, Maria makes it possible for Evelyn to marry her husband and frees herself to share her life with another woman. Described in terms of self-sacrifice, Maria's act seems at least as much a means toward self-gratification. To understand the double edge to the novel's conclusion, it is helpful to explore Freeman's depiction of Maria's relationship with the insightful and eccentric dwarf Rosa Blair.

Rosa Blair describes herself as someone who "happened to bloom outside the pale," and she feels an instant affinity when she meets Maria whom she senses is "also outside the pale in some way." Recognizing that Maria "has escaped from the garden of life," Rosa gives Maria a new name, in essence helping Maria to change identities (483). She explains to Maria that "it is not so very bad outside when one becomes accustomed to it," and helps Maria see the life that may be available to her "outside" of her society, separated from the expectation of heterosexuality and marriage. Maria's response to Rosa is an intriguing description of female bonding; Freeman allows the relationship to blossom into a "marriage" only in a realm that is completely divorced from a society dominated by heterosexuality. First, Maria gazes at Rosa Blair and is surprised by the attraction she feels:

Maria gazed at her as she sat so, with an odd, inverted admiration. It seemed extraordinary to her she should actually admire any one like this deformed little creature, but admire her she did. It was as if she suddenly had become possessed of a sixth sense for an enormity of beauty beyond the usual standards. (485)

Freeman establishes a new standard of beauty as she describes Rosa through Maria's eyes. Rosa tells her that she must come back to her home to live with her. Explaining to Maria that they will "shelter" each other, she decides to support Maria financially and emotionally, to help her discover and come to terms with a new identity.

The home of Rosa Blair, a place Maria sees as full of "bizarre splendor," is a microcosm for both women. It is a world in which a female relationship can flower without restrictive heterosexual definitions of passionate love. Surrounded by Eastern hangings and rugs, "and dark gleams of bronzes and dull lights of brass, and the sheen of silken embroideries," Maria recognizes that she has entered another plane of existence. Rosa no longer appears to be "deformed" in these surroundings: "she fitted into this dark, rich, Eastern splendor as a misformed bronze idol might have done" (487).

In "Old Woman Magoun," Lily's grandmother determines that Lily must literally die in order to live in the female heaven of her imagination, an idealized place of maternal love. Here, Freeman allows her character life on earth and creates a "heaven" in the home of a woman whose physical appearance has banished her from society. Rosa's home is a utopian, self-made heaven devoid of male standards of beauty and acceptability:

The walls were hung with paper covered with sheafs of white lilies; white fur rugs—wolf-skins and skins of polar bears—were strewn over the polished white floor. All the toilet articles were ivory and the furniture white, with decorations of white lilies and silver. In one corner stood a bed of silver with white draperies. Beyond Maria had a glimpse of a bath in white and silver, and a tiny dressing-room which looked like frost-work. (487–88)

Despite the images of lily-white virginity, this heaven is full of female sensuality. Maria realizes "a sort of delight in externals which she had never had before. The externals seemed to be farther-reaching." One is reminded of the "farther-reaching" capacity of women to love each other that Freeman described in "The Tree of Knowledge."

The rooms Freeman loved when she lived with Mary Wales may have been the model for the descriptions of Rosa's home. In her letter to Kate Upson Clark from the home of Mary Wales, Freeman wrote:

> I am taking a lot of comfort in these new rooms—had a fire in my hearth just now. It must have been about all our ancestors could do to keep the hearth fires a-going. I don't see how they got time to do anything else. But when the fire blazes up, it looks beautiful. I light this room with candles in old brass candlesticks. I have dull blue and gilt paper on the walls, and a striped Madagascar rug over a door, and a fur rug before the hearth. It is one of the queerest looking places you ever saw, I expect. You ought to see the Randolph folks when they come in. They look doubtful in the front room, but they say it is "pretty." When they get out into the back room, they say it "looks just like me." I don't know when I shall ever find out if that is a compliment.[60]

When she had moved in with Mary Wales, Freeman was given the entire north portion of the house, which included a small sitting room with a study behind it. Edward Foster comments on the "curious old fireplace" and notes that the rooms were "decorated in her own taste."[61] The clear pleasure Freeman took in her letter to Clark when she described her writing haven is the very satisfaction of being, as Rosa says, "outside the pale," set apart from the "Randolph folks." It is in what Freeman called this "queerest looking" place, with its exotic rugs and candlesticks, that she was able to create her own world apart.

Freeman's description of Rosa's bedroom symbolically remakes the world in Rosa's terms:

> To Maria's utter amazement, she [Rosa] no longer seemed in the least deformed, she no longer seemed a dwarf. She was in perfect harmony with the room, which was low-ceiled, full of strange curves and low furniture with curved backs. It was all Eastern, as was the first floor of the house. Maria understood with a sort of intuition that this was necessary. The walls were covered with Eastern hangings, tables of lacquer stood about filled with squat bronzes and gemlike ivory carvings. The hangings were all embroidered in short curve effects. Maria realized that her hostess, in this room, made more of a harmony than she herself. She felt herself large, coarse, and common where she should have been tiny, bizarre, and according to the usual standard, misformed. Miss Blair had planned for herself a room wherein everything was misformed, and in which she herself was in keeping. (489)

It is in this room that Maria realizes her love for Rosa Blair and sees as well her beauty. As Rosa explains, "beauty is only a matter of comparison, you know." The room Rosa has created, the realm she will inhabit with Maria, is a place that is designed to create images of harmony, a world apart and a world of Rosa's creation, a place where Rosa's size and curved spine become irrelevant, where the choice of "differentness," of women living together instead of with husbands, is acceptable and even beautiful. A model for Freeman's own artistry, Rosa has designed her home with the eye of an artist, and this is the setting Freeman chooses for her heroine's final resting place.

Rosa acknowledges that "the world is right and I am wrong, but in here I seem to be right." Similarly, Freeman recalled the reactions of visitors to her back room when she lived with Wales and their comments that it "looks like me." Wishing that she could make herself over "to suit the world," Rosa chooses instead to create a place in which she is "in harmony after I have been out of tune." Freeman knew that heterosexual standards had influenced her own choice to leave Wales and marry Charles. She has her dwarf Rosa exclaim to Maria, "what a pity I cannot make the whole earth over to suit me . . . instead of only this one room. Now I look entirely perfect to you, do I not?" (489). By the time Freeman was writing this novel, she could only achieve such harmonious images in her fiction, for the home in which she was *now* living was a great distance from Mary Wales. To envision a female "marriage" for Maria, Freeman had to create a character "outside the pale," a world in which deformity *is* a standard of beauty. Furthermore she had to remove her heroine from her familiar world through a feigned death, destroying the possibility of her survival within society.

In a moment of weakness, Maria thinks she would like to reclaim her life in the world by revealing that she had not died and arranging a divorce from her husband. She attempts to visit Evelyn and sees her at a distance in the window with her husband. Rosa warns Maria that to reveal her existence and request a divorce will destroy reputations. Perhaps this was Freeman's fear as she remained in a marriage that was so clearly a disaster. Nevertheless Maria temporarily attempts to find a solution through divorce. When she stands outside the window, on the outside looking in at an image of marriage, she longs not for her lost husband but for Evelyn and then for Rosa Blair. She watches her former husband kiss Evelyn and realizes that "Evelyn

looked to Maria more beautiful than she had ever seen her." In the
next instant, she thinks of Rosa Blair.

> She seemed to suddenly sense the highest quality of love: that which
> realizes the need of another, rather than one's own. The poor little dwarf
> seemed the very child of her heart. She looked up at the stars shining
> through the plumy foliage of the trees, and thought how many of them
> might owe their glory to the radiance of unknown suns. . . . She ques-
> tioned no longer the right or wrong of what she had done, as she hurried
> on and reached the little Amity station in time for the last train. (497)

Choosing finally to live with Rosa Blair and let the world assume she
has died, Maria abandons heterosexual love, takes "the last train"
away from the question of "right or wrong," and feels "radiance"
rather than terror in the choice. It is not surprising that one reviewer
dismissed the novel with vehemence, claiming that it is "repellent"
and "disagreeable." [62]

By the Light of the Soul is the only work Freeman completed that
tapped so candidly, and in such a stark comparison, the choice between heterosexuality and the possibility of spending one's life with
another woman, an option Freeman had had with Mary Wales. It is
likely that as Freeman wrote this unusual conclusion, she was evaluating and imagining another life for herself. Her decision to have
Maria feign death in order to live with Rosa suggests the danger she
saw in ending her own marriage, her fear of public humiliation and
ostracism. Freeman allows Maria a way out of her marriage through
a sort of death and rebirth. Through her pretense of death, the
possibilities of heterosexuality are closed to Maria, and she can only
live in the cloistered world of Rosa's creation. This novel is a tribute
to Freeman's courage to present such a life as blissful and radiant
rather than tragic.

The Shoulders of Atlas

The Shoulders of Atlas (1908) focuses still more precisely on a single
relationship between two women, Sylvia Whitman and the young,
distant relative who comes to live with her, Rose Fletcher. When Rose
is courted by Horace Allen, Sylvia does all she can to interfere with
their romance. Despite the many other aspects of the plot, this
strand is by far the most intriguing and the most highly developed.
The relationship between Sylvia and Rose seems to mirror that of

Mary Wilkins Freeman and Mary Wales in its maternal quality and intensity. It is possible that when Freeman wrote about the difficulties of Rose's separation from Sylvia she was reflecting on the decision she had made in 1902 to leave Mary Wales in order to marry Charles Freeman.

The plot of *The Shoulders of Atlas* begins with Sylvia's unexpected inheritance from a distant relation, Abrahama White, and becomes increasingly complex. Sylvia is surprised that all of Abrahama's savings and property have been left to her rather than to Abrahama's niece, Rose Fletcher. She is told by her lawyer, however, that Abrahama had cut off all ties to Rose's mother (who has since died) because of their bitter rivalry over a man. Sylvia feels guilty about the inheritance, but enjoys the new financial gains. Rose eventually comes to live with Sylvia and her husband, Henry, when Rose's guardian, Eliza Farrell, dies. Sylvia's initial guilt grows stronger when she discovers the existence of an earlier will, written before the rift between Abrahama and Rose's mother. Sylvia becomes convinced that because of this will (which it later becomes clear is not legally valid and was superseded by the second will), the inheritance must belong to Rose. Although she mistakenly believes that Rose is the rightful heir through most of the novel, Sylvia hides this information from Rose.

The awkward explanation for Sylvia's excessive interference in Rose's marriage possibility is that she wishes to keep Rose under her roof so that she too can reap the benefits of the inheritance. This twist in the plot, however, is one of the most glaring failures in the novel and becomes an unconvincing disguise for Sylvia's passionate involvement with Rose. Her guilty secret about the discovery of an earlier will fails to account for the degree of Sylvia's rage when she finds that Rose is attracted to Horace Allen.

When she sees Rose's "smile of ecstasy" after she has been with Horace in the orchard, Sylvia "turned deadly pale."[63] Her argument against Rose's marriage is charged with possessiveness and jealousy. Through the twist in the plot concerning the inheritance, Freeman avoids the more interesting psychological dimensions of the novel, the threat that Rose's suitor represents to Sylvia. The "quasi-lesbian, quasi-mother-daughter" relationship, as Donovan terms it, that forms between Rose and Sylvia mirrors that of Ellen and Cynthia in *The Portion of Labor* but goes much further.[64] Whereas Cynthia drops out of the story as a viable contender for Ellen's affections after

Robert becomes her serious suitor, Sylvia almost prevents Rose's marriage. Having been married for six years at the time, Freeman may have been working through the very arguments against marriage that she had considered in her own years of hesitation. Her words about Sylvia's sense of the inadequacy of marriage might easily have applied to her own situation: "Nobody knew how on occasions Sylvia longed for another woman to whom to speak her mind. She loved her husband, but no man was capable of entirely satisfying all her moods" (63).

Sylvia's affection is not initially an obstacle to Rose's happiness. She showers Rose with unconditional love. Although she would like to express affection physically, Sylvia holds back. Parting with her before she goes to sleep, Sylvia "did not touch her, but she was quivering with maternal passion which seemed to embrace without any physical contact" (197). Perhaps more clearly than in any of her other work, Freeman broadens her definition of "maternal passion" and its scope. It was a passion she had felt in her relationship with her mother and transferred in many respects to her relationship with Wales. Sylvia's love for Rose captures that process of transference well:

> She adored the girl to such an extent that the adoration fairly pained her. Rose herself might easily have found this exacting affection, this constant watchfulness, irritating, but she found it sweet. She could scarcely remember her mother, but the memory had always been as one of lost love. Now she seemed to have found it again. She fairly coquetted with this older woman who loved her, and whom she loved, with that charming coquettishness sometimes seen in a daughter towards her mother.... She affronted Sylvia with a delicious sense of her own power over her and an underlying affection.... (109)

Much as she sets the love in maternal terms, Freeman also suggests a love that is romantic and potentially physical. As an expression of gratitude for Sylvia's many acts of kindness, Rose kisses Sylvia "with such vehemence that the elder woman started back" (207). On another night, she kisses Sylvia again "with such effusion" that Sylvia once again "started back." The kiss takes on great meaning for Sylvia: "The soft impetuous kiss caused her cheek to fairly tingle as she went downstairs and about her work. It should have been luminous from the light it made in her heart" (210).

The relationship between Sylvia and Rose grows in intensity until Rose responds to the advances of Horace Allen, the young man who wishes to marry her. It is at this point that Sylvia hardens and attempts to interfere. In Sylvia's reaction, Freeman portrays the quiet rage she may have imagined Mary Wales harbored during her own period of engagement to Charles. She captures as well the dilemma for Rose, who longs for the "normal" life that she associates with marriage although she fears losing Sylvia's affection. Sylvia's husband, Henry, discusses with a friend Sylvia's obsessive desire to interfere with Rose's opportunity to marry. The friend shrewdly questions whether Sylvia is in love with Rose, and Henry replies affirmatively but translates the love in purely maternal terms. At the same time, he describes her fear of Rose's marriage as though Sylvia were a jealous lover.

In a conversation with Rose about another young woman, Lucy Ayres, Sylvia makes a convincing argument against marriage for financially independent young women. Her words may reflect what Freeman had come to feel about her own mistaken choice:

> "What a girl is so crazy to get married for, anyway, when she has a good mother and a good home, I can't see," said Sylvia, leading directly up to the subject in the secret place of her mind.
>
> Rose blushed, with apparently no reason. "But she can't have her mother always, you know, Aunt Sylvia," said she.
>
> "Her mother's folks are awful long-lived."
>
> "But Lucy is younger. In the course of nature, she will outlive her mother, and then she will be all alone."
>
> "What if she is? 'Ain't she got her good home and money enough to be independent? Lucy won't need to lift a finger to earn money if she's careful."
>
> "I always thought it would be very dreadful to live alone," Rose said, with another blush.
>
> "Well, she needn't be alone. There's plenty of women always in want of a home. No woman need live alone if she don't want to."
>
> "But it isn't quite like"—Rose hesitated.
>
> "Like what?"
>
> "It wouldn't seem quite so much as if you had your own home, would it as if . . ." Rose hesitated again.
>
> Sylvia interrupted her. "A girl is a fool to get married if she's got money enough to live on," said she. (201–2)

Rose stresses fear of living alone and the desire to have "her own home" with whatever undefinable privileges accompany marriage. But Sylvia's counterargument points to the very options that were available to Freeman at the time of her marriage to Charles: financial independence, motherly love, and sharing a home with another woman. Furthermore, Sylvia stresses the sufficiency of maternal love in place of heterosexual love. Sylvia assures herself and attempts to convince Rose that "all a girl needs in this world to make her happy and free from care is a woman to be a mother to her" (209).

Despite the elaborate and awkward mechanics of the plot of the novel and Rose's ultimate marriage, the subject of *The Shoulders of Atlas* is the nature of relationships between women and the complexity of "maternal passion." This is at the root of any of the actions in the novel, even before the relationship between Sylvia and Rose develops. Rose has come to Sylvia after having lived with Eliza Farrell, her guardian. Eliza was said to have "loved women better than a woman usually does." She kept Rose from attending a boarding school for fear that she would enter "one of those erotic friendships which are really diseased love affairs, with another girl or teacher" (158). Freeman may have protected her characters against the full development of "erotic friendships" because of her own fear that such liaisons are in fact "diseased love affairs." This may be the explanation for Freeman's awkward disguise for Sylvia's passion, her attempt at some rational explanation for Sylvia's behavior. The conclusion of the novel is an idyllic wedding scene in which Sylvia learns that her worries were unnecessary, that in fact she was not in possession of money that belonged to Rose and could therefore part with Rose without guilt. The earlier emphasis on her intense and possessive love of Rose fades as the relationship becomes secondary to that of the bride and groom. As Donovan puts it, "it is as if no explanation were needed, as if no one would or could question the superiority of the male claim to women's affection, attention, and commitment." [65]

While depicting "unresolved female liaisons" more openly than most other women writers, Freeman's packaged conclusion suggests that she "seems to have imbibed a moral atmosphere which assumes the male prerogative." [66] It is possible as well that when Freeman found herself writing passionate scenes of love between women, whether the exchanges between Ellen and Cynthia, Maria and Rosa, or Sylvia and Rose, she came too close to the heart of her own ambivalence and longing. She was at the edge of a truth that may have been too difficult to acknowledge. Written on the brink of the decay of her marriage, her elaborate descriptions of Sylvia's love for Rose seem to reflect how deeply she felt Mary Wales's absence.

7

"IF YOU DON'T SEE THE OLD ME"

∞

IN A LETTER to Harriet Randolph Hyatt Mayor written in 1900, Freeman expressed an anxiety which proved to be valid. Fearing the change that marriage would bring, Freeman wrote, "If you don't see the old me, I shall run and run until I find her."[1] Kate Upson Clark, the woman who had introduced Mary to Charles, wrote years later of the failed marriage that "we had warned her, but she probably felt that her influence could make him keep his promises,—the rock on which so many fair young lives have been wrecked."[2] From the moment that she decided to marry Charles Freeman until her death in 1930, Freeman's life became what she called in another letter written in 1900, "a hopeless sort of chase of myself."[3] She had completed her best work by the year 1908, and yet she would continue to write almost frenetically while struggling to sustain a marriage that showed signs of its disastrous end almost from the beginning.

Ironically, public honor and recognition came her way at the same time that her fiction became increasingly cumbersome and unreadable by today's standards. In 1917, the Committee on Nominations of the National Institute of Arts and Letters nominated Freeman for membership. Although she was not elected at that time which, as Brent Kendrick explains, was a result of the committee's concern about admitting women, the nomination itself was a notable honor.[4] Perhaps because of the increasing recognition she received, Freeman seemed relatively unaware of the awkwardness and excessive sentimentality in her late work. She knew, however, that writing did not come as easily to her. When she learned in 1915 that her novel *Jerome* might be made into a film, she considered herself ready "at last to tiptoe along on the summit."[5] Her volume *Edgewater People* (1918) was her last collection of short fiction and her weakest. Here she did acknowledge self-doubt. She wrote in the preface that she had hoped to delineate the way in which communities resemble individuals: "I may have succeeded in making this evident in this volume . . . I may have failed."[6]

The publication of *Edgewater People* occurred at a time when Freeman's personal life had become more desperate than ever before. Since none of Freeman's letters offers specific indications of how Charles's alcoholism must have been affecting the marriage, one can only imagine the effort it took to tolerate married life, especially after Charles had been hospitalized for alcoholism in 1909. She had been married for sixteen years when she finally acknowledged the disaster her marriage had become. In all those years of struggle, she may have hoped to turn things around or at least to avoid the humiliation of divorce. By 1918, there was every indication that Charles would never reverse his behavior. Along with his alcoholism he had developed a serious drug addiction, and in 1918 he suffered a complete breakdown from which he never recovered. Kendrick notes that at work, Charles had begun to abuse customers and to make frivolous purchases that might have driven him into bankruptcy had it not been for his business manager, John Breen, who placed the corporation in trust. His illness took the form of extreme paranoia. He began to experience hallucinations and his behavior "bordered on being violent."[7] Charles went off on sprees for weeks at a time. One of the few revealing letters from Freeman in this period suggests the impact of Charles's illness. She wrote to Samuel Schenck in November 1918 about one of Charles's disappearances:

> Charles did not come down to get me. I have not seen him, nor personally received one letter, or message from him, since I left. No, no quarrels, conditions such it seems impossible than they can ever be changed. But that does not lie with me, nor does my ability to return, when I am well again, lie with me.[8]

Despite the enigmatic references to the situation, Freeman does mention in the letter the impossibility of recovery and refers indirectly to the dissolution of her marriage. She describes her nervous condition as having worsened, particularly when she attempts to sleep, and explains, "I have real reason to be anxious."[9] And of course, she did. As Kendrick notes, both of Charles's parents had died and his sisters had moved away. This left all the responsibility for Charles's care in Mary's hands. She arranged for his treatment at Belle Meade Sanitorium in New Jersey in 1919. His condition worsened however, partly as a result of prohibition. Charles began to drink bootleg liquor, his health declined still further, and on 2 August 1920 he entered the New Jersey State Hospital for the Insane at Trenton. The treatment was ineffective largely because of Charles's resistance to it. He was diagnosed as a man in the "advanced stages of chronic alcoholism."[10] Suffering from delirium tremens and delusions, he escaped from the hospital after several weeks.[11] His condition continued to decline. When she returned from a trip to the White Mountains in the summer of 1921, Mary felt her safety jeopardized and decided she could not live in the same house with him. It became necessary for her to commit him, since he would not go voluntarily, to the institution from which he had escaped, New Jersey State Hospital, on 23 August 1921. Although his sister Sallie visited him at the hospital and urged him to remain because of the seriousness of his condition, Charles was determined to leave once again. This time Mary signed papers for his release (3 October), and then followed the advice of her lawyer to temporarily separate from Charles. Her only comfort at the time appears to have been an almost obsessive attention to her garden which Edward Foster describes as a "superb circular clump of rose bushes." Her own emotional state in this period comes across in a poem she published in 1922.

> Save for the roses I am blest to hold
> Sweeter than love and lovely as the day,
> If I were made of precious beaten gold
> I'd count myself as dross to fling away.[12]

Mary later explained the final sequence of events in an interview published in the *New Brunswick* (N.J.) *Sunday Times* on 18 March 1923: "Things became so unbearable that I was forced to obtain a legal separation which was filed by former Senator Brown about the same time that Dr. Freeman was removed from Trenton. I did this

not because of any family trouble but only as a protection for myself
and servants and my property interests." [13] Oddly enough, even at
this point, Mary defended the merits of the marriage.

The conclusion of the marriage and of Charles's life is curious
and much has been left unexplained. The separation agreement
involved a weekly payment to Mary of fifty dollars. At the same time,
Charles drew up a hurtful, even vengeful will. Rather than live with
his sister, who had offered to take care of him, Charles moved in
with his chauffeur William Breen. He then moved in with a new
secretary, chauffeur and mechanic he had hired, twenty-seven year-
old Harry B. Mohring, whom he hardly knew. He lived with Mohring,
his wife, and two children for nearly fourteen months. According to
Kendrick, Freeman "thought he might get well and wish to resume
living with her." [14] She continued to live in their home and to maintain his room.

On 7 March 1923, Charles died in the home of the Mohrings of
heart failure. The shock of Charles's will soon followed. The will
dictated that a thousand dollars would go to Lettie Patterson, two
hundred dollars to each of his four sisters, and one dollar to Mary
Wilkins Freeman. He gave Harry Mohring, whom at the time the will
was written he had known for only six months, $10,000 in cash and
the "rest, residue and remainder" of the entire Freeman estate, the
value of which was estimated to be $225,000.

His comment in doing so aimed to hurt Mary still further: "in
appreciation of a loyalty and devotion which I have appreciated
and which I have failed to receive from those nearer by ties of
blood, marriage and business." [15] After her years of dedication and
patience with Charles, these words and his cruel gesture of leaving
her a token dollar must have come as a tremendous blow. The law
suit that followed was enormously painful for Mary. Perhaps in a
feeble effort to protect her reputation, Mary defended the merits of
her marriage and of Charles even after this. In the *Sunday Times*
interview of 1923, she said, "I have suffered nothing but grief since
my husband's tragic end, which seems like a double tragedy to me
because of our separation and then his death. He was a thoroughly
good man, but worried much about his business and I have an idea
that the war had done much to bring on a breakdown. We lived in
idyllic happiness for twenty-two years until 1921, when my husband

became mentally ill, and became so bad that in August 1921, he was removed to the New Jersey State Hospital for the Insane at Trenton."[16]

Despite her effort to present an image of marital bliss destroyed only after twenty-two years, Mary had to face public humiliation in court. She said, "one thing that hurts is in order to contest the will, you will have to say things you hardly have the heart to mention in public."[17] Because the value of the Freeman estate was $225,000, the case was highly publicized. The hearing went into elaborate detail about Charles's deterioration, clarifying the fact that he was not in a rational state of mind when he composed the will. James Lawless, a saloon keeper, noted that Charles had been under the influence of alcohol for the twenty years that he had known him.[18] Witness after witness, friends and those who knew him through business transactions, testified to the horrors of Charles's condition. One witness revealed that Charles would go to sleep holding a hay knife and would walk on the roof of the porch, "saying he was looking for something, but was unable to tell what." His sister Nellie described her last visit to see her brother when "he did not know me." She had thought he had suffered a stroke. All of the medical testimony supported the views of the witnesses that Charles was not in his "right mind." Doctors verified that he suffered from extensive "hallucinations of eye, sight and hearing."[19] Harry Mohring explained that Charles had left Mary one dollar because "he resented his wife for committing him to the asylum and additionally he felt that the income from her books had made her as wealthy or more so than he was." Mohring referred to Charles's "dissatisfaction with home affairs" and insisted that Charles had stopped drinking while he lived with him. The Mohrings argued that Charles was completely sane when he drew up the will. After many appeals of the initial decision that Charles was in fact unable to make a valid and effectual will because "he lacked the necessary mental capacity," a final judgment came in 1925, two years after litigation had begun. Freeman would receive one hundred dollars a month.[20] Ultimately she was allotted the total sum of $78,000.

In a letter she wrote to her friend Evelyn Sawyer Severance two years after this decision, Mary sums up the crisis with an almost uncanny calm:

My husband died four years ago next March. He had been in Trenton
Insane Asylum. The Volsted Act did him harm. He would have partaken
of the ardent in any case, but would not have gone blind or insane. Of
course it was not altogether hilarious for the poor man or me. I was forced
to obtain a separation, not a divorce, a separation for protection. My
doctors told me I must. Then after his death came a litigation of two years.
He left a considerable estate which he had bequeathed to a chauffeur who
was not an angel of light. My four in-laws and I broke that will. Then I,
in order to avoid further litigation sold my rights in the estate which
comprehended, of course, the whole to the sisters. I incline to believe the
in-laws felt that I ought to have nothing, but I differed and so did my
lawyers. I got a little.[21]

Her tone here, even in a letter to a close friend, hardly captures the
emotional strain of these years of litigation and how they seem to
have affected her health. It is as though she wished to sum up these
years of struggle as a series of facts to be recorded and then dismissed. The letter concludes humorously in reference to her
strength: "I must have a very tough streak in me. I did not look so
but time has proved it or else a queer diet, mostly buttermilk. I am
not strong but I live along and fear I shall continue until I look like
John D. Rockefeller, in spite of the cold cream."[22]

Indeed, Mary survived, and survived with considerable energy, a
series of illnesses. Her letters between 1918 and 1925 all indicate
her declining physical strength. She wrote in 1919, however, about
her slow recovery from influenza despite failing eyesight. Although
she devoted hours to thinking about writing or attempting to write,
she felt frustrated about her increasing inability to produce manuscripts. According to one of her friends, it was impossible for her to
write effectively in this period as she was so deeply hurt by the
outcome of her marriage: "Her typing was all corrections and her
plots confused. . . . Her manuscripts were returned and although she
had fits of crying and despondency every time they came back, she
kept on writing. . . . at the time of her death they filled a filing
cabinet."[23]

In 1919, Freeman wrote an interesting letter to Professor Fred
Lewis Pattee who had devoted a portion of his text, *Sidelights on
American Literature,* to an analysis of her role in American literary
history. She described her compulsion to write in terms of "circumstances" that made it "imperative for me to do that one thing, and

no other." She sadly acknowledged in the letter her own sense of unfulfilled potential: "I do know, and have always known, my accomplished work is not the best work of which I am capable, but it is too late now."[24] In 1920, she described her ailing health which included "nervous prostration, three attacks of Spanish influenza for which I hope the Kaiser will have to sizzle, Conjunctivitis, three acute attacks, my never rabbit-built-ears lopping dreadfully, then bronchitis, and a close squeak from pneumonia."[25]

In her last years, Freeman felt the aging process acutely. She seemed angriest about how hampered she was by age and failing eyesight in her efforts to write. In 1927 she wrote, "I have been prevented by the exigencies of existence from writing much for several years and have wondered if I have not lost my key-note."[26] She continued in these years, however, to communicate with editors, to arrange for reprints of her work, to stay on top of the public reception of her work, and to compose new stories. She also attempted to revise some of her work. Even as late as 1928, when she was seventy-six, she was composing a story that she hoped to publish in England.[27] She sent another story out in 1929, though with great hesitation.[28] In November of that year, she was working on several additional stories which she hoped to send and mentioned in her last letters to Lois Schenck Lord (23 and 25 November 1929). She described her struggle to write in these years in a letter in 1928, and she wrote of her habit in this period of "being afraid the work was not good and placing it in my file, and not sending anywhere."[29] She worried about "the life of my work," as she put it in another letter written in 1928. "I feel it is all I came into the world for, and have failed dismally if it is not a success."[30] As Kendrick states, she produced nothing notable in her last period aside from occasional poems and stories published in *Harper's Magazine* or *Woman's Home Companion*. She spent much time uncovering some of her unpublished stories, protecting her future. "I am trying to eliminate worthless work," she wrote, "if I can identify it. I do not wish a lot of trash to appear after me."[31]

Freeman received much recognition in her late years. When she was first informed in 1917 that the National Institute of Arts and Letters might be divided on the question of admitting women, Freeman wrote with characteristic acquiescence but ambiguity: "I can very readily see that many would object." She offered the Academy a graceful way out of her election by saying that she "shall not fail to understand if I am not admitted because of the division among the membership as to the advisability of admitting women."[32] But understanding the men in the Academy and their motives was not necessarily agreeing with their position, nor does understanding suggest acceptance. She proposed at the time that they consider "honorary membership" if actual membership could not be arranged. In 1926, The National Institute of Arts and Letters did elect Freeman to membership along with Agnes Repplier, Margaret Deland, and Edith Wharton, and the bronze doors of the Academy still carry the inscription "Dedicated to the Memory of Mary E. Wilkins Freeman and the Women Writers of America." In the same year, the American Academy of Arts and Letters awarded her the Howells Medal for distinction in fiction.

Freeman's early depictions of aging women focus on the role of work in their lives and on the importance of the opportunity to define oneself in the context of one's work, even in old age. She herself attempted to make work central to her life well into her seventies despite her physical weakness and its interference in her ability to write. Like her portrayal of Hetty in "A Church Mouse," Freeman's sharp analysis of Candace Whitcomb's dilemma in "A Village Singer" anticipated her own struggle to continue to be taken seriously in the literary world. The community gives Candace a photo album, her "golden parachute," and a letter of dismissal from her position as soprano in the church choir. She is to be replaced by the younger Alma Way. Candace's response becomes a celebration of the spirit to rebel against the injustice of minimizing the contributions of aging women.

On the Sunday when the young and conventionally pretty Alma must sing for the first time, the feisty heroine plays her organ and sings so loudly in her cottage near the church that her "shrill clamor" can be heard above Alma's sweet, thin voice.[33] Criticized by the minister and the choir leader, Candace rebels still further, using language as her weapon. She defiantly exclaims that she uses the retirement gift, the photo album, as a footstool. She challenges as well the discrimination against her gender by reminding the minister that William Emmons is allowed to continue as the choir leader despite the fact that he is three years older than she is. As Marjorie Pryse explains, "Mary Wilkins Freeman describes a village which finds aging offensive in women but acceptable in men. Candace's 'song' protests the unfairness of this view of women, and in retaining her sense of personal triumph into death, Candace mirrors for her community the way they have lost but must regain their own humanity."[34]

Freeman's approach to aging and death resembled that of the spirited elderly heroines in her best fiction. All her letters from these late years indicate the pride she took in her autonomy, her capacity to continue working at what she cared about (despite her frustration with the quality of what she produced), her love of storytelling, and her appreciation of women friends. Freeman had an intuitive understanding in her younger years of the inner strength that would carry her through as she aged. The stories that best capture these aspects of her later life were written when she was much younger. The old women in her fiction reflect the spirit that she herself would later develop to rebel against stereotypical definitions of aging women who submit to circumstances and depend on others for their own survival. Early on, Freeman was praised for her capacity to capture the experience of aging. She was fascinated by the paradox of the aging process, the growth of wisdom and the decline of physical strength. In a letter to Kate Upson Clark in 1889, she mentioned having met an elderly "theosophist, in an old gold plush wrap, a cinnamon brown dress, and a green bonnet, who said that I did write such beautiful stories that she thought I must have passed through many incarnations, and must be—a very old soul." With her touch of humor, Freeman added that "she felt a little indignant, not knowing rightly whether it was a compliment or not to be told that I was several thousand years old." She then came to the conclusion that "age in the soul means eternal youth, and I am awfully set up and expect that respect and veneration which is due me."[35] Some of the finest stories which go right to the heart of her analysis of the aging process and its demands are "A Mistaken Charity," "An Innocent Gamester," "On the Walpole Road," "A Village Singer," "An Independent Thinker," and "An Object of Love."

A home of one's own, self-sufficiency, and control over one's fate in the later years of life were, to Freeman's mind, critical to meaningful survival. This is what she worked at arranging for herself in the last decade of her life, and she wrote about these needs beginning in her thirties when she published *A Humble Romance and Other Stories* and *A New England Nun and Other Stories.* She recognized even then the threat to autonomy that was especially acute for older unmarried women. One story from each collection will serve as examples of how effectively Freeman anticipated these concerns.

"A Mistaken Charity" focuses on the struggle of two aging sisters to resist the well-meaning but "mistaken" efforts of a neighbor who attempts to have them comfortably cared for in an "Old Ladies' Home." Harriet and Charlotte live in relative poverty, but take pride in their ability to care for each other, to "keep a roof over their heads, covering on their backs, and victuals in their mouths."[36] The women have never had lovers, nor have they wished for marriage. Their delight in living comes from the bond they share and in their self-sufficiency. As they get older, Harriet begins to lose her hearing and Charlotte becomes blind. Still, the two women communicate remarkably well, support themselves through tailoring work, and maintain their garden impeccably.

> The delight the two poor old souls took in their own pumpkins, their apples and currants, was indescribable. It was not merely that they contributed largely towards their living; they were their own, their private share of the great wealth of nature, the little taste set apart for them alone out of her bounty, and worth more to them on that account, though they were not conscious of it, than all the richer fruits which they received from their neighbor's gardens. (45)

Despite the poor condition of their home, with drafts and leaks everywhere, the pleasure the women take in what is "their own" is the most important survival tool in their old age.

The delight they share in each other is equally important. For Charlotte, there is also the simple joy which she tries to describe to Harriet, the meaning she finds in the glimmers of light that seem to pass before her unseeing eyes when she thinks of the simple things that they share, whether it's "pork an' greens," or an unexpected breeze. Charlotte calls these odd moments of unexpected light in the midst of continuous darkness "chinks."

> "if you was in the dark, as I am, Harriet, you wouldn't make fun an' turn up your nose at chinks. If you had seen the light streamin' in all of a sudden through some little hole that you hadn't known of before when you set down on the door-step this mornin', and the wind with the smell of the apple blows in it came in your face, an' when Mis' Simonds brought them hot doughnuts, an' when I thought of the pork an' greens jest now

—O Lord, how it did shine in! An' it does now. If you was me, Harriet, you would know there was chinks." (48)

When the sisters are removed from their home and taken to an old people's home, Charlotte is no longer able to see these chinks of light. They had everything to do with her contentment in the world that she and her sister had created for themselves. Charlotte tells Harriet that if only they could return to their home "how the light would stream in!" In the institution they are cared for, fed, dressed, and given comforts that were unavailable to them previously. Yet both sisters cry; they mourn their lost autonomy.

With a remarkable sensitivity to the needs of women as they age, Freeman captures the heroism of their final act of self-determination. The women "gleefully" escape the institution, prepared to walk over fourteen miles in order to live peacefully once again in their own home. A man in a covered wagon gives them a ride, and they go unrecognized by those from the institution who are out searching for them. The last scene in which the two women creep across a field and reenter their old home is perhaps one of the most beautiful in all of Freeman's fiction.

> "The clover is up to our knees," said Harriet; "an' the sorrel and the white-weed; an' there's lots of yaller butterflies."
> "O Lord, Harriet, thar's a chink, an' I do believe I saw one of them yaller butterflies go past it," cried Charlotte, trembling all over, and nodding her grey head violently.
> Harriet stood on the old sunken door-step and fitted the key, which she drew triumphantly from her pocket, in the lock, while Charlotte stood waiting and shaking behind her. Then they went in. Everything was there just as they had left it. Charlotte sank down on a chair and began to cry. Harriet hurried across to the window that looked out on the garden.
> "The currants air ripe," said she; "an' them pumpkins hev run all over everything."
> "O Lord, Harriet," sobbed Charlotte, "thar is so many chinks that they air all runnin' together!" (55–56)

The sisters share a vision together, each one offering the other a description of the freedom they now share with those yellow butterflies. Their garden is ready to harvest and the "chinks" on which Charlotte thrives, streams of light in the home that is their own, are everywhere.

The struggle of Harriet and Charlotte to resist "mistaken charity"

reflects Freeman's fear that aging would invite the unwanted attention of well-meaning friends or relatives. To come and go as she
pleased, to be in charge of her present and future, to maintain
dignity even as her body weakened with age, these are the rights
Freeman treasured in her late years. Despite the many years that
Freeman thrived on feeling nurtured and cared for by Mary Wales
and others, her need to maintain her autonomy was always central.
This became more intensely apparent in her later years. Letters
she wrote to her editors suggest her fear of losing control over the
appearance and distribution of her texts. She was horrified when she
learned of old friends whose autonomy seemed threatened by their
experiences in old age homes.

To the end, she lived in her home in Metuchen. Helpful visitors
were welcomed, but she always remained in charge of the way she
spent her time, whom she would visit, and what she did each day.
She knew early in her life that the efforts of others to take care of
the elderly in a way that stripped them of self-possession must be
vigorously resisted. Her story "An Innocent Gamester" is a splendid
rendering of the struggle involved. In her old age, Lucinda Moss
faces the tyranny of her well-organized, controlling niece who is
determined to dictate the shape of Lucinda's life:

> Lucinda Moss's household plan had been revolutionized since her niece
> had come to live with her. She had no longer any voice in anything, and
> she had come almost to forget what her own original note had been. She
> was growing deprecatory and shamefaced about herself, and she no
> longer openly confessed in many cases her preferences.[37]

The one source of joy in Lucinda's life is fortune-telling. She tries
to explain her pleasure in telling her fortune with cards to her niece
Charlotte: ". . . when anybody ain't had any more change than I've
had 'most all their life, it's kind of comfortin' to spread out the cards
an' try to calculate if there ain't somethin' different comin' " (366).
Thriving on the promise of "somethin' different comin' " through
her fortune-telling, Lucinda is crushed to see Charlotte's reaction.
Her niece essentially rearranges her life, showing disdain for her
pleasures, organizing her menu so that it no longer includes the
rich cupcakes she loves, and stripping her of all control over her
environment. Finally, Lucinda disappears, escaping on a train to
visit her cousin. The escape is her way of clarifying the need for

self-direction and autonomy. Through Lucinda, Freeman captures the importance of empowerment for aging women, a need too frequently overlooked. In the end, Charlotte has to recognize that her love for her aging aunt must incorporate some understanding of her need for freedom. In the concluding scene, Charlotte gives Lucinda a deck of cards to tell her fortune as her gesture of respect and acceptance.

Freeman felt an almost desperate need to keep her creativity alive as she aged, and to convince others that this was possible. She knew that the impulse to tell stories, to pass along her vision of scenes and events in people's lives, had only grown more intense with age. She seems to have anticipated this need in her story "On the Walpole Road." Miss Green, a woman of seventy, tells her younger friend Almiry a family legend, a story which Almiry finally reminds her she has told to her (with variations), every time they pass Walpole.

Perhaps Freeman's philosophy when she reached her seventies is best summarized in a letter she wrote in 1928 after seeing her friend Harriet Mayor's mother, Mrs. Hyatt, who was ninety years old and had become blind that that year:

> Annihilation to me is unimaginable. Change is not, but nothing really ceases to exist. . . . Such tremendous vitality as is in Mrs. Hyatt cannot become nothing any more than fire can. Her body, even, cannot cease to exist in some form. I think her soul deserves a splendid new house of flesh, and I know it will have it. Her tired little body will become violets, but she herself is a separate, elemental thing, which has climbed for years. She will not descend from her heights. Of course you will understand that I believe in transmigration—almost.[38]

Freeman had established her own sense of religion, quite different from her early Calvinistic training. Her spirituality assured her that "nothing really ceases to exist." She trusted in womanly "vitality" of the sort she saw in Mrs. Hyatt and recognized in herself.

A letter she wrote to Allie Morse, an old Brattleboro friend who was now at the Brattleboro Home for the Aged with Evelyn Sawyer Severance, is full of nostalgia for her adolescent years in Brattleboro:

> Oh how wonderfully beautiful it was in Brattleboro. I used to walk to the head of High Street, and stand and look at the mountain in winter. The beauty in Brattleboro made a great difference in my life. And summer nights, when the moon rose over the mountain and the whipperwills sang on the river bank, and the river sang! Joy of youth outside that beauty—

so I made the most of it, and I think it became a part of myself that
remains young and defies time.[39]

The part of Freeman that "defied time" comes through quite clearly
in this letter. It had everything to do with her connection to her
work, evident here when she attempts to recapture Brattleboro
through the images of her prose. Writing now at age seventy-seven,
Freeman would not part with that youth in herself. Even as she
described her physical pain, she wrote of the ongoing effort to
create:

> We live a lonely life here. I am trying to write again, but have not been
> well enough for three or four years. Am a bit better now. I have been
> entertaining facial neuralgia, and could not satisfactorily do so and write.
> Now my doctor has given me something which seems to quiet the rather
> awful pain and I hope I can accomplish something.[40]

In the same letter, she bemoaned the fate of her friends in "The
Home for the Aged": "I hate it, don't you, if you tell the exact truth?
I really think the human body is not such a very good job. They
simply do not match souls, out of alignment." Expressing the rebellious spirit so characteristic of the older women in her fiction, Freeman revolted against the limitations of the body. At the same time,
her own description celebrated the essence of the soul that goes
beyond any "house of flesh," and is necessarily "out of alignment."

Mary visited her friend Hattie Belcher in Randolph in the autumn
of 1929. Belcher recorded that she insisted on going to a nearby
lake which she had loved as a girl. Belcher recalled the words Freeman spoke at the shore of the lake: "You don't know what this means
to me." She also returned to Brattleboro where she met with the
friend she had kept for sixty years, Evelyn Sawyer Severance. According to Foster, Mrs. Severance recalled that they drove to a hilltop
where they could look together at the Connecticut River and "the
curve of Mount Wantastiquet."[41] This reunion and revisiting of old
haunts must have helped Freeman sustain, even in her last painful
year, that "joy of youth" she described in an earlier letter.

Freeman's last recorded letter, a fragment written to Marion Boyd
Allen, captures her ongoing capacity for hope in the face of hardship. She was seventy-eight when she wrote it and in very poor health.

> I am stronger but do not yet count too much on my strength. My heart
> may suddenly rebel, and I feel out of the scheme. . . . As near as I can

make out I have been tearing around for years when I was unable. Then the crash came and now I shall be better.[42]

Feeling "out of the scheme" and recognizing that she had simply fought off the reality of the effects of aging for years, Freeman still believed she would regain her health. On March 13, however, she died of a heart attack at 7:45 P.M. She suffered a serious illness for two weeks before her death and died in her bed with a volume of Kipling's poetry beside her.[43]

8

FREEMAN AND TWO NEW ENGLAND CONTEMPORARIES

∞

IN THE RANGE of nineteenth- and early twentieth-century American women writers, Freeman's voice resonates as an odd mixture of traditions: sentimentalist, regionalist, subtle feminist, supernaturalist. In all of these categories, she was one of the most significant precursors of twentieth-century psychological fiction about women. Set alongside New England women writers of her time, Freeman provides a fascinating middle ground. She is neither an outspoken and committed feminist, the unambivalent "new woman" who began to emerge most visibly in the 1890's, nor the passive promoter of the status quo so evident in women's advice books and journals of her time.

A glance at Sarah Orne Jewett, Mary Wilkins Freeman and Charlotte Perkins Gilman together, is a glance at the spectrum of women's strategies and responses to social conditions at the turn of the century. The three voices offer varying degrees of protest. In Jewett, we hear protest through the communal voices of women in a world where men play a very small part in things, protest through utopian omission. Freeman, in contrast, dwells in the realm of social realities, incorporating her form of protest in the willful assertion of her women characters and in the unjust interpretations of such assertions by men in power. Unlike Jewett, then, Freeman does not avoid the reality of male power. In works such as "Christmas Jenny" or "A Church Mouse" she asks her readers to hear the mistaken male assumption of female madness when women rebel against traditional expectations. Gilman takes her readers even further, pushing beyond the mere exposure of injustice. While Freeman focused on revealing and analyzing the inequities, Gilman outlined specific proposals to eliminate them.

Freeman is most often read alongside Sarah Orne Jewett, whose regionalist prose has a comparable emphasis on women and their environment, but Freeman's connection to her more overtly feminist contemporary, Charlotte Perkins Gilman, is in some sense far more interesting. As Amy Kaplan explains, Freeman "stayed within domestic regional boundaries while subverting them as centers of social protest."[1] Freeman empowers her women characters within the constraints of the domestic realm and asserts a radical critique of the oppression of women, but she never asks her characters to step outside of the system that oppresses them or to attempt to bring about widescale social change. Her stories offer women strategies of subterfuge, methods of coping and surviving through seeming compromise. Her insightful feminist analysis does not take Gilman's next step, toward feminist conclusion. Yet Freeman does invite a level of protest comparable to Gilman's.

The intense level of protest evident in Freeman's descriptions of conflict between men and women (though often hidden beneath layers of sentimentality) is only barely visible in Jewett's fiction. For the most part, Jewett manages to lift characters such as her narrator in *The Country of the Pointed Firs* out of the context of the oppressive restrictions of nineteenth-century womanhood, to spare them the rage we see in Freeman's "The Revolt of 'Mother' " or the agony of "Old Woman Magoun." To a large extent, Jewett avoids most of the tensions that both Freeman and Gilman expose by offering her readers feminine males, men who seem to know from the start that women's values are superior. In this respect, she too frames a world that quietly challenges the accepted norms for women of her time. What saves Jewett's characters from the outrage and potential destruction we see in the fates of some of Freeman's and Gilman's heroines (the grandmother's murder of her grandchild in "Old Woman Magoun" or the woman's painful 'rest cure' and consequent madness in "The Yellow Wallpaper") is her capacity to create an alternative world, a consistent pastoral and utopian ideal in which men do not have the power to shape women's lives. The community in *The Country of the Pointed Firs* is a matriarchy in which men such as

Elijah Tilley are in fact feminized and women have an implicit autonomy that they do not seem to have to fight for.

Later women writers such as Edith Wharton were often dismayed
by the "rose and lavender pages" of Sarah Orne Jewett and Mary
Wilkins Freeman, but Cecelia Tichi makes clear in her essay "Women
Writers and the New Woman" that Jewett and, to a greater extent,
Freeman paved the way for the idea of the new woman who in fact
"occupies an incipient, covert place in their careers and writing" and
in the subtly subversive messages of so much of their work. Tichi
defines the contributions of Freeman and Jewett not in the conventional context of local color but in terms of "women's regionality."
This is a critical distinction. Although some nostalgia for the culture
and geography of New England accounts for the traditional categori-
zation of both Jewett and Freeman as "memorialists of a faded New
England," these writers moved beyond this focus by concentrating
on women's lives. As Tichi clarifies, "their essential agenda in the
era of the new woman was to map the geography of gender. . . . The
geography of America formed an important part of their work, but
essentially, they charted the regions of women's lives, regions both
without and within the self."[2] Their fiction, seen in this context,
offers a somewhat muted yet powerful echo for the more explosive
and didactic statements Gilman was vocalizing in the same period. A
comparison of Freeman with Gilman and then Freeman with Jewett
suggests that Freeman's work embodies the sensibilities of both
Jewett and Gilman in a unique blend of Gilman-like passion and
Jewett-like calm.

Freeman, like Gilman, was working to establish what Tichi calls
"alternative bases of consciousness" and "to show how consciousness
itself could be deployed for women's empowerment."[3] But Freeman
chose to do so within the safe arena of women's magazines; by
allowing the revolt of her women characters to succeed within the
home she was able to reach that wider audience of women who lived
within the restrictive boundaries of nineteenth-century patriarchy.
Interestingly, Gilman expressed disdain for the women's magazines
in which Freeman published—insisting that they were "not truly for
women at all, but only for dressmakers, cooks, nurses, houseservants,
and those who need books on etiquette." She complained that
"these housekeepers' manuals are not the literature for the new
woman."[4] She chose to voice her feminism freely in magazines such

as *The Forerunner* where she could present her most radical view-points without mask or sentiment. What makes Freeman so intriguing is that, although she shared many of Gilman's feminist views, she managed to convey them without an ideological framework, to voice rage in a paradoxically "pleasing" way, and thereby to reach a larger audience of women. Both writers spoke in women's voices, but by writing in the women's magazines which Gilman deplored, Freeman was able to be heard by the audience Gilman rejected, the "dressmakers, cooks, nurses, houseservants," the wives who felt compelled to conform to the very advice books and "books of etiquette" that enraged Gilman.

Understanding the obstacles to open protest, Freeman did not share in Gilman's condemnation of women who submitted to subservient positions in the home. Gilman felt that women ought "to burn with shame, deep scorching shame, at the pitiful limitations with which so many of them are still contented," but Freeman suggested that these limitations could not be overthrown without ambivalence or cost.[5] Freeman's and Gilman's were sister voices, which when heard together, complement each other with counterbalanced themes. At her best, Freeman's fiction explores and indirectly bemoans the experience of those Gilman described as "house slaves" in *Women and Economics*. Whereas Gilman concludes her critique with proposals to lift women out of the home, Freeman revolutionized the mother in the kitchen and demanded that her readers hear that voice and recognize its worth. Because Freeman was working at all times to find the right mask for the rage she shared with Gilman, and to offer revolution without seeming to threaten society, it is not surprising that she apologized after creating a rebel mother and wife such as Sarah Penn.

A comparison of Gilman and Freeman offers an intriguing puzzle. Freeman's implicit fear of the open expression of feminism and Gilman's articulation of her feminist goals are equally problematic in their shaping of characters. In her least readable and most cumbersome fiction, Freeman strayed so far from Gilman-like protest that she allowed her women characters to acquiesce and become subservient. The more extreme her resistance to feminist ideology in her fiction, the less credible her characters seem to become. This is clear in stories such as "A Humble Romance," where a woman's power and capacity to manage a business and gain autonomy is abruptly eliminated with the cheerful and sentimental return of her missing husband. Gilman's fiction also presents aesthetic difficulties, but they occur when she inserts her feminist ideology to such an extent that a credible character becomes an exemplum of her political goals. Gilman wanted to write "good stories," as she stated in the early 1890s, which could become "powerful addition[s] to [her] armory." As Denise Knight explains, Gilman's greatest concern was to "proselytize the reader by infusing her stories with socialist and feministic ideology."[6] Critics today recognize that her stress on using her stories to promote her vision for women's equality often detracted from characterization and dialogue.[7] Moreover, the prose of both Gilman and Freeman was weakest when the authors succumbed to their instincts for rather opposite sorts of "happy endings." While Freeman made the deliberate effort in her conclusions to counter her own moments of rebellion by creating acceptable images of women, Gilman made the deliberate effort to overturn such conformity. In a sense, their aesthetic failures have in common an obsession with audience. Gilman's goal was to provoke radical change; Freeman wanted both to reach the widest possible audience of women in safely coded language and to succeed financially by attempting to please all readers.

When Freeman and Gilman were able to show less concern for audience, they created their strongest and most interesting fiction. In those works, albeit with different voices, they presented the ambiguities of women's experiences in the late nineteenth century, explored psychological complexity, and allowed their stories complicated and inconclusive endings. At her most interesting, Freeman develops characters such as Wheatcroft in her supernatural story, "The Hall Bedroom," or Polly in "Sister Liddy," figures who become social outcasts and stray so significantly from acceptability that they are unable to return to the New England village that has shaped them. Gilman's fiction is similarly powerful when she incorporates some of the ambiguity and ambivalence we see in Freeman's work. Her darkest and most inconclusive story, "The Yellow Wallpaper," is in fact her most successful. A comparison of "The Yellow Wallpaper" with Freeman's supernatural fiction suggests a surprisingly powerful parallel between these otherwise dissimilar writers.

In these works, Freeman and Gilman uncover the most complicated women's issues and offer no resolution. At the heart of their seemingly supernatural tales, there is an exploration of a fundamental dilemma for women: the inevitable link between sexuality, reproduction, and motherhood. As Kate Chopin's *The Awakening* makes so clear, the concept that dominated women's lives at the turn of the century was that indulgence in sexual pleasure was only acceptable when accompanied by devoted motherhood as one's single form of meaningful work. In their most interesting fiction, both Gilman and Freeman suggest that such a fate of necessity represented a loss of self.

Despite their awareness of the obstacles to autonomy that marriage would bring, both Freeman and Gilman married. Each expressed her hesitation poignantly in the context of its interference with work. Two years before marrying Walter Stetson, Gilman wrote to him about her fear: "As much as I love you I love *WORK* better, & I cannot make the two compatible. . . . It is no use, dear, no use. I am meant to be useful & strong, to help many and do my share in the world's work, but not to be loved."[8] Gilman's words reflect her knowledge that loving one's work and loving a man required antithetical energies. As I have indicated in Chapter 6, Freeman's long hesitation before marrying Charles was based on the similar fear that marriage would "swallow her up," that she would lose her "old self," the self who Charles acknowledged was "not used to a man taking charge of her business."[9] Freeman avoided motherhood by marrying late in life, but Gilman became pregnant shortly after her marriage to Stetson. The complexities of evading or succumbing to motherhood were powerful for both writers.

In their most effective portrayals of the impact of marriage and motherhood or spinsterhood and childlessness, Freeman and Gilman wrote stories that merged the supernatural and the psychological. Just as "The Yellow Wallpaper" is unlike much of Gilman's less ambiguous fiction, supernatural stories such as "The Wind in the Rosebush," "The Lost Ghost," and "The Hall Bedroom" represented a divergence for Mary Wilkins Freeman. In a letter to Fred Lewis Pattee, Freeman wrote ". . . most of my own work, is not really the kind I myself like. I want more symbolism, more mysticism. I left that out, because it struck me people did not want it, and I was forced to consider selling qualities."[10] As Beth Wynne Fisken explains, "the conventions of ghost fiction as a less 'serious' literary form, the supernatural machinery, melodramatic episode and exaggerated emotion that defined the genre, enabled Wilkins Freeman to give oblique expression to disturbing personal issues without fear of exposure." [11]

Freeman explores the choice to remain childless and the psychological ramifications of that choice in three supernatural stories which were all written shortly after her marriage to Charles Freeman: "The Wind in the Rosebush," "The Lost Ghost," and "The Hall Bedroom." Conversely, Gilman explores the possible consequences of submitting to early motherhood and wifely obedience in "The Yellow Wallpaper," a story based on her own "rest cure" after having had a baby. At the heart of these works is the sense that existence itself is threatened by either choice. As Alfred Bendixen suggests in his introduction to *Haunted Women*, "supernatural fiction opened doors for American women writers, allowing them to move into otherwise forbidden regions." By lifting the experience of their characters into the supernatural realm, both Gilman and Freeman were able to explore more freely "such 'unladylike' subjects as sexuality, bad marriages, and repression." [12]

The difficult bind for women becomes evident in these texts. In "The Wind in the Rosebush," Freeman suggests that to avoid motherhood is to be haunted by maternal impulses and by the ghosts of children one has never had; to give into the maternal desire to care for a child, as Abby Bird does in "The Lost Ghost," is to risk losing self entirely. To experience a sexual awakening, as in "The Hall Bedroom," and yet to detach one's sexuality from the accompanying expectation of domesticity and motherhood, is to leave the realm of reality, and to live in complete exile—in effect, to vanish. To have a baby is to put aside one's hopes for autonomy and intellectual satisfaction and possibly to seek an escape into madness, as we see in "The Yellow Wallpaper."

In "The Wind in the Rosebush," Rebecca, some time after the death of her sister, hopes to become a surrogate mother to her niece, Agnes. Without the knowledge that her niece has died because of the neglect of her stepmother, Rebecca travels to visit Agnes with the intention of bringing her home with her. When she arrives, her niece's shadow and the wind in the rosebush from which a rose has been picked and placed on her niece's nightgown become haunting reminders of the opportunity of motherhood that has passed Rebecca by. The ghost in the story is, as Fisken explains, "the ghost of the child that had never been in [Rebecca's] life, and that now would never be; she is haunted by her own unfulfilled needs."[13]

Much as Freeman may have expressed her own "unfulfilled needs" through the haunted consciousness of a childless woman in "The Wind in the Rosebush," she also recognized that fulfilling the maternal impulse was an extraordinarily dangerous undertaking for women. Perhaps having observed her own mother's selfless attention to her needs as a child, Freeman saw motherhood as an insurmountable threat to self-possession. This insight is evident in works such as "The Selfishness of Amelia Lamkin," but she captured the complexity of the conflict between the desire to nurture a child and the fear of its cost more powerfully in her ghost tale "The Lost Ghost."

The haunted Abby Bird is a woman who exhibits the characteristics of Freeman's mother. Her sister explains that it is lucky Abby never had children, for "she would have spoilt them."[14] Abby Bird, "a real motherly sort of woman," self-sufficient and childless, is haunted by the appearance and voice of a child who once inhabited the house in which she lives. The child, who had died after having been abandoned and abused by her mother, now appears before Abby and utters in eerie repetition, "I can't find my mother, I can't find my mother" (214). The child's death is attributed to her mother's neglect, as her mother had clearly rejected the maternal role. While the child's father was away, her mother had an affair with a married man and neglected to feed or care for her child. Her behavior was completely self-serving, and this brought about the child's death. In this story, self-indulgence is synonymous with child abuse. Leaving her child locked in a room to die of starvation, the mother ran away. She was ultimately killed by the child's father.

Abby's conflicted response to the ghost is fascinating. She notes that the child's appearance "would have been very beautiful if she had not been so dreadful." She explains to her sister how painful she finds it to see the child and be unable to take care of her, essentially to be unable to respond as the child's mother: "It seems to me sometimes as if I should die if I can't get that awful little white robe off that child and get her in some clothes and feed her and stop her looking for her mother" (235). Shortly after this statement, Abby's sister sees the shadow of Abby's figure beside that of the child's, "walking off over the white snow-path with that child holding fast to her hand, nestling close to her as if she had found her own mother." Abby's body is found in her bed, "smiling as if she was dreaming, and one arm and hand was stretched out as if something had hold of it; and it couldn't be straightened even at the last—it lay out over her casket at the funeral." The paralyzing image of the outstretched arm, the hand reaching out to care for the child, captures the level of danger Freeman associated with maternal giving. Beth Wynne Fisken sees this story as the "most direct fictional expression of ambivalence toward motherhood."[15] It captures both the sense that Freeman was haunted by the child she never had and the idea that by giving to a child, one loses one's capacity to give to oneself. Alfred Bendixen's summary is useful: "Thus in this tale we find a strong sympathy for the deprived child combined with the suggestion that motherhood may require self-sacrifice to the point of sacrifice of self."[16] The child's appearance evokes an understandable dread. Her cry, "I can't find my mother," comes across as demand for Abby to respond as mother, and then to give up self. Becoming mother also requires giving up childhood. "To have a child, one must give up one's primary image of oneself as a child," as Fisken puts it. During Freeman's childbearing years, this would have meant parting with the maternal nurturance she enjoyed in the care of Mary Wales. It was such nurturance that relieved her of adult responsibilities and enabled her to focus on her craft and on her own needs.

Given the dangerous consequences of Abby's response to the calling of motherhood, it is interesting to turn to Freeman's depiction of the equally dangerous lure of sexuality without motherhood. If succumbing to motherhood requires the loss of self, the self-nurturance of a sexual awakening without motherhood requires complete exile from the narrow limitations of the nineteenth-century New England village. Just as Freeman found it necessary to kill off Abby at the height of her longing to give to a child, she created the supernatural disappearance of Wheatcroft in "The Hall Bedroom" at the height of his sexual self-indulgence. "The Hall Bedroom" presents yet another layer of complexity. Sexual awakening without the accompanying consequence of reproduction cannot exist in the New England village Freeman knew so well. Hence her character experiences a nightly hallucination which awakens all of the senses and ends in annihilation.

Mrs. Jennings, the narrator of "The Hall Bedroom," is a childless widow who "graduated from a young ladies' seminary" (much like the one Freeman failed to graduate from) and describes herself as "highly respectable." Just as Freeman felt abandoned when her parents died, Mrs. Jennings feels herself to be utterly alone upon the death of her parents. She runs a boardinghouse and takes in a boarder whose experience she relates from the journal she discovers after his disappearance. Her attraction to the mysterious and ultimately frightening freedom she finds in this journal has much to do with the limitations of her own experience. Her sharp, almost defensive opening descriptions of herself as having been "well brought up" and having "also married well" provide a contrasting prelude to the world she is to discover in the journal. Her mention of the seminary is a reminder of all the restrictions that Freeman found difficult in her year at Mount Holyoke Female Seminary with its "hammering away at the collective student conscience at prayer meetings and church services." [17] Mrs. Jennings feels her own "prosperity in life" to be shadowed by Wheatcroft's experience in the hall bedroom. In effect, Wheatcroft becomes the shadow or double for the socially conventional Mrs. Jennings. In his male voice, Mrs. Jennings's longings are mirrored. It is interesting that Freeman found it necessary to transfer these desires to a male character. Like Mrs. Jennings, Mr. Wheatcroft is alone in the world. He comes to the hall bedroom to escape the reality of all the limitations which have prevented him from experiencing the adventure and freedom he desires. Wheatcroft is recovering from an undefined illness which requires nightly medication (similar to the sedatives Freeman was taking shortly after her marriage and at the time that she wrote this story).

Although he has the "soul of an explorer," Wheatcroft comes to Mrs. Jennings's boardinghouse to recover from his perpetual "defeats." [18] Having "lost sight of his horizons," Wheatcroft becomes obsessed with the horizons of the landscape painting on his wall. He studies the pair of lovers sitting in their boat on a winding river. As he reaches for his medication each night, waking as if still in a dream, Wheatcroft finds that the boundaries of his room dissolve; he wanders into the landscape on his wall until he strikes a "safety match" and returns to his bed. Within the realm of art, inside the landscape painting, he is "awakened from his state of quiescence," as Freeman may have been through the creation of this story. Feeling "buoyancy and stimulation" with each step, Wheatcroft is ecstatic and frightened. In "a rapture of sublimated sense" and "giddiness," the intensity of his awakening becomes overwhelming (31). His stimulation is pitted against the reality of existence on the other side of the wall where he denies himself a desirable pudding in order to meet the restrictions of his diet. As his sense of taste and touch are aroused, he cries out: "I have lived my life and always have I gone hungry until now" (32). On one of his nightly excursions into the canvas, Wheatcroft meets a beautiful young woman who had once come to the same boardinghouse to recover from a "love disappointment" only to disappear from the same hall bedroom. On his last excursion, Wheatcroft experiences the sense of touch most palpably as his "groping hands to right and left touched living beings" (36).

The effect of such forbidden arousal is cumulative and moves from pleasure to terror at the possibility of his own obliteration. With each reference to touch, "the soft texture of their garments as they swept around me," "a hand closed, softly over mine," "an arm passed around me," Wheatcroft's response builds in intensity until the terror of near annihilation and the ecstasy of tactile sensation drive him again to light the safety match and return for the last time to the bedroom (36–37). In his last entry, Wheatcroft notes the river "upon which one could sail away" and wonders "what it would all be if all my senses together were to grasp it" (37). The story abruptly shifts back to Mrs. Jennings's narration, for Wheatcroft disappears, never to be found again.

"The Hall Bedroom" is Freeman's most striking description of the effects of sexual repression on the psyche. Through the shadowed figures of Wheatcroft and Jennings, she relays the difficult, if not impossible, options: the unbearable sense of restriction and denial in the world inhabited by Mrs. Jennings or the fulfillment of one's senses and the consequence of complete exile. The world on the other side of Mrs. Jennings's wall, though it brings about irreversible obliteration, is an escape from the boundaries of the "respectability" which Mrs. Jennings, as childless widow, must accept. With Wheatcroft's annihilation after the description of his sexualized responses, Freeman captures the dilemma she faced in her own choice to avoid motherhood. Sexual elation such as Wheatcroft's is both forbidden and unattainable within Mrs. Jennings's world. Only the flight of the imagination, Freeman's journey into the consciousness of Wheatcroft, can grant such gratification. Wheatcroft describes his nightly journeys as though they are waking dreams. Part of the power of the story builds on the subtle indications that his supernatural experience is in fact psychological.

Gilman's "The Yellow Wallpaper," like Freeman's supernatural stories, depicts the realities that haunted women of the nineteenth century. Although she described the work to William Dean Howells as "pure propaganda," "The Yellow Wallpaper" moves well beyond a polemical exposure of oppression. Here Gilman explores not only the damage of passivity as a prescription for stability in women, but also the conflict between the need for love which women could win through obedient conformity and the desire for freedom from the constraints required to win such acceptable love. The parallels to Freeman's "The Hall Bedroom" are striking, though the terms of imprisonment and freedom differ. Recovering from childbirth and the new demands of motherhood, the narrator of "The Yellow Wallpaper" is brought by her husband to a house in the country for her "rest cure" and is confined to the room of her husband's choice, a nursery. Infantalized in her marriage, the narrator turns to her forbidden journal to assert a voice of her own. She must turn to her journal without her husband's knowledge, for part of the prescription for her recovery is to resist all efforts at thinking or writing. Just as Wheatcroft's obsession with the canvas on the wall stems from his own sense of confinement and limitation, the narrator of "The Yellow Wallpaper" studies the patterns on the wall until she too drifts out of the realm of the realities that oppress her.

For Wheatcroft, sexuality without a consequent imprisonment can only exist on the other side of the wall. For Gilman's narrator, sexuality has already brought her to a state of imprisonment as mother and wife. Escaping into the patterns on the wallpaper evokes a terror and ecstasy similar to Wheatcroft's. As she detects a woman, her double, trapped behind the patterned bars on the ghostly wallpaper, she becomes determined to free the figure. Freedom comes to the narrator in the form of madness, for in this state her husband has no power to control her fate. She parts with the identity of the woman her husband knew by tearing apart the wallpaper, freeing her double, and proceeding to creep around the room in an animal/child posture. Both Freeman and Gilman found it necessary to free characters who were imprisoned by a set of impossible restrictions on self-expression and self-nurturance. While Gilman stated often that she wrote "The Yellow Wallpaper" as a protest against the specific "rest cure" she herself had been forced to endure in the care of Dr. Weir Mitchell after the birth of her child, the story goes beyond this level. The connection between the needed departure from reality and the narrator's role as a woman is implicit throughout the story. Designed to hide imperfections and to offer an orderly appearance, wallpaper becomes the symbol for the narrator's entrapment as a woman. As she studies the paper, the narrator sees the bars of her own existence, the impediments to freedom. Unable to control her own destiny, to read, to write, to think, or to take pleasure in herself, the world she creates is one in which she can be powerful because she can be free of her husband's expectations. Wheatcroft's journey into a landscape of the senses is a comparably powerful escape from equally oppressive restrictions in unmarried life. Unlike Gilman's narrator, however, Wheatcroft has left all rage behind. His disappearance is almost ethereal. The angry narrator of "The Yellow Wallpaper" concludes by creeping right over her estranged husband, deliberately unconcerned.

Recognizing the restrictions imposed upon women, whether married or unmarried, Freeman and Gilman dramatized in their most unusual fiction the need for escape to an alternative plane of existence. Both women wrote these works after having married, and both wrote out of a consequent awareness of the inequities that limited their choices and denied them the freedom to experience self-fulfillment.

It is interesting that the desperation Freeman and Gilman depict is not present in Jewett's work, and to note that Jewett is the only writer of the three who never married. By feminizing the men in *The Country of the Pointed Firs,* Jewett was able to provide women who chose to reject marriage and motherhood a world in which they could thrive. When she wrote *The Country of the Pointed Firs,* Sarah Orne Jewett created a realm of possibility for women within the idyllic community of Dunnet Landing. Unlike Wheatcroft and the narrator of "The Yellow Wallpaper," Jewett's narrator finds that she can achieve both a needed artistic isolation and a loving sense of connection to a community without any punishment for her autonomy.

As she writes in a separate space, a deserted schoolhouse, the

narrator of *The Country of the Pointed Firs* achieves a distance within
the community itself that both Wheatcroft and the narrator of "The
Yellow Wallpaper" lack. It is a space of her own choice; from its
windows she can observe the community and remain separate and
yet connected. Her closest companion, Mrs. Almira Todd, presents
an alternative way of being. Mrs. Todd nurtures others and sees this
as her primary source of pleasure. But the narrator derives pleasure
from observing Mrs. Todd's interaction with others, and keeps her
focus on her writing without guilt or fear of rejection. The narrator's
choice is respected and valued as much as Mrs. Todd's. Even Joanna,
the woman whose choice of isolation is most extreme, receives the
support of the men and women in the community. Suffering from a
disappointment in love, not unlike Wheatcroft's, Joanna moves to
the remote and inaccessible Shell-Heap island where she lives alone.
She asks that the community accept her desire to be alone, and in
return "all the folks about the bay respected her an' her feelings;
but as time wore on . . . one after another ventured to make occasion
to put somethin' ashore for her if they went that way." [19] No one
assumes that because Joanna has rejected marriage and motherhood
she is mad, and consequently she does not vanish or transform as
Gilman's and Freeman's comparable characters must. Jewett's narrator observes that Joanna's choice to be an "uncompanioned hermit"
is acceptable in Dunnet's Landing: "I had been reflecting upon a
state of society which admitted such personal freedom and a volun-
tary hermitage" (69).

Although members of the community refer to Joanna as "poor
Joanna," she is never seen as mad or undeserving of affection. What
makes it possible for Jewett to envision such a "state of society" is her
deliberate transformation of male behavior. In essence, men become
women by experiencing women's lives. Elijah Tilley, the old seafarer
whose wife has died, takes on the life his wife had lived. He knits,
tends to the kitchen chores, and gazes out the window imagining
what it was like for his wife to wait for his return: "She used to say
the time seemed long to her, but I've found out all about it now. I
used to be dreadful thoughtless when I was a young man and the
fish was bitin' well. I'd stay out late some o' them days, an' I expect
she'd watch an' watch an lose heart a-waitin' " (123). Now Elijah
Tilley sheds a tear as he describes the beauty of his wife's companionship and conversation, and he proudly shows the narrator "her best

tea things" (123–24). Tilley lives a woman's life and adopts women's values, recognizing the importance of women's work and women's experiences.

In Freeman's favorite Jewett story, "A White Heron" (1886), Jewett did address the process of rejecting men who, unlike Elijah Tilley, represent conventional male aggression. The starting point in so much of Freeman's work was this necessary rejection and its consequences. In this sense, Freeman moved beyond both Jewett and Gilman to analyze the difficulty inherent in seeking empowerment by turning away from heterosexual love. A comparison of "A White Heron" and Freeman's "A Symphony of Lavender" will capture an important distinction. In "A White Heron," a young girl relinquishes the world of men when she decides to resist revealing the location of a beautiful heron in response to a hunter's request. Although Sylvia "would have liked him vastly better without his gun" and "could not understand why he killed the very birds he seemed to like so much," she is drawn to this man and is attracted to the "dream of love" that he evokes in her newly discovered "woman's heart." [20] Tempted by the man's plea, she establishes instead a renewed relationship with the white heron and they "watched the sea and the morning together. . . ." Jewett poetically depicts the choice to live in nature, free of male domination. If regret or ambivalence is voiced, it is subtle and barely recognized by Sylvia. The narrator poses the concluding question: "Were the birds better friends than their hunter might have been,—who can tell? Whatever treasures were lost to her, woodlands, and summertime, remember! Bring your gifts and graces and tell your secrets to this lonely country child!" (239). With only this acknowledgment of "treasures lost," Jewett still leaves readers with a confirmation of the choice. In "A Symphony of Lavender," an equally mystical story in which the young heroine Caroline turns away from a man, Freeman explored the same theme in greater depth. Here she described a woman's fear of and longing for sexual fulfillment. Her rejection of male love, like Sylvia's rejection of the hunter's overtures, spares Caroline inevitable subjugation. But Freeman leaves readers with a greater sense of ambiguity and more clearly sets the rejection in psychological terms.

Bringing her readers almost immediately into a psychological framework, Freeman describes the heroine's decision first in the context of an unsettling dream in which she is carrying a basket of flowers when she meets a young man: "When he reached me he stopped and looked down into my face and then at my basket of flowers. I stopped too—I could not seem to help it in my dream—and gazed down at the ground. I was afraid to look at him, and I trembled so that the lilies and roses in my basket quivered." [21] At first the dreamer's response reveals all the passion she has learned to hide in her conscious existence. Caroline's basket of flowers embodies her conflict, for it contains the lilies we associate with purity and virginity as well as the rich red roses of heightened sensuality. The quivering flowers suggest the intensity of Caroline's desires, yet her trembling also suggests her fear of the consequences. When the young man requests a flower, the dreamer gathers courage: "When his eyes met mine it did seem to me that I wanted to give him one of those flowers more than anything else in the world" (44). Her resistance is set in terms of enormous conflict, unlike the simplicity of Sylvia's decision in "A White Heron." For Sylvia, the mere memory of the white heron and her love of its beauty prevents her from "giving the heron's secret" away. Freeman allows her character to experience and voice a dramatic ambivalence for she "wanted at once to give him the lily and would have died rather than give it to him." (44) This is a remarkable description of the conflict between socially unacceptable fulfillment and acceptable self-denial.

Caroline must struggle against her own sensuality. As she gazes at the young man's face, it suddenly begins to transform to mirror her painful conflict: "As I gazed, his face changed more and more to me till finally . . . it looked at once beautiful and repulsive" (45). In the face of her possible freedom and consummation, horror mixes with longing. While Caroline craves sexual pleasure, she recognizes the danger of succumbing and even internalizes her society's equation of female sexuality with evil. Accordingly, her vision of the man's face reflects an understandable fear. She flees, firmly gripping her basket of flowers and feeling "a great horror of something, I did not know what, in my heart" (45). Caroline acts out, in her dream, the drama of a conflict that ultimately causes her to suppress her desire for passion. The conflict between her inner compulsion and desire and her fearful recognition of its consequences shapes her destiny. When a young man does appear in her life, one year after the dream, the dreamlike horror returns. He courts her, and clearly takes over her life as he "would come here at all hours of the day" and "sit beside me in the parlor and watch me sew, and in the kitchen and watch me cook." When he proposes marriage, she sees the same transforming visage of the man in her earlier dream, both beautiful and evil, and she runs again. She poses a crucial question for readers when she later wonders whether "my dream was really sent to me as a warning, or that I fancied it all, and wrecked—no, I won't say wrecked—dulled the happiness of my whole life for a nervous whim" (47). To her credit, Freeman never minimized the conflict or the cost involved in Caroline's choice.

As we look at Freeman in the context of women writers of her period and region, it is useful to conclude with her own interpretation of the woman writer's dilemma in the nineteenth century. Her story "Sister Liddy" offers a fictionalized exploration of the artistic process that might have been at work when Freeman wrote sentimental stories or added the sentimental conclusion to stories such as "A Humble Romance." Reading "Sister Liddy" helps us understand these intrusions of sentimentality in a broader context. "Sister Liddy" is a powerful story depicting the desperation of a woman for whom "the world had seemed simply standing ground; she had gotten little more out of it."[22] Here Freeman avoids the trap of sentimentality as she paints the portrait of Polly, a woman who spends her life within the narrow corridors of an insane asylum for the poor. Given how often Freeman's villagers label as insane heroines who refuse to conform, it is interesting that in this story the heroine is in fact locked away. Much like Gilman's narrator in "The Yellow Wallpaper," Polly creates an imaginary double. But her double is far from the rebellious, creeping image behind the bars of the wallpaper. On the contrary, Polly creates an almost painfully conventional imaginary "Sister Liddy" to compensate for what is an essentially unlived life. She tells the other women patients the "story" of her imaginary sister's life in a "flood" of rich details. She equips her fictive sister with all that she lacks: happy marriage, baby, silk-lined cradle. For Sister Liddy, all things end well: she is conventionally "pretty" while Polly is not; she has the love of the husband and child Polly has never had; she is accepted, free from the corridors of Polly's asylum. Polly's story becomes appallingly flowery, a parody of Freeman's sentimental prose at its worst.

In "Sister Liddy," Freeman offers readers a way of interpreting her own work. It is an analysis of her own ambivalence. Whenever

Polly begins to drift into her dreams of conventional bliss, Sally, a figure of rebellion and violence, flies down the hallway in a rage. Sally rips her bed sheets to shreds every day, an act of desperation. She acts out the repressed violence that is in Polly, and perhaps in Freeman as well. Sally is, in this sense, the other sister, the other Freeman. Sister Liddy is the self that society encourages, the one who marries "early and well," as Freeman's father had wished for her, who belongs, who conforms. Sister Sally is the "madwoman" whom society rejects; she can only fly down the hallway with all the anger that must remain trapped within the asylum.

The story concludes with Polly's confession on her deathbed. But as she confesses to the "sin" of having lied to create Sister Liddy, Freeman describes Sally's wild actions: "Sally trotted past . . . she had just torn her bed to pieces. As soon as she got her breath enough, Polly Moss finished what she had to say. I s'pose I was dretful wicked, she whispered, but I never had any Sister Liddy" (98). The connection between the rebel Sally and the passive Polly is implicit. It is quite similar to the connection between Gilman's narrator in "The Yellow Wallpaper" and the creeping woman who gets out. Polly must gather her breath for the confession almost as though she herself had just finished tearing her bed apart. Perhaps it is not "never having had a Sister Liddy" but never having *been* a Sister Liddy that has made Polly think of herself as "dretful wicked." Women writers who, like Freeman, would not completely conform to the model of a Sister Liddy were left with exactly this conflict. Writers such as Gilman, Jewett, and Freeman were defying the Liddy stereotype both in their own life choices and in their creation of unconventional heroines. Even as Freeman expressed her anger through Sally, her longing to be the acceptable Liddy remained. Freeman's life and work is in fact a fascinating interweaving of Liddy's and Sally's, an often brilliant expression of a conflict that is still with us today. Caught between the idealized model of Liddy and the horrifying image of mad Sally, Mary E. Wilkins Freeman had to struggle to move beyond such definitions of self and to create heroines who could move beyond these limitations.

NOTES

∞

Preface

1. I refer to her as Freeman rather than Wilkins because this was her preference as a published writer.

2. Mary E. Wilkins Freeman, "A Maiden Lady," *Century* 30 (August 1885):
654.

3. Mary E. Wilkins Freeman, "The Girl Who Wants to Write: Things to Do
and Avoid," *Harper's Bazaar* (June 1913).

4. Margaret Hamilton Welch, "American Authoresses of the Hour: Mary E.
Wilkins," *Harper's Bazaar* (January 1900): 69–70; cited by Monika Elbert, "Mary
Wilkins Freeman's Devious Women, *Harper's Bazaar*, and the Rhetoric of Adver-
tising," *Essays in Literature* 20 (Fall 1993): 269.

5. Edward Foster, *Mary E. Wilkins Freeman* (New York: Hendricks House,
1956), 87.

6. *New York Times*, 24 April 1926, sec. 1, 7.

7. Mary E. Wilkins Freeman, "Mary E. Wilkins," in *My Maiden Effort: The
Personal Confessions of Well-Known Authors,* ed. Gelett Burgess (New York: Doubleday, Page, 1921), 267.

1. "Nurtured in Repression"

1. Letter to Sarah Orne Jewett, 10 December 1889, #50 in *The Infant
Sphinx: Collected Letters of Mary E. Wilkins Freeman,* ed. Brent L. Kendrick (Metuchen, N.J.: Scarecrow Press, 1985), 99. Subsequent letters from this collection
will be cited with their number and the page in Kendrick, e.g., (#50), Kendrick,
99.

2. Fred Lewis Pattee, *A History of American Literature since 1870.* (New York:
Century Company, 1915), 236.

3. See Edward Foster, *Mary E. Wilkins Freeman* (New York: Hendricks House,
1956), and Perry Westbrook, *Mary Wilkins Freeman* (New York: Twayne, 1967),
28. I have drawn many of the general facts about Freeman's life from these early

biographies, but both biographers include very limited references to Freeman's early years.

4. See Brent L. Kendrick's introductory sections in *The Infant Sphinx,* 1–31, 39–54, 111–24, 197–209, 259–81, 361–78.

5. Foster, *Mary E. Wilkins Freeman,* 69–70.

6. Elizabeth Meese, "Signs of Undecidability: Reconsidering the Stories of Mary Wilkins Freeman," in *Critical Essays on Mary Wilkins Freeman,* ed. Shirley Marchalonis (Boston: G.K. Hall, 1991), 160.

7. Josephine Donovan, *New England Local Color Literature: A Women's Tradition* (New York: Ungar, 1983), 8.

8. Kendrick, *The Infant Sphinx,* 42.

9. This pleasure in constructing the details of an architectural plan or describing the interior and exterior of homes is most apparent in her novel *Pembroke* (New York: Harper and Brothers, 1894), where the structure of houses provides a significant index for understanding Freeman's characterizations. All references are to this edition; page numbers are cited parenthetically in the text.

10. Westbrook, *Mary Wilkins Freeman,* 23.

11. Foster, *Mary E. Wilkins Freeman,* 5.

12. Westbrook, *Mary Wilkins Freeman,* 23.

13. Foster, *Mary E. Wilkins Freeman,* 19.

14. According to Foster, Warren's role in Mary's life waned as financial pressures mounted: "Warren Wilkins began to slip into the background" (ibid., 37).

15. Ibid., 11. Foster describes Eleanor's overprotection as a consequence of Mary's fragility, yet it is difficult to determine whether Eleanor's behavior was based on a realistic assessment of Mary's physical health or on her extreme fear of losing another child.

16. Letter to Sarah Orne Jewett, 12 August 1889 (#47), Kendrick, 97.

17. See Beth Wynne Fisken's "The Faces of Children that had Never Been," in *Haunting the House of Fiction: Feminist Perspectives on Ghost Stories by American Women,* ed. Lynette Carpenter and Wendy Kolman (Knoxville: University of Tennessee Press, 1991), 43–47. Fisken's interpretation of "A Gentle Ghost" has a somewhat different focus. Fisken places the "forlorn little girl" in the context of Freeman's unresolved tensions not only in relation to her sense of displacement and then abandonment with the loss of her sister and the ultimate death of her mother ("the lost and abandoned girl was she [Freeman] as well as her sister"), but also in view of her own ambivalence about never having had children of her own. The ambiguity of this story invites these multilayered associations. The primary focus of the story, however, is on the relationship between Flora and her mother, and it clearly parallels the complexities of Freeman's relationship with her own mother. See also my discussion in Chapter 8 of stories in which Freeman's ambivalence about her evasion of motherhood is far more central.

18. Freeman, "A Gentle Ghost," in *A New England Nun and Other Stories* (New York: Harper and Brothers, 1891), 241. All future references are to this edition; page numbers are cited parenthetically in the text. See physical descriptions of

Mary Wilkins Freeman as a young woman at Mount Holyoke Female Seminary. Miss Hufford records remembering her as "rather small," with "light auburn hair and the delicate pink and white complexion that goes with it" (Hufford, MS undated, Mount Holyoke College Archives).

19. Foster, *Mary E. Wilkins Freeman*, 8.

20. Ibid., 9.

21. Kendrick, *The Infant Sphinx*, 11–12.

22. Carroll Smith-Rosenberg, "The Female World of Love and Ritual: Relations between Women in Nineteenth-Century America." *Signs* 1, no. 1 (1975): 15. See also Mary Reichardt's analysis in "The Web of Self-Strangulation: Mothers, Daughters and the Question of Marriage in the Short Stories of Mary Wilkins Freeman," in *Joinings and Disjoinings: The Significance of Marital Status in Literature*, ed. JoAnna S. Mink and Janet D. Ward (Bowling Green: Bowling Green State University Popular Press, 1991), 109–19. Reichardt notes that Freeman's stories often focus on "problems of separation and differentiation of the self, both mother from daughter and daughter from mother" (110).

23. Kendrick, *The Infant Sphinx*, 11. Kendrick notes Freeman's ability to "see into the heart of childhood" in her fiction and relates this to her own "childlike nature."

24. Smith-Rosenberg, "The Female World," 17, 16.

25. Mary Wilkins Freeman, "Old Woman Magoun," in *The Winning Lady and Other Stories* (New York: Harper and Brothers, 1909), 245. All references are to this edition; page numbers are cited parenthetically in the text.

26. Julia Bader, "The Dissolving Vision: Realism in Jewett, Freeman, and Gilman," *American Realism: New Essays*, ed. Eric Sundquist (Baltimore: Johns Hopkins University Press, 1982), 190. See also Monika Elbert, "Mary Wilkins Freeman's Devious Women, *Harper's Bazaar*, and the Rhetoric of Advertising," *Essays in Literature* 20 (Fall 1993): 251–72. Elbert sees "Old Woman Magoun" as Freeman's "most pessimistic story," one that implies that "if woman is to establish her own economic system, she must choose separatism and literally sever the bridge between the sexes" (267).

27. *New York Times*, 24 April 1926, sec., 1, 7.

28. Foster, *Mary E. Wilkins Freeman*, 15.

29. Kendrick, *The Infant Sphinx*, 42.

30. Foster, *Mary E. Wilkins Freeman*, 15.

31. See my essays "She Is the One You Call Sister: Discovering Mary E. Wilkins Freeman," in *Between Women: Biographers, Novelists, Critics, and Artists Write about Their Work on Women*, ed. Carol Ascher, Louise DeSalvo, and Sara Ruddick (1984; reprint, New York: Routledge, 1993), 187–211; "Mary E. Wilkins Freeman: 'The Stranger in the Mirror,' " *Massachusetts Review* 25 (Summer 1984): 323–39; and "Profile: Mary E. Wilkins Freeman," *Legacy: A Journal of Nineteenth Century American Women Writers* 22, no. 2 (Spring 1987): 3–11. In these early essays I began to address the paradox of the pressure placed upon Mary to marry, her bond with her mother, and her choice to reject the life her mother had lived. As I suggested in these essays, many of Freeman's short stories seem to have been attempts to address the conflict between her own needs and

the expectation that she would follow her mother's path. See also Reichardt's "The Web of Strangulation," which explores this idea in the context of stories such as "The Buckley Lady" in *Silence and Other Stories* (New York: Harper and Brothers, 1898), 65–129. For a full discussion of Freeman's resistance to marriage and its reflection in her fiction, see Chapter 3: "Sometimes I Think I Am a Monster."

32. Foster, *Mary E. Wilkins Freeman*, 23.

33. Ibid., 15.

34. Anna L. Hufford recounts Helen French Gulliver's recollections of Mary Wilkins Freeman as a student at Mount Holyoke (1870–71), MS undated, Mount Holyoke College Archives.

35. Letter to Helena L. Todd, 6 March 1907 (#386), Kendrick, 324.

36. M. D. E. Morse, "Reminiscences of the Early 'Seventies,' " May 1931, *Mount Holyoke Alumnae Quarterly*, Mount Holyoke College Archives. Morse explains that the strict rules and regulations from 37 years before "were in full force" (26).

37. Ibid.

38. Hufford's recounting, Mount Holyoke College Archives. Mary Nutting's recollections refer to Mary as "very shy and very quiet"; E. Isabel Williams's recollections describe her as "quiet and retiring with no special elements of popularity." Manuscripts undated. Mary E. Wilkins Freeman folder, Mount Holyoke College Archives.

39. *One Hundred Year Biographical Directory of Mount Holyoke College*, 136–37, Mount Holyoke College Archives. At the twenty-fifth reunion of the class of 1871, Freeman was elected an honorary member of the class. She responded by accepting the honor appreciatively. Freeman folder, Mount Holyoke College Archives.

40. Lillian Faderman, *Surpassing the Love of Men: Romantic Friendship and Love Between Women from the Renaissance to the Present* (New York: William Morrow, 1981). Faderman explores the pattern common to so many women of Freeman's period and clearly applicable to Freeman, of forming close relationships with women and resisting the oppressive consequences of heterosexual love.

41. Foster, *Mary E. Wilkins Freeman*, 35.

42. Quoted in ibid., 38.

43. Ibid., 194.

44. Ibid., 42.

45. Michele Clark, Afterword to Freeman, *The Revolt of "Mother" and Other Stories* (New York: Feminist Press, 1974), 177.

46. Anna Hufford recounts Helen French Gulliver's recollections of Freeman as a student at Mount Holyoke Female Seminary, MS undated, Mount Holyoke College Archives. These are reported to be the words Freeman wrote to Gulliver after the death of her parents.

47. Letter to Evelyn Sawyer Severance, January 1893 (#113), Kendrick, 145.

48. Freeman, "The Revolt of 'Mother,' " in *Selected Stories of Mary E. Wilkins Freeman*, ed. Marjorie Pryse (New York: Norton, 1983), 297. All future references are to this edition; page numbers are cited parenthetically in the text.

49. "The Revolt of 'Mother,' " along with "A New England Nun," has become a pivotal piece in feminist criticism on Freeman in the last decade. See my analysis in "She Is the One You Call Sister,"199–203. See also Elbert, "Mary Wilkins Freeman's Devious Women"; Elizabeth Meese, *Crossing the Double Cross: The Practice of Feminist Criticism* (Chapel Hill: University of North Carolina Press, 1986), 34–38; Elaine Orr, "Reading Negotiation and Negotiated Reading: A Practice with/in 'A White Heron' and 'The Revolt of "Mother," ' " *CEA-Critic* 63 (1991): 19–65; Patricia Dwyer, "Diffusing Boundaries: A Study of Narrative Strategies in Mary Wilkins Freeman's 'The Revolt of "Mother," ' " *Legacy* 10 (1993): 120–27. Martha Cutter's "Frontiers of Language: Engendering Discourse in 'The Revolt of "Mother," ' " *American Literature* 63 (1991): 279–91, is one of the most interesting recent theoretical discussions of the story.

50. Cutter, "Frontiers of Language," 279–80. Cutter offers an interesting linguistic analysis of the story.

51. Ibid., 282. See also Alice Glarden Brand, "Mary Wilkins Freeman: Misanthropy as Propaganda," *New England Quarterly* 50 (1977): 91.

52. Cutter, "Frontiers of Language," 288.

53. Ibid.

54. Ibid., 290–91.

55. Freeman, Untitled article, *Saturday Evening Post,* 8 December 1917, 25.

2. "The Art of My Work"

1. Mary E. Wilkins Freeman, "The Girl Who Wants to Write: Things to Do and Avoid," *Harper's Bazaar* (June 1913): 272. I refer to this quote in my preface to clarify my attraction to Freeman's way of looking at writing as a source of power and freedom for women.

2. Letter to Edward Everett Hale, Randolph, Mass., 2 September 1875 (#1), Kendrick, 57.

3. Perry Westbrook, *Mary Wilkins Freeman* (New York: Twayne, 1967), 29.

4. *New York Times,* 24 April 1926, sec. 1, 7.

5. See Edward Foster, *Mary E. Wilkins Freeman* (New York: Hendricks House, 1956), and *The Infant Sphinx: Collected Letters of Mary E. Wilkins Freeman,* ed., Brent L. Kendrick (Metuchen, N. J.: Scarecrow Press, 1985), 51.

6. Freeman, *Harper's* (December 1892): 148. Freeman also wrote to Mrs. Gulliver of her "wish that they [her parents] might have been spared to her" and that "she longed to make some return to them for their love and care." (Recounted by Miss Hufford, MS undated, Mount Holyoke College Archives).

7. Foster, *Mary E. Wilkins Freeman,* 141, 62.

8. Letter to Mary Louise Booth, before 28 April 1886 (#12), Kendrick, 68.

9. Mary Wilkins Freeman, "Mary E. Wilkins," in *My Maiden Effort: The Personal Confessions of Well-Known Authors,* ed. Gelett Burgess (New York: Doubleday, Page, 1921), 267.

10. David Hirsch, "Subdued Meaning in 'A New England Nun,' " *Studies in Short Fiction* 2 (Winter 1965): 124–36. See also Freeman's reference to her discovery of a chained dog and its effect upon her in her letter to Mary Louise

Booth, 28 April 1886 (#13), Kendrick, 69. Apparently the sight of the chained dog plagued her when she "went a-hunting material" and came upon "a poor old dog" at "an old lady's birthday-party." She described it as the only thing "worth writing about" at the event and complained: "I have felt like crying every time I have thought of him. He wagged his tail, and looked so pitiful, he is half blind too." Most likely this dog was the model for Caesar in "A New England Nun." The dog Freeman described in her letter had been "chained thirteen years, because he bit a man once, in his puppy-hood."

11. Essays that reflect this controversy are best read chronologically to capture the unfolding of a feminist perspective. Hirsch's essay of 1965 can be read in conjunction with Aliki Barnstone's "Houses within Houses: Emily Dickinson and Mary Wilkins Freeman's 'A New Nun,' " *Centennial Review* 28(Spring 1984): 129–45; both are cited as "negative readings" of the text by Martha Cutter ("Mary E. Wilkins Freeman's Two New England Nuns," *Colby Quarterly* 26 [December 1990]: 213–25). In a study similar to Hirsch's, Linda Brown more recently examines the imagery of "fluttering wings" in the context of "the sexuality the New England spinster shuns" in her note "Anderson's Wing Biddlebaum and Freeman's Louisa Ellis," *Studies in Short Fiction,* 27 (Summer 1990): 113–14. Hirsch is particularly detailed in his reading of the text, suggesting a Freudian view of the story that underscores "a dynamic tension between conscious desire and unconscious, repressed fears" (127). Feminist criticism interprets Louisa's rejection of marriage as "a fulfillment of greater desires" and "a strong, authentic choice leading to Freedom." See Emily Toth, "The Independent Woman and 'Free' Love," *Massachusetts Review* 16 (Autumn 1975): 656–57. The following key essays outline the feminist perspective: Susan Allen Toth, "Defiant Light: A Positive View of Mary Wilkins Freeman," *New England Quarterly* 46 (March 1973): 82–93; Marjorie Pryse, "An Uncloistered 'New England Nun,' " *Studies in Short Fiction* 20 (Fall 1983): 289–95; Leah Blatt Glasser, "Mary E. Wilkins Freeman: The Stranger in the Mirror," *Massachusetts Review* 25 (Summer 1984): 323–39, and "She Is the One You Call Sister: Discovering Mary Wilkins Freeman," in *Between Women: Biographers, Novelists, Critics, and Artists Write about Their Work on Women,* ed. Carol Ascher, Louise DeSalvo, and Sara Ruddick (1984; reprint, New York: Routledge, 1993); Josephine Donovan, "Silence or Capitulation: Prepatriarchal 'Mothers' Gardens' in Jewett and Freeman," *Studies in Short Fiction* 23 (Winter 1986): 43–48; in "Some Reflections on the Spinster in New England Literature," *Regionalism and the Female Imagination: A Collection of Essays,* ed. Emily Toth (New York: Human Sciences, 1985), Barbara Johns notes that women such as Louisa "regard personal integrity as an essential value that marriage ought not to violate" (36); Elizabeth Meese, *Crossing the Double-Cross, the Practice of Feminist Criticism* (Chapel Hill: University of North Carolina Press, 1986), 27–29; Lorne Feinberg, "Mary E. Wilkins Freeman's 'Soft Diurnal Commotion': Women's Work and Strategies of Containment," *New England Quarterly* 62 (1989): 483–501. (Feinberg is particularly astute on the question of the centrality of work in women's lives, stating that Louisa "has translated the work process into a ritual that manifests her self-mastery and her

mastery of her environment" [485]). Cutter, "Mary E. Wilkins Freeman's Two New England Nuns," offers an interesting comparison of Louisa Ellis and Louisa Britton (from the story "Louisa"), arguing that Freeman was in fact "theorizing a way that women of this time period can achieve self-definition" as "active participants in their self-construction rather than passive victims of external circumstances and the demands of others." Cutter sees the choice of celibate autonomy for both characters as positive and unambiguous (225). See also Kate Gardner, "The Subversion of Genre in the Short Stories of Mary Wilkins Freeman," *New England Quarterly* 65 (1992): 462–65, and Anne Romines, *The Home Plot* (Amherst: University of Massachusetts Press, 1992), 108–12.

12. Hamlin Garland, *Roadside Meetings* (New York, 1952), 33.

13. Freeman, "A New England Nun" in *Selected Stories of Mary E. Wilkins Freeman*, ed. Marjorie Pryse (New York: Norton, 1983), 110. All future references are to this edition; page numbers are cited parenthetically in text.

14. Letter to Hale, 2 September 1875.

15. Hirsch, ("Subdued Meaning," 124–36) and Pryse ("An Uncloistered 'New England Nun,' " 289–95) offer interesting alternative interpretations of Louisa's celibacy and the image of the chained dog.

16. Mary Wilkins Freeman, "Good Wits, Pen and Paper," in *What Women Can Earn*, ed. G. H. Dodge et al. (New York, 1899), 28–29.

17. The poem, which opens this chapter, was included in a letter from Freeman to Henry Mills Alden on his seventieth birthday, 1906. It is used with permission of the Alfred Williams Anthony Collection, Rare Books and Manuscripts Division, The New York Public Library, Astor, Lenox and Tilden Foundations.

18. William Dean Howells spoke of a "certain degree of gentility" expected in magazines to be read by "young girls." See Thomas Knipp, "The Quest for Form: The Fiction of Mary E. Wilkins Freeman," (diss., Michigan State University 1966). Knipp refers to Freeman's willingness to satisfy her market by adding sentiment "like sugar to a cake recipe" (310).

19. Henry Alden specified the commitment of the magazine to a "pledge" of morality in *Magazine Writing and the New Literature* (New York, 1908), 68.

20. Letter to Elizabeth Garver Jordan, 12 July 1904 (#350) Kendrick, 301.

21. See Monika Elbert, "Mary Wilkins Freeman's Devious Women, *Harper's Bazaar*, and the Rhetoric of Advertising," *Essays in Literature* 20 (Fall 1993): 251–72. Elbert argues further that both the female market which *Harper's* aimed to attract and Freeman's heroines "all have this in common—the love affair with a commodity. However, by the end of Freeman's tales, the enlightened heroine learns to despise the commodity and to find pleasure or solace in something beyond consumer culture—whether that be through sisterhood (e.g., "Mistaken Charity"), economic self-reliance (e.g., "A New England Nun"), or triumph over the man who would deceive her (e.g., "Old Woman Magoun"). . . . In many ways, the male mastermind who creates the need for a woman's market is debunked and outwitted by the positive heroine's actions, and so Freeman quite subversively undermines the objective of *Harper's Bazaar* and certainly of the ads

which support it" (254). See also Leah Blatt Glasser, "Mary E. Wilkins Freeman," in *The Instructor's Guide for the Heath American Literature,* ed. Judith A. Stanford, (Lexington, Mass.: Heath, 1990), 299–304.

22. Letter to Mary Louise Booth, 17 February 1885 (#5), Kendrick, 61.

23. Elbert notes that Booth was herself a "bundle of contradictions." Citing William Leach (*True Love and Perfect Union: The Feminist Reform of Sex and Society* [New York: Basic, 1980], 252), Elbert highlights Booth as a "fashionable feminist," someone who tried to "establish standards of behavior for feminists and fashionables alike" (Elbert, "Mary Wilkins Freeman's Devious Women," 257).

24. Marjorie Pryse, "Mary E. Wilkins Freeman," in *Modern American Women Writers,* ed. Elaine Showalter, Lea Baechler, A. Walton Litz (New York: Scribner's and Sons, 1991), 143; quotation from 144. Pryse discusses Freeman's relationship with Booth and its influence on her development as a writer.

25. Letter to Mary Louise Booth, 21 April 1885 (#6), Kendrick, 62.

26. Freeman, "The Girl Who Wants to Write," 272.

27. Ibid.

28. Mary Wilkins Freeman, Preface to *A Humble Romance and Other Stories* (Edinburgh, 1890).

29. Hamlin Garland, *Roadside Meetings* (New York: Macmillan, 1952), 33.

30. Margaret Hamilton Welch, "Mary E. Wilkins," *Harper's Bazaar* 33 (January 1900): 68.

31. Freeman, "Mary E. Wilkins," 266.

32. Kendrick, *The Infant Sphinx,* 24.

33. Letter to Mary Louise Booth, 31 March 1886 (#10), Kendrick, 66.

34. Letter to William Harlowe Briggs, Metuchen, N.J., 1 February 1928 (#495), Kendrick, 424.

35. Letter to Hale, 2 September 1875.

36. Freeman, "A Poetess" (1880) in Pryse, *Selected Stories,* 194–95, 198. All future references are to this edition and will be cited parenthetically in the body of the text.

37. Charles Miner Thompson, "Miss Wilkins: An Idealist in Masquerade," *Atlantic Monthly* 83 (May 1899): 670. See also Virginia L. Blum's review of other problematic assessments of Freeman's work in "Mary Wilkins Freeman and the Taste of Necessity," *American Literature* 65 (March 1993): 69–94. Blum notes the irony of the frequent references to Miner's review as a "positive" or "serious" treatment of her work. She also analyzes the role of the marketplace in Freeman's approach to her fiction.

38. Linda Grasso, "Thwarted Life, Mighty Hunger, Unfinished Work": The Legacy of Nineteenth-Century Women Writing in America," *American Transcendental Quarterly* 8 (June 1994): 106. Grasso offers an interesting analysis of "A Poetess" and Constance Fenimore Woolson's "Miss Grief" (97–118) in the context of nineteenth-century sentimentality and "the angered anxiety that a number of late nineteenth-century women writers were feeling when they began to assert their right to become 'artists' in male defined terms" (97). See also Blum, "Mary Wilkins Freeman and the Taste of Necessity," 81–82; Elbert, "Mary Wilkins Freeman's Devious Women," 255–57; Romines, *The Home Plot,* 112–15.

39. Letter to Booth, 21 April 1885.

40. Letter to Hale, 2 September 1875.

41. Letter to Evelyn Sawyer Severance, early January 1893 (#111), Kendrick, 144.

42. Letter to Eliza Anna Farman Pratt, Brattleboro, Vt. Summer 1884 (#3), Kendrick, 59.

43. Letter to Booth, 17 February 1885.

44. Letter to Hamlin Garland, Randolph, Mass., 23 November 1887 (#28), Kendrick, 83.

45. Quoted by Kendrick, *The Infant Sphinx,* 464.

46. Mary Wilkins Freeman, "A Humble Romance," in *A Humble Romance and Other Stories* (New York: Harper and Brothers, 1887), 2. All references are to this edition; page numbers are cited parenthetically in the text.

47. Knipp, "Quest for Form," 310.

48. See interpretations of this story in Glasser, "She Is the One You Call Sister," 203–6; see also Kate Gardner, "The Subversion of Genre," 464–65 and Romines, *The Home Plot,* 102–6.

49. Mary Wilkins Freeman, "A Church Mouse," in *The Revolt of "Mother" and other Stories* (New York: Feminist Press 1974), 150. All references are to this edition; page numbers are cited parenthetically in the text.

50. Letter to Fred Lewis Pattee, Metuchen, N.J., 5 September 1919 (#441), Kendrick, 382.

51. See Chapter 8 for a full discussion of "Sister Liddy."

3. "Sometimes I Think I Am a Monster"

1. See Josephine Donovan, *New England Local Color Literature: A Women's Tradition* (New York: Ungar, 1983), 119–38. See also Mary Reichardt, "Web of Self-Strangulation: Mothers, Daughters and the Question of Marriage in the Short Stories of Mary Wilkins Freeman," in *Joinings and Disjoinings: The Significance of Marital Status in Literature,* ed. JoAnna S. Mink and Janet D. Ward (Bowling Green: Bowling Green State University Popular Press, 1991), 109–19.

2. Anthony quoted in Barbara Levy Simon, *Never Mind Married Women* (Philadelphia: Temple University Press, 1987), 29. See also *Old Maid to Radical Spinster: Unmarried Women in the Twentieth Century Novel,* ed. Laura Doan; foreword by Nina Auerbach (Urbana: University of Illinois Press, 1991), 1–16.

3. See the discussion of Freeman's attraction to Tyler in Chapter 1. Most likely, Freeman sensed from the start that Tyler would not return her love.

4. Mary Wilkins Freeman, undated, untitled manuscript given to Edward Foster by Mrs. A. B. Mann, Randolph, Mass.; see Edward Foster, *Mary E. Wilkins Freeman* (New York: Hendricks House, 1956), 142–44.

5. Foster, *Mary E. Wilkins Freeman,* 143. See also Elizabeth Meese's critique of Foster's approach in "Signs of Undecidability: Reconsidering the Stories of Mary Wilkins Freeman," in *Critical Essays on Mary Wilkins Freeman,* ed. Shirley Marchalonis (Boston: G. K. Hall, 1991), 160.

6. Letter to Kate Upson Clark, December 1889 (#51), Kendrick, 100.

7. Charlotte Wolff, *Love between Women* (New York: Harper and Row, 1971), 211.

8. Letter to Harriet Randolph Hyatt Mayor, 28 August 1900 (#288), Kendrick, 243–44.

9. Letter to Carolyn Wells, Metuchen, N.J., 19 January 1910 (#399), Kendrick, 334.

10. Barbara A. Johns, "Some Reflections on the Spinster in New England Literature," in *Regionalism and the Female Imagination,* ed. Emily Toth (University Park: Human Sciences, Press, Inc., 1985), 29–30.

11. Ibid., 36.

12. George Napheys, *The Physical Life of Woman: Advice to the Maiden, Wife and Mother* (Philadelphia: George Maclean, 1870), 39–40.

13. Susan Koppelman, ed. *Old Maids: Short Stories by Nineteenth-Century U.S. Women Writers* (Boston: Pandora Press, 1984), 3.

14. Lee Chambers-Schiller, "Woman is Born to Love: The Maiden Aunt as Maternal Figure in Literature," *Frontiers* 10, no. 1 (1988): 41. Chamber-Schiller cites "The Hygienic Relations of Celibacy," *The Nation* 5 (1867): 357–58. In many of Freeman's stories, rebellious spinsters such as Hetty in "The Church Mouse" or Jenny in "Christmas Jenny"—those who lived alone and were happy about that choice—are considered insane at the height of their rebellion. Males in the community visit them to consider what can be done.

15. Ruth Freeman and Patricia Klaus, "Blessed or Not? The New Spinster in England and the United States in the Late Nineteenth and Early Twentieth Centuries," *Journal of Family History* 9 (Winter 1984): 396.

16. Koppelman, *Old Maids,* 3.

17. Freeman and Klaus, "Blessed or Not?" 395.

18. Quoted in ibid., 409, from "Autobiography of an Old Maid," *Everybody's* 13 (1905): 843–44.

19. Sandra Gilbert and Susan Gubar, *The Madwoman in the Attic: The Woman Writer and the Nineteenth-Century Literary Imagination* (New Haven: Yale University Press, 1979), 77–78.

20. See my discussion of this story in "Mary Wilkins Freeman: 'The Stranger in the Mirror,' " *Massachusetts Review* 25 (Summer 1984): 323–39.

21. Freeman, "A Moral Exigency," in The *Revolt of "Mother" and Other Stories* (New York: Feminist Press, 1974), 19. All future references are to this edition; page numbers are cited parenthetically in the text.

22. Freeman, *Madelon* (New York: Harper and Brothers, 1896), 171–72. There is a full discussion of this novel in Chapter 5.

23. George Eliot, *The Mill on the Floss,* ed. Gordon S. Haight (Boston: Houghton Mifflin, 1961), 269–70.

24. Letter to Evelyn Sawyer Severance, January 1893 (#113), Kendrick, 145.

25. See Freeman, "The Hall Bedroom" in *Collected Ghost Stories by Mary Wilkins Freeman* (Sauk City, Wisc.: Arkham House, 1974). The hero escapes the narrow boundaries of his room through a series of hallucinatory excursions in which he actually enters the landscape of the painting on his wall. There is a full discussion of the story in Chapter 8.

26. Quoted by Foster, *Mary E. Wilkins Freeman*, 32.

27. Mary E. Coleridge, "The Other Side of the Mirror" in *Poems by Mary E. Coleridge* (London: Elkin Matthews, 1908), 8–9.

28. Freeman, "The Stranger," unpublished handwritten manuscript, 15 February 1901. Mary Wilkins Freeman Collection [#7407], Clifton Waller Barrett Library, Special Collections Department, University of Virginia Library.

29. Foster, *Mary E. Wilkins Freeman*, 42.

30. Clark, Afterword to Mary Wilkins Freeman, *The Revolt of "Mother" and Other Stories* (New York: Feminist Press, 1974), 185.

31. Letter given to Edward Foster by Mrs. John Steele Tyler. Quoted by Foster, *Mary E. Wilkins Freeman*, 44.

32. Helene Deutsch, *Psychology of Women*, vol. 1 (New York: Grune and Stratton, 1944), 250.

33. Jean Baker Miller, *Toward a New Psychology of Women* (Boston: Beacon Press, 1976), 120.

34. Ibid.

35. Eunice's need for acceptance from Ada, her childhood schoolmate, and her fear of alienation may be linked to Freeman's childhood experience. See Perry Westbrook, *Mary Wilkins Freeman* (New York: Twayne, 1967), 25. Freeman was alienated from other children at school who "hated her." Westbrook notes that "Mary Wilkins must have suffered ostracism, however bravely she shrugged it off," and that when Freeman presents "strong willed individualists in a disapproving and jeering community, she offers them peace only when they return to the village norm" (25). This pattern is striking in Freeman's work where the "individualists" are generally women who have broken some code of feminine behavior. The return to the village norm results in some cost to the heroine's self-conception.

36. The triple indications of "want" can be translated as: "I need," "I lack," or "I desire." See Meese, "Signs of Undecidability," 158: Freeman's "own experience of sexual politics led her to represent the interplay of forces through undecidable or purposefully 'unreadable' images that both affirm and negate, . . . always resisting a determination of the text's meanings."

37. See other analyses of "Louisa" in Martha Cutter, "Mary E. Wilkins Freeman's Two New England Nuns," *Colby Quarterly* 26 (1990): 220–25; Thomas A. Maik, "Dissent and Affirmation: Conflicting Voices of Female Roles in Selected Stories by Mary Wilkins Freeman," *Colby Quarterly* 26 (1990): 59–68; Johns's "Some Reflections," 35–36; Kate Gardner, "The Subversion of Genre in the Short Stories of Mary Wilkins Freeman," *New England Quarterly* 65 (1992): 460–62. Like Cutter, Gardner compares Louisa Britton in "Louisa" with Louisa Ellis in "A New England Nun."

38. Freeman, "Louisa," in *A New England Nun and Other Stories* (New York: Harper and Brothers, 1891), 396. All references are to this edition; page numbers are cited parenthetically in the text.

39. See Zora Neale Hurston, *Their Eyes Were Watching God* (Urbana: University of Illinois Press, 1978). See concluding passage (286).

40. Freeman, "Arethusa," in *Understudies* (New York: Harper and Brothers,

1901), 148. All references are to this edition; page numbers will be cited parenthetically in the text.

41. Susan Toth argues that Freeman concludes this story "with an ironic thrust at Lucy's self-satisfied husband"; Elizabeth Meese sees this as a limited interpretation. She views Lucy's husband as "Freeman's ideal male," noting his "sensitive perseverance" and suggesting that although he doesn't understand Lucy's visits, he allows her the freedom to be "true to her own nature." See Toth, "Defiant Light: A Positive View of Mary Wilkins Freeman, *New England Quarterly*" 46 (March 1973): 92 and Meese, "Signs of Undecidability," 33–34.

42. Freeman, "One Good Time," in *The Love of Parson Lord and Other Stories* (New York: Harper and Brothers, 1900), 209. All references are to this edition; page numbers are cited parenthetically in the text. See also Monika Elbert's discussion of this story in "Mary Wilkins Freeman's Devious Women, *Harper's Bazaar*, and the Rhetoric of Advertising," *Essays in Literature* 20 (Fall 1993): 263–64.

43. Donovan, "Mary Wilkins Freeman and the Tree of Knowledge," in *New England Local Color Literature*, 134.

44. Ibid., 132.

45. Freeman, "Christmas Jenny," in *A New England Nun and Other Stories*, 164. All references are to this edition; page numbers are cited parenthetically in text.

46. Barbara Johns, "Love-Cracked: Spinsters as Subversives in 'Anna Malann,' 'Christmas Jenny,' and 'An Object of Love,' " *Colby Library Quarterly* 23 (March 1987): 1, 4–15.

47. Ibid., 11.

48. Ibid., 11–12.

49. Ibid.

50. This position is supported in ibid., 12.

51. Sarah Sherman, "The Great Goddess in New England: Mary Wilkins Freeman's 'Christmas Jenny,' " *Studies in Short Fiction* 17, no. 2 (1980): 160, 161.

52. Freeman, "The Lombardy Poplar," in *Six Trees* (New York: Harper and Brothers, 1903), 147. All references are to this edition; page numbers are cited parenthetically in the text.

53. Freeman, "The Girl Who Wants to Write: Things to Do and Avoid," *Harper's Bazaar* (June 1913): 272. In Chapter 2, I discussed Freeman's reference to a foreign hat as a means of rebelling against the village norm.

54. Barbara Welter, "The Cult of True Womanhood: 1820–1860," in *Dimity Convictions: The American Woman in the Nineteenth Century* (Athens: Ohio University Press, 1976).

55. Freeman, "The Selfishness of Amelia Lamkin," in *The Winning Lady and Others* (New York: Harper and Brothers, 1909), 127.

56. Chambers-Schillers, "Woman Is Born to Love," 42–43.

57. Cutter argues for an alternative interpretation of Freeman's depiction of Jane Strong's role in relation to Amelia Lamkin in "Beyond Stereotypes: Mary Wilkins Freeman's Radical Critique of Nineteenth-Century Cults of Femininity," *Women's Studies* 21 (1992): 383–95. Seeing the story as a demonstration of

Freeman's awareness of "the constraining and ultimately destructive nature of later nineteenth- and early twentieth-century feminine stereotypes," Cutter suggests that Freeman deconstructs two stereotypes: that of the "Domestic Saint" (through Amelia), and that of the "New Woman" (through Jane); in Cutter's analysis, Freeman's description of the limits of Jane's role as unmarried sister is Freeman's way of critiquing the positive stereotype which was emerging at the time, of the self-accepting, progressive spinster. In this way, the story expresses "Freeman's understanding of the debilitating nature of *all* patriarchal images of femininity" (383).

58. Alfred Bendixen, introduction to *The Whole Family: A Novel by Twelve Authors* (New York: Ungar, 1987), xii. All references are to this edition; page numbers are cited parenthetically in the text. In 1907, Freeman joined with William Dean Howells, Henry James, and other contemporaries in constructing this novel about a family in a small town.

59. Cited by Bendixen (introduction to *The Whole Family*) from the letters in Elizabeth Jordan Papers in the Rare Books and Manuscripts Division of the New York Public Library.

60. Letter to Elizabeth Jordan, Metuchen, N.J., 24 July 1906 (#369), Kendrick, 312.

61. Letter to Jordan, Metuchen, N.J., August 1906 (#371), Kendrick, 313.

62. Ibid.

4. Sexual Politics in *Pembroke*

1. Deborah Lambert, "Rereading Mary Wilkins Freeman: Autonomy and Sexuality in *Pembroke*," in *Critical Essays on Mary Wilkins Freeman*, ed. Shirley Marchalonis (Boston: G. K. Hall, 1991), 197.

2. Ibid., 198.

3. In the *New York Herald*'s announcement of her marriage to Charles Freeman, Mary gave her age as thirty-five, although she was fourteen years older (*New York Herald*, 3 January 1902, 6). See also expressions of her concerns about her appearance in letters to Hayden Carruth (November 1915 [#417], Kendrick, 347) and to Edith Porter Tolman (December 1916 [#434], Kendrick, 355).

4. Lambert, "Rereading," 198.

5. Freeman, "Introductory Sketch" to *Pembroke*, Biographical edition (New York: Harper and Brothers, 1899). Quoted in full in Perry Westbrook, *Mary Wilkins Freeman* (New York:Twayne, 1967), 95–96.

6. Westbrook, *Mary Wilkins Freeman*, 92.

7. Marjorie Pryse, "Mary E. Wilkins Freeman," in *Modern American Women Writers*, ed. Elaine Showalter, Lea Baechler, A. Walton Litz (New York: Scribner's and Sons, 1991), 146, 147. Pryse argues that *Pembroke* is an example of Freeman's concept of the role of outside intervention in the lives of troubled individuals.

8. Freeman, *Pembroke* (New York: Harper and Brothers, 1894), 3–4. All references are to this edition; page numbers will be cited parenthetically in the text.

9. Letter to Harriet Randolph Hyatt Mayor, Summer 1912 (#407), Kendrick, 340.

10. Lambert, "Rereading," 205. Lambert's interpretation is perceptive as she notes "Freeman's painful exploration of women's possibilities" (204). Early criticism of *Pembroke* failed to take into account the depth of Freeman's analysis of women's lives. Larzer Ziff complained in *The American 1890's: Life and Times of a Lost Generation* (New York: Viking Press, 1966) that in *Pembroke* Freeman "launches a massive attack on New England religion with its pinched, dehumanized narrowness leading to sexual frustration or illegitimate relations or psychosomatic crippling, but denies the tale the validity it cries for by refusing to give it a psychological dimension" (294–95). While Edward Foster acknowledged that Freeman delves into the human psyche in her "deeply felt plea for the natural expression of normal feeling" (*Mary E. Wilkins Freeman* [New York: Hendricks House, 1956], 126), he never touches on the complexities Freeman uncovers as she grapples to define just what "normal feeling" might be for the nineteenth-century woman. Perry Westbrook also recognized the psychological focus of the novel, but offered no detail in his discussion of it. See also Melissa McFarland Pennell, "The Liberating Will: Freedom of Choice in the Fiction of Mary Wilkins Freeman," in Marchalonis, *Critical Essays on Mary Wilkins Freeman*, 207–21.

11. I discuss this passage in Chapter 1 in the context of Freeman's childhood.

12. Lillian Faderman, *Surpassing the Love of Men: Romantic Friendship and Love between Women from the Renaissance to the Present* (New York: William Morrow, 1981), 158.

13. See Alice Garden Brand, "Mary Wilkins Freeman: Misanthropy as Propaganda," *New England Quarterly* 50 (1977), on the way in which "women's anger distorted their perception because it could not be confronted and examined" (99).

14. See Susan Allen Toth, "Defiant Light: A Positive View of Mary Wilkins Freeman," *New England Quarterly* 46 (1973): 82–93.

15. See Freeman, "Introductory Sketch," in Westbrook, *Mary Wilkins Freeman,* 95–96. Freeman refers to the tragedy of her characters' inability to comprehend their own unhappiness.

16. I discuss dream texture in "The Hall Bedroom" and "A Symphony in Lavender" in Chapter 8.

17. Lambert, "Rereading," 204.

5. "Savage Squaw" and "Fair Angel" in *Madelon*

1. Edward Foster, *Mary E. Wilkins Freeman* (New York: Hendricks House, 1956), 139.

2. Letter to Evelyn Sawyer Severance, early January 1893 (#111), Kendrick, 144.

3. Letter to Fred Lewis Pattee, Metuchen, N.J., 5 September 1919 (#441), Kendrick, 382.

4. Letter to Eunice McDaniel Dana, 20 January 1896 (#191), Kendrick, 184–85.

5. Letter to Asa P. French, 26 July 1896 (#199), Kendrick, 187.

6. Brent L. Kendrick, ed., *The Infant Sphinx* (Metuchen, N.J.: Scarecrow Press, 1985), 117.

7. Foster, *Mary E. Wilkins Freeman*, 138.

8. Perry Westbrook, *Mary Wilkins Freeman* (New York: Twayne, 1967), 109.

9. Susan Harris, "But Is It Any Good? Evaluating Nineteenth-Century American Women's Fiction," *American Literature* 63, no. 1 (1991): 44.

10. Kendrick, *The Infant Sphinx*, 24, 118–19.

11. Harris, "But Is It Any Good?" 52–53. Harris poses some significant questions: "What needs did they [nineteenth-century women's novels] serve for their intended audience? . . . Did they give hope to readers, let them know that there were other questing souls out there? What effect does the text's structure have on its theme or themes? What kinds of cognitive or emotional discrepancies exist, and how might contemporary readers have responded to them? What is the power of fascination the texts hold? Is it the same power that holds us (those of us who read them) today? If so, can we describe it? Is it sexual?—moral?—aesthetic?—affective?"

12. George Preston, "Concerning Good English," *The Bookman* (1896): 361–62. See also Horace Scudder, *Atlantic Monthly* 78 (August 1896): 269–70; Scudder's piece is a rare example of a positive review of the novel. He commented on Freeman's "most artistic portrayal of the idée fixe of the psychologist," and noted that to read *Madelon* is "to enter the domain of the pathologist, yet we would point out to the reader how much of Miss Wilkins's skill seems to lie in stopping just short of insanity in her characters." Although he praised Freeman's "extraordinary concentration of language" as an example of "an art which makes language have the cold splendor of a winter sunset," Scudder's comments did little to promote the novel because of his emphasis on her portrayal of "insanity." He wrote, somewhat sardonically, that "a little more and every mother's son and daughter of them would be in the madhouse."

13. Virginia Woolf discusses the effect of Freeman's sort of anger in *A Room of One's Own* (1929; New York: Harcourt, Brace Jovanovich, 1957), 76. Woolf refers to Charlotte Brontë's anger, but much of what she says applies to Freeman: "She remembered that she had been starved of her proper due of experience—she had been made to stagnate in a parsonage mending stockings when she wanted to wander free over the world. Her imagination swerved from indignation and we feel it swerve . . . we constantly feel an acidity which is the result of oppression, a buried suffering smouldering beneath her passion, a rancour which contracts those books, splendid as they are, with a spasm of pain." This "spasm of pain" emerges in Freeman's portrayal of Madelon, although if we apply Harris's argument, it can become the very thing that compels us to read the novel.

14. Charles Miner Thompson, "Miss Wilkins: An Idealist in Masquerade," *The Atlantic Monthly* 83 (May 1899): 674.

15. Westbrook, *Mary Wilkins Freeman*, 106.

16. Mr. J. Edgar Chamberlain, quoted by Foster, *Mary E. Wilkins Freeman*, 134–35.

17. Freeman, "Emily Brontë and *Wuthering Heights*," in *The World's Great Women Novelists*, ed. T. M. Parrott (Philadelphia: The Booklovers Library, 1901), 88–89.

18. Freeman, *Madelon* (New York: Harper and Brothers, 1896). All references are to this edition; page numbers are cited parenthetically in the text.

19. F. O. Matthiessen, "New England Stories," in *American Writers on American Literature*, ed. John Macy (New York: Horace Liveright, 1931), 406–7. Matthiessen suggests that the circumstances of Freeman's early life are almost "exactly parallel" to Emily Brontë's. He notes similarities in her own description of Emily Brontë where Freeman sees her "hedged about by great spaces of loneliness and insuperable barriers of religion in an isolated parsonage with more of the dead than the living for neighbors" (88–89). Matthiessen made a rare acknowledgment of Freeman's capacity to portray the "secrets of others." For an opposite and more negative response to her work, see Grant Overton, *Women Who Make Our Novels* (New York: Moffat Yard and Co., 1922). Overton says that Freeman's work is "unimportant," "of no permanent value" and that this is an "assertion of fact" rather than an "expression of opinion" (198). Unlike Matthiessen, Overton claims "her stories are cordially welcome and likable . . . without having the slightest relation to the business of living" (199).

20. Charlotte Brontë, " 'Editor's Preface,' to the New Edition of *Wuthering Heights* (1850)," in *Wuthering Heights* (New York: Norton, 1972), 11. Brontë continues: "Whether it is right or advisable to create beings like Heathcliff, I do not know. I scarcely think it is" (12).

21. Letter to Kate Upson Clark, before May 1896 (#193), Kendrick, 185.

22. In *Madelon*, Freeman adds the element of marginality; applying the stereotypes of her time to her part-Indian heroine, she accentuates Madelon's primitive "savagery" and links it to her Native American heritage. Although she was not intolerant or consciously racist, Freeman did embrace the nineteenth-century stereotypes of the "savage Indian" in this novel. While this may disturb modern readers initially, Freeman's imagery in *Madelon* must be seen in the context of her position as a nineteenth-century writer. A similar dilemma, to a greater extent, arises in Harriet Beecher Stowe's depictions of African Americans in *Uncle Tom's Cabin*.

23. Sandra M. Gilbert and Susan Gubar, *The Madwoman in the Attic: The Woman Writer and the Nineteenth-Century Literary Imagination* (New Haven: Yale University Press, 1979), 77–78.

24. Ibid., 78.

25. Freeman's untitled, undated manuscript given to Foster by Mrs. A. B. Mann; quoted by Foster, *Mary E. Wilkins Freeman*, 142–44. Jane Lennox sees herself as a "graft on the tree of human womanhood." See my discussion of this text in Chapter 3.

26. Gilbert and Gubar, *Madwoman in the Attic*, 78.

27. The contrast between dark and light heroines is a significant pattern in the use of doubles. See Claire Rosenfield, "The Shadow Within: The Conscious

and Unconscious Use of the Double," in *Stories of the Double,* ed. Albert J. Guerard (Philadelphia: Lippincott, 1967), 314. Rosenfield explains that "when the passionate uninhibited self is a woman, she more often than not is dark." The links and contrasts between Madelon and Dorothy are not unlike the connection between the dark Bertha and the fair Jane Eyre. This doubling (fair and dark heroine) relates to a tradition in American letters of character pairs like Dorothy and Madelon (e.g., Lucy and Isabelle in Melville's *Pierre;* similar use of doubles in Hawthorne's *The Marble Faun*). The way in which Madelon and Dorothy are juxtaposed throughout the novel may be explained by Rosenfield's statement that use of psychological doubles often involves the juxtaposition of "two characters, the one representing the socially acceptable or conventional personality, the other externalizing the free, uninhibited, often criminal self" (314). Madelon's criminal act and Dorothy's initial obedience create this effect.

28. Edward Wasiolek, "Raskolnikov's Motives: Love and Murder," in *The Practice of Psychoanalytic Criticism,* ed. Leonard Tennenhouse (Detroit: Wayne State University Press, 1976). Wasiolek discusses Raskolnikov's mare-beating dream and states that it "shows us Raskolnikov who is killing himself, who is tormenter and tormented. . . . The mother, landlady and pawnbroker exist as meanings within him. . . . In killing them, he attempts to kill what they mean in him" (125). Raskolnikov's hostility, according to Wasiolek, is directed not only against his "real or imagined tormenters," but also against himself.

29. Helene Deutsch's chapter, "The Active Woman: Masculinity Complex" (*Psychology of Women,* vol. 1 [New York: Grune and Stratton, 1944), applies to Madelon's behavior. Madelon's masochistic actions which follow the stabbing stem from the "predominance of active and aggressive tendencies" in her personality "that lead to conflicts with the woman's environment and above all with the remaining feminine inner world," which Dorothy represents (288–89). Deutsch notes that a "woman's aggression can constitute a flight and a mask for deeply feminine instinctual desires that are dangerous for her and are therefore repressed." Her example of Carmen is especially interesting in connection with Madelon's actions: "Sadistically enjoying the torment of others, she at the same time masochistically enjoys her own panic fear of the ultimate outcome that she herself prepares with iron fatality" (288).

30. Harris, "But Is It Any Good?" 61.

31. There are other parallels between the two novels. The women characters are similarly paired and contrasted (Madelon and Dorothy, Maggie and Lucy). Maggie shares Madelon's self-destructive impulses and, in the end, seeks to "save" Tom just as Madelon is obsessed with saving Burr's life through her self-destruction.

32. Gilbert and Gubar, *Madwoman in the Attic,* 17–18.

33. Ibid., 57.

34. In this poem, a woman sees a male stranger and recognizes that he "abides" in her own flesh and soul. I discuss this poem in Chapter 3 in the context of the mirror scene in " A Moral Exigency."

35. Foster, *Mary E. Wilkins Freeman,* 113.

36. Ibid.

37. Michele Clark, Afterword to Freeman, *The Revolt of "Mother" and Other Stories* (New York: Feminist Press, 1974), 174.

38. Ibid., 197.

6. "The Tenderness of One Woman for Another"

1. See Mary R. Reichardt's study of women's relationships in Freeman's short stories in *A Web of Relationships: Women in the Short Stories of Mary Wilkins Freeman* (Jackson: University of Mississippi Press, 1992). See also Reichardt's " 'Friend of My Heart': Women as Friends and Rivals in the Short Stories of Mary Wilkins Freeman," *American Literary Realism* 22, no. 2 (Winter 1990): 54–68. Reichardt argues that Freeman's depictions of women's friendships more often focus on "women friends as unequal and thus competitive. One of the women is the other's superior in strength, beauty, wealth, or even morality; the other woman envious, strives to imitate her" (58). As this chapter will illustrate, I differ with this assessment of Freeman's portrayal of women's relationships.

2. Carroll Smith-Rosenberg, "The Female World of Love and Ritual: Relations between Women in Nineteenth-Century America," *Signs* 1, no. 1 (1975): 2.

3. Smith-Rosenberg, *Disorderly Conduct: Visions of Gender in Victorian America* (New York: Alfred A. Knopf, 1985), 59–60.

4. Edward Foster, *Mary E. Wilkins Freeman* (New York: Hendricks House, 1956), 141. The relationship of Freeman and Wales is briefly discussed in Chapter 2.

5. Letter to Mary Louise Booth, after 17 March 1886 (#9), Kendrick, 66.

6. Letter to Mary Louise Booth, 5 November 1887 (#27), Kendrick, 81.

7. Edith Somerville quoted in Lillian Faderman. *Surpassing the Love of Men: Romantic Friendship and Love between Women from the Renaissance to the Present* (New York: William Morrow, 1981), 205.

8. Letter to Mary Louise Booth, before 28 April 1886, Randolph, Mass. (#12), Kendrick, 68.

9. *Hamlin Garland's Diaries*, ed. Donald Pizer, (San Marino, Calif.: Huntington Library, 1968).

10. Foster, *Mary E. Wilkins Freeman*, 133.

11. Brent L. Kendrick, ed., *The Infant Sphinx: Collected Letters of Mary E. Wilkins Freeman* (Metuchen, N.J.: Scarecrow Press, 1985), 203.

12. Ibid., 204, 205.

13. Foster, *Mary E. Wilkins Freeman*, 141.

14. Quoted by Kendrick, *The Infant Sphinx*, 206; from "Miss Wilkins Wedding Postponed to Allow her to Finish 'The Lion's Share,' " (unidentified newspaper clipping, fall 1900; collection of Brent L. Kendrick).

15. Kendrick, *The Infant Sphinx*, 206–7, 208. Kendrick quotes many articles in tracing the record of engagement announcements, including those to which I refer: *Boston Herald*, 19 October 1899, 2; *New York Tribune*, 19 October 1900, 9; 16 November 1901, 1; 18 November 1901, 1. Kendrick also cites the *New York Telegraph* and *New Brunswick Home News* from "Newspapers Urged Wedding on Him," *New Brunswick Home News*, 27 September 1939.

16. Letter to Harriet Randolph Hyatt Mayor, 28 August 1900 (#288), Kendrick, 243.

17. Letter to Harriet Randolph Hyatt Mayor, 22 December 1901 (#316), Kendrick, 256.

18. Letter to Frederick Atherton Duneka, Randolph, Mass., 23 February 1908 (#390), Kendrick, 328.

19. Letter to Annie Isabel Willis McCullough, 21 November 1908 (#394), Kendrick, 330.

20. Letter to Harriet Randolph Mayor, 23 December 1908 (#395), Kendrick, 331.

21. Letter to Carolyn Wells, Metuchen, N.J., 19 January 1910 (#399), Kendrick, 334.

22. Kendrick, *The Infant Sphinx,* 14.

23. Letter to Harriet Randolph Hyatt Mayor, Summer 1912 (#407), Kendrick, 339.

24. Letter to Carolyn Wells, 19 January 1910 (#399), Kendrick, 334.

25. Quoted by Kendrick, *The Infant Sphinx,* 464.

26. Foster, *Mary E. Wilkins Freeman,* 33, 34, 38.

27. Letter to Evelyn Sawyer Severance, January 1893 (#113), Kendrick, 145.

28. Ibid., 145, 146

29. Letter to Evelyn Sawyer Severence, 22 December 1901 (#317), Kendrick, 257.

30. Letter to Evelyn Sawyer Severence, 25 April 1902 (#323), Kendrick, 286–87.

31. Letter to Mary Louise Booth, 21 April 1885 (#6), Kendrick, 62.

32. Letter to Mary Louise Booth and Anna W. Wright, 17 March 1886 (#8), Kendrick, 65.

33. Letters to Mary Louise Booth: undated fragment traced by Kendrick to have been written after 17 March 1886 (#9), 66; 31 March 1886 (#10), 67; 28 April 1886 (#12), 68–69; undated letter traced by Kendrick to have been written before 15 November 1886 (#18), 75; 26 November 1886 (#19), 76; 27 January 1888 (#31), 87; 28 April 1886 (#13), 69. See the discussion of Booth as Freeman's maternal mentor and editor in Chapter 2; see also Pryse's discussion of their relationship in "Mary E. Wilkins Freeman," in *Modern American Women Writers,* ed. Elaine Showalter, Lea Baechler, A. Walton Litz (New York: Scribner's and Sons, 1991), 143–44.

34. Reichardt, *A Web of Relationships,* 14.

35. Letter to Mary Louise Booth, 27 December 1887 (#30), Kendrick, 85.

36. Foster, *Mark E. Williams Freeman,* 161–162.

37. Kendrick, *The Infant Sphinx,* 261. Kendrick cites Henrietta W. Silzer's letter to Thomas Schuler Shaw, 20 February 1932, in Shaw's scrapbook of letters written to him (1930–1932) about Freeman (Library of Congress, Rare Book and Special Collections Division, Washington, D.C.).

38. Letter to Kate Upson Clark, 25 April 1902 (#322), Kendrick, 286.

39. Kendrick, *The Infant Sphinx,* 261–62.

40. Letter to Evelyn Sawyer Severance, 25 April 1902 (#323), Kendrick, 287.

41. Letter to Harriet Randolph Hyatt Mayor, 23 December 1908 (#395), Kendrick, 331.

42. Cited by Kendrick *The Infant Sphinx*, 264, from the collection of Brent L. Kendrick.

43. Kendrick, *The Infant Sphinx*, 267; see also letter to Severance, 25 April 1902.

44. Kendrick, *The Infant Sphinx*, 362, 271.

45. Ibid., 280

46. Letter to Jeanette Leonard Gilder, 9 April 1915 (#414), Kendrick, 345.

47. Letter to Florence Morse Kingsley, June 1916 (#430), Kendrick, 353–54. Her letter refers to "two dear friends who are dangerously, mortally ill." Kendrick explains that the reference is to Mary Wales and Carolyn Alden (*The Infant Sphinx*, 515).

48. Kendrick, *The Infant Sphinx*, 17. As Kendrick explains, "the fate of that collection . . . is unknown."

49. Letter to Edith Porter Tolman, 29 December 1916 (#434), Kendrick, 355.

50. "The Love of Parson Lord," in *The Love of Parson Lord and Other Stories* (New York: Harper and Brothers, 1900), 4. All references are to this edition; page numbers are cited parenthetically in the text.

51. Martha Satz, "Going to an Unknown Home: Redesign in *The Portion of Labor*," in *Critical Essays on Mary E. Wilkins Freeman*, ed. Shirley Marchalonis (Boston: G. K. Hall, 1991), 192.

52. Josephine Donovan, *New England Local Color Literature: A Women's Tradition* (New York: Ungar, 1983), 120.

53. Letter to Elizabeth Porter Tolman, after 15 October 1925 (#457), Kendrick, 394.

54. Satz, "Going to an Unknown Home," 185–86.

55. Freeman, *The Portion of Labor* (New York: Harper and Brothers, 1901), 121. All references are to this edition; page numbers are cited parenthetically in the text.

56. Satz, "Going to an Unknown Home," 185.

57. See Sara Ruddick, *Maternal Thinking: Toward a Politics of Peace* (New York: Ballantine Books, 1989), 13–27.

58. Donovan, *New England Local Color Literature*, 125; Satz, "Going to an Unknown Home," 193.

59. Freeman, *By the Light of the Soul* (New York: Harper and Brothers, 1907), 352. All references are to this edition; page numbers are cited parenthetically in the text.

60. Letter to Kate Upson Clark, 12 August 1889 (#46), Kendrick, 96–97.

61. Foster, *Mary E. Wilkins Freeman*, 60.

62. "Comments on Current Books," *Outlook*, 4 July 1908, 532.

63. Freeman, *The Shoulders of Atlas* (New York: Harper and Brothers, 1908), 268. All references are to this edition; page numbers are cited parenthetically in the text.

64. Donovan, *New England Local Color Literature,* 128.

65. Ibid., 129.

66. Ibid.

7. "If You Don't See the Old Me"

1. Letter to Harriet Randolph Hyatt Mayor, 28 August 1900 (#288), Kendrick, 243.

2. Quoted by Brent L. Kendrick, ed., *The Infant Sphinx: Collected Letters of Mary E. Wilkins Freeman* (Metuchen, N.J.: Scarecrow Press, 1985), from Kate Upson Clark, "Mary Eleanor Wilkins Freeman," unpublished biographical sketch, June 1932, in Thomas Schuler Shaw's unclassified scrapbook, Library of Congress, Rare Books and Special Collections Division, Washington, D.C.

3. Letter to Robert Underwood Johnson, 21 October 1900 (#291), Kendrick, 245.

4. Kendrick, *The Infant Sphinx,* 281.

5. Letter to Florence E. Bate, 17 December 1915 (#418), Kendrick, 348.

6. Quoted by Perry Westbrook, *Mary Wilkins Freeman* (New York: Twayne, 1967), 171.

7. Kendrick, *The Infant Sphinx,* 362.

8. Letter to Samuel Schenck, 21 November 1918 (#439), Kendrick, 358–59.

9. Ibid.

10. Kendrick, *The Infant Sphinx,* 362, 363.

11. Testimony of Dr. William Ramsay, brain specialist of Perth Amboy, N.J., reported in "Expert Decision in Freeman Will Case within Ten Days," *Metuchen Review,* 14 September 1923, 1; cited in ibid., 363.

12. "The Vase," *The Literary Digest,* 19 August 1922, 38; cited in Edward Foster, *Mary E. Wilkins Freeman* (New York: Hendricks House, 1956), 187.

13. Kendrick, *The Infant Sphinx,* 365, 518.

14. Ibid., 364.

15. Ibid. Kendrick quotes from "Text of Will Tells Loyalty of Harry Mohring," *New Brunswick* (N.J.) *Daily Home News,* 7 April 1923. See also 366, 368.

16. "Mrs. Freeman, in Interview Insists Husband was Mentally Unbalanced," *New Brunswick* (N.J.) *Sunday Times,* 18 March 1923. Quoted by Kendrick, *The Infant Sphinx,* 365.

17. "Mrs. Freeman Insists Husband Was Not Himself when Will Was Made Cutting Her Off with Only One Dollar," *Metuchen Recorder,* 27 April 1923, 1.

18. Kendrick, *The Infant Sphinx,* 366–68.

19. Dr. Henry Cotton, superintendent of the New Jersey State Hospital for the Insane. See ibid.

20. Ibid., 368.

21. Letter to Evelyn Sawyer Severance, 15 January 1927 (#479), Kendrick, 412.

22. Ibid.

23. Helen C. Carvalho to Thomas Schuler Shaw, authograph letter signed [ALS], 14 April 1932, cited by Kendrick, *The Infant Sphinx*, 375, 520.

24. Letter to Fred Lewis Pattee, 25 September 1919 (#442), Kendrick, 383–84.

25. Letter to Carolyn Wells, 2 May 1920 (#444), Kendrick, 387.

26. Letter to John Hutchinson, 8 April 1927 (#483), Kendrick, 415–16.

27. Freeman refers to this story in a letter to Edith O'Dell Black, 16 December 1928 (#502), Kendrick, 428.

28. Letter to Henry Goddard Leach, 14 January 1929 (#503), Kendrick, 428.

29. Letter to William Harlowe Briggs, 22 November 1928 (#501), Kendrick, 426.

30. Letter to William Harlowe Briggs, Metuchen, N.J., 1 February 1928 (#495), Kendrick, 424.

31. Ibid.

32. Letter to Ashley Horace Thorndike, 25 October 1917 (#437), Kendrick, 357.

33. Mary Wilkins Freeman, "A Village Singer," in *A New England Nun and Other Stories* (New York: Harper and Brothers, 1891), 19.

34. Marjorie Pryse, "The Humanity of Women in Freeman's 'A Village Singer' " *Colby Library Quarterly* 19 (June 1983): 70. See also Kate Gardner, "The Subversion of Genre in the Short Stories of Mary Wilkins Freeman," *New England Quarterly* 65 (1992): 459.

35. Letter to Kate Upson Clark, 5 March 1889 (#43), Kendrick, 95.

36. "A Mistaken Charity," in *Selected Stories of Mary E. Wilkins Freeman,* ed. Marjorie Pryse (New York: Norton, 1983), 43. All references are to this edition; page numbers are cited parenthetically in the text.

37. Freeman, "An Innocent Gamester," in *A New England Nun and Other Stories,* 366–67.

38. Letter to Marion Boyd Allen, 3 April 1928, after a visit with Mrs. Hyatt in which they discussed death (#497), Kendrick, 425.

39. Letter to Allie Morse, 13 December 1929 (#509), Kendrick, 431–32.

40. Ibid.

41. Foster, *Mary E. Wilkins Freeman,* 194.

42. Letter to Marion Boyd Allen, 2 February 1930 (#510), Kendrick, 432.

43. Kendrick cites Margaret Durick, "New England's Portrayer at Rest Beside Graves of Alden Sisters," *New Brunswick* (N.J.) *Sunday Times,* 23 March 1900, 8; "Noted Authoress Passes Away," *Metuchen Recorder,* 13 March 1930, 1; Kendrick, *The Infant Sphinx,* 376.

8. Freeman and Two New England Contemporaries

1. Amy Kaplan, "Nation, Region, and Empire," in *Columbia History of the American Novel,* ed. Emory Elliott (New York: Columbia University Press, 1991), 254.

2. Cecelia Tichi, "Women Writers and the New Woman" in *Columbia Literary History of the United States*, ed. Emory Elliott (New York: Columbia University Press, 1988), 590, 598. See the introducton by Judith Fetterley and Marjorie Pryse in *American Women Regonalists, 1850–1910*, ed. Fetterley and Pryse (New York: W. W. Norton, 1992) for a useful discussion on women regionalists. See also Judith Fetterley's insightful work on nineteenth-century women writers in her introduction to *Provisions: A Reader from 19th-Century American Women*, ed. Fetterley (Bloomington: Indiana University Press, 1985).

3. Tichi, "Women Writers and the New Woman," 590.

4. Charlotte Perkins Gilman, "Coming Changes in Literature," *The Forerunner* 6 (September 1915): 235; quoted by Denise Knight in her thoughtful critical introduction to *"The Yellow Wallpaper" and Selected Stories of Charlotte Perkins Gilman*, ed. Knight (Newark: University of Delaware Press; London: Associated University Presses, 1994), 28.

5. Charlotte Perkins Gilman, *The Forerunner* 7 (December 1916): 327; cited in Knight, introduction to *"The Yellow Wallpaper,"* 24.

6. Quoted by Knight from a folder in Charlotte Perkins Gilman Papers (Arthur and Elizabeth Schlesinger Liibrary at Radcliffe College, Cambridge, Mass.) titled "Thoughts and Figgerings," (ibid., 22, 23).

7. See Knight's discussion of Gilman's tendency in some of her fiction to "emphasize her message at the expense of her characters, many of whom are underdeveloped or stereotyped" (*"The Yellow Wallpaper,"* 23). My discussion of Gilman focuses on comparing "The Yellow Wallpaper" with some of Freeman's supernatural fiction. For more detailed analysis of Gilman's life and work, in addition to Denise Knight's introduction, see Elaine R. Hedges's afterword to *The Yellow Wallpaper* (New York: Feminist Press, 1973), 37–60; Mary A. Hill, *Charlotte Perkins Gilman: The Making of a Radical Feminist* (Philadelphia: Temple University Press, 1980); Gary Scharnhorst, *Charlotte Perkins Gilman* (Boston: Twayne, 1985); Sheryl L. Meyering, ed., *Charlotte Perkins Gilman: The Woman and Her Work* (Ann Arbor: UMI Research Press, 1989); Anne J. Lane, *To Herland and Beyond: The Life and Work of Charlotte Perkins Gilman* (New York: Pantheon, 1990).

8. Mary A. Hill, ed., *Endure: The Diaries of Charles Walter Stetson* (Philadelphia: Temple University Press, 1985), 63; cited by Knight, *"The Yellow Wallpaper,"* 13.

9. Brent L. Kendrick, ed., *The Infant Sphinx: Collected Letters of Mary E. Wilkins Freeman* (Metuchen, N.J.: Scarecrow Press, 1985), 206.

10. Letter to Fred Lewis Pattee, 5 September 1919 (#441), Kendrick, 382.

11. Beth Wynne Fisken, "The 'Faces of Children That Had Never Been' " in *Haunting the House of Fiction: Feminist Perspectives on Ghost Stories by American Women*, ed. Lynette Carpenter and Wendy Kolmar (Knoxville: University of Tennessee Press, 1991), 60.

12. Alfred Bendixen, Introduction, *Haunted Women: The Best Supernatural Tales by American Women Writers*, ed. Bendixen (New York: Ungar, 1984), 2.

13. Fisken, "The 'Faces of Children,' " 57.

14. Freeman, "The Lost Ghost," in *The Wind in the Rose-bush and Other Stories of the Supernatural* (New York: Doubleday, 1903), 212. All references are to this edition; page numbers are cited parenthetically in the text.

15. Fisken, "The 'Faces of Children,' " 58.

16. Alfred Bendixen, Afterword in *The Wind in the Rose-bush and Other Stories* (Chicago: Academy Chicago Publishers, 1986), 249.

17. Perry Westbrook, *Mary Wilkins Freeman* (New York: Twayne, 1967), 27.

18. Freeman, "The Hall Bedroom," in *Collected Ghost Stories by Mary Wilkins Freeman,* ed. Edward Wagenknecht (Sauk City, Wisc.: Arkham House, 1974), 24. All references are to this edition; page numbers are cited parenthetically in the text. First published in *Collier's,* 28 Mar. 1903.

19. Sarah Orne Jewett, *Country of the Pointed Firs and Other Stories,* (New York: Norton, 1981), ed. Mary Ellen Chase, with an introduction by Marjorie Pryse, 77. All future references are to this edition, with page numbers cited parenthetically in the text.

My discussion of Sarah Orne Jewett focuses on comparing some aspects of her work to Freeman's. For more detailed analysis of Jewett's life and work, see Marjorie Pryse's introduction; Josephine Donovan, *Sarah Orne Jewett* (New York: Ungar, 1980); Gwen Nagel, ed., *Critical Essays on Sarah Orne Jewett* (Boston: G. K. Hall, 1984); Margaret Roman, *Sarah Orne Jewett: Reconstructing Gender* (Tuscaloosa: Unviersity of Alabama Press, 1992); Elizabeth Silversthorne, *Sarah Orne Jewett: A Writer's Life* (Woodstock, N.Y.: Overlook Press, 1993); Paula Blanchard, *Sarah Orne Jewett: Her World and Her Work* (Reading, Mass.: Addison-Wesley, 1994).

20. Jewett, "A White Heron," in *The Country of the Pointed Firs and Other Stories,* 233.

21. Freeman, "A Symphony of Lavender" in *A Humble Romance and Other Stories* (New York: Harper and Brothers, 1887), 44. All references are to this edition; page numbers are cited parenthetically in the text.

22. Freeman, "Sister Liddy," in *A New England Nun and Other Stories* (New York: Harper and Brothers, 1981), 93. All references are to this edition and are cited parenthetically in the text.

SELECTED BIBLIOGRAPHY
OF THE WORKS OF
MARY E. WILKINS FREEMAN

∞

I have limited this bibliography to works most pertinent to my study of Freeman's life. Freeman's oeuvre includes 14 novels, 250 short stories, 15 short story collections, several plays, children's works, and essays. This selected list cites the original rather than more recent collections of Freeman's work. Her uncollected fiction has been recently republished in *The Uncollected Stories of Mary Wilkins Freeman,* ed. Mary R. Reichardt (Jackson: University Press of Mississippi, 1992).

"Amanda and Love." In *A New England Nun and Other Stories* (1891). 288–304.
"Amarina's Roses." In *The Fair Lavinia and Others* (1907). 43–83.
"The Apple-Tree." In *Six Trees* (1903). 169–207.
"Arethusa." In *Understudies* (1901). 147–69.
"The Balsam Fir." In *Six Trees* (1903). 101–27.
The Best Stories of Mary E. Wilkins. Edited by Henry Wysham Lanier. New York: Harper and Brothers, 1927.
"Brakes and White Vi'lets." In *A Humble Romance and Other Stories* (1887). 107–17.
"The Buckley Lady." In *Silence and Other Stories* (1898). 55–110.
"The Butterfly." In *The Givers* (1904). 229–65.
The Butterfly House. New York: Dodd, Mead and Company, 1912.
By the Light of the Soul. New York: Harper and Brothers, 1907.
"Calla-Lilies and Hannah." In *A New England Nun and Other Stories* (1891). 99–120.
"Catherine Carr." In *The Love of Parson Lord and Other Stories* (1900). 143–81.
"Christmas Jenny." In *A New England Nun and Other Stories* (1891). 160–77.
"A Church Mouse." In *A New England Nun and Other Stories* (1891). 407–25.
"Cinnamon Roses." In *A Humble Romance and Other Stories* (1887). 164–79.
"A Conflict Ended." In *A Humble Romance and Other Stories* (1887). 382–98.

"A Conquest of Humility." In *A Humble Romance and Other Stories* (1887). 415–36.

"The Copy-Cat." In *The Copy-Cat and Other Stories* (1914). 1–31.

The Copy-Cat and Other Stories. New York: Harper and Brothers, 1914.

The Debtor. New York: Harper and Brothers, 1905.

Edgewater People. New York: Harper and Brothers, 1918.

"Eglantina." In *The Givers* (1904). 93–131. Republished in *Fair Lavinia and Others* (1907). 87–108.

Eglantina: A Romantic Parlor Play. Ladies' Home Journal 27 (July 1910): 13–14, 38.

"The Elm-Tree." In *Six Trees* (1903). 1–40.

"Emily Bronte and *Wuthering Heights.*" In *The World's Great Woman Novelists.* Edited by T. M. Parrott, 85–93. Philadelphia: The Booklovers Library, 1901.

"Evelina's Garden." In *Silence and Other Stories* (1898). 111–83.

"The Fair Lavinia." In *The Fair Lavinia and Others* (1907). 3–39.

The Fair Lavinia and Others. New York: Harper and Brothers, 1907.

"A Far-Away Melody." In *A Humble Romance and Other Stories* (1887). 208–18.

"Flora and Hannah." In *The Winning Lady and Others* (1909). 307–17.

"A Gala Dress." In *A New England Nun and Other Stories* (1891). 37–53.

"A Gatherer of Simples." In *A Humble Romance and Other Stories* (1887). 280–95.

"Gentian." In *A Humble Romance and Other Stories* (1887). 250–65.

"A Gentle Ghost." In *A New England Nun and Other Stories* (1891). 234–52.

Giles Corey, Yeoman: A Play. New York: Harper and Brothers, 1893.

"The Girl Who Wants to Write: Things to Do and Avoid." *Harper's Bazaar* 47 (June 1913): 272.

The Givers. New York: Harper and Brothers, 1904.

"Good Wits, Pen and Paper." In *What Women Can Earn: Occupations of Women and Their Compensation.* Edited by G. H. Dodge et al., 28–29. New York: Frederick A. Stokes Co., 1899.

"The Hall Bedroom." *Collier's* 30 (28 March 1903), 19, 22–23. Reprinted in *Collected Ghost Stories by Mary Wilkins Freeman.* Edited by Edward Wagenknecht, 21–38. Sauk City, Wisc.: Arkham House, 1974.

The Heart's Highway, A Romance of Virginia in the Seventeenth Century. New York: Doubleday, Page and Company, 1900.

"An Honest Soul." In *A Humble Romance and Other Stories* (1887). 78–91.

"A Humble Romance." In *A Humble Romance and Other Stories* (1887). 1–24.

A Humble Romance and Other Stories. New York: Harper and Brothers, 1887.

"In Butterfly Time." In *A Humble Romance and Other Stories* (1887). 315–29.

"An Independent Thinker." In *A Humble Romance and Other Stories* (1887). 296–314.

"An Innocent Gamester." In *A New England Nun and Other Stories* (1891). 363–83.

"Introductory Sketch." In Biographical Edition of *Pembroke.* New York: Harper and Brothers, 1899.

The Jamesons. New York: Doubleday and McClure Company, 1899.

Jane Field. New York: Harper and Brothers, 1893.

Jerome, A Poor Man. New York: Harper and Brothers, 1897.

"A Kitchen Colonel." In *A New England Nun and Other Stories* (1891). 427–47.

"Life Everlastin'." In *A New England Nun and Other Stories* (1891). 338–62.

"The Lombardy Poplar." In *Six Trees* (1903). 129–67.

"The Lost Ghost." In *The Wind in the Rose-Bush and Other Stories of the Supernatural* (1903). 201–37.

"Louisa." In *A New England Nun and Other Stories* (1891). 384–406.

"The Love of Parson Lord." In *The Love of Parson Lord and Other Stories* (1900). 3–81.

The Love of Parson Lord and Other Stories. New York: Harper and Brothers, 1900.

"A Lover of Flowers." *A Humble Romance and Other Stories* (1887). 192–207.

"Luella Miller." In *The Wind in the Rose-Bush and Other Stories of the Supernatural* (1903). 75–104.

Madelon. New York: Harper and Brothers, 1896.

"Mary E. Wilkins." In *My Maiden Effort: Being the Personal Confessions of Well-Known Authors as to Their Literary Beginnings.* 265–67. Garden City: Doubleday, Page and Company, 1921.

"A Mistaken Charity." In *A Humble Romance and Other Stories* (1887). 234–49.

"A Modern Dragon." In *A Humble Romance and Other Stories* (1887). 60–77.

"A Moral Exigency." In *A Humble Romance and Other Stories* (1887). 219–33.

"A New England Nun." In *A New England Nun and Other Stories* (1891). 1–17.

A New England Nun and Other Stories. New York: Harper and Brothers, 1891.

"An Object of Love." In *A Humble Romance and Other Stories* (1887). 266–79.

"An Old Arithmetician." In *A Humble Romance and Other Stories* (1887). 368–81.

"Old Lady Pingree." In *A Humble Romance and Other Stories* (1887). 148–63.

"Old Woman Magoun." In *The Winning Lady and Others* (1909). 243–77.

"One Good Time." In *The Love of Parson Lord and Other Stories* (1900). 195–233.

"On the Walpole Road." In *A Humble Romance and Other Stories* (1887). 134–47.

"A Patient Waiter." In *A Humble Romance and Other Stories* (1887). 399–414.

Pembroke. New York: Harper and Brothers, 1894.

The People of Our Neighborhood. Philadelphia: Curtis Publishing Company, 1898.

"A Poetess." In *A New England Nun and Other Stories* (1891). 140–59.

The Portion of Labor. New York: Harper and Brothers, 1901.

"A Pot of Gold." In *A New England Nun and Other Stories* (1891). 178–97.

"The Revolt of 'Mother.' " In *A New England Nun and Other Stories* (1891). 448–68.

"Robins and Hammers." In *A Humble Romance and Other Stories* (1887). 118–33.

"The Scent of Roses." In *A New England Nun and Other Stories* (1891). 198–214.

"The Secret." In *The Fair Lavinia and Others* (1907). 187–228.

"The Selfishness of Amelia Lamkin." In *The Winning Lady and Others* (1909). 125–72.

The Shoulders of Atlas. New York: Harper and Brothers, 1908.

"Silence." In *Silence and Other Stories* (1898). 1–54.

Silence and Other Stories. New York: Harper and Brothers, 1898.

"Sister Liddy." In *A New England Nun and Other Stories* (1891). 81–98.

Six Trees. New York: Harper and Brothers, 1903.

"A Solitary." In *A New England Nun and Other Stories* (1891). 215–33.

"The Southwest Chamber." In *The Wind in the Rose-Bush and Other Stories of the Supernatural* (1903). 107–64.

"A Souvenir." In *A Humble Romance and Other Stories* (1887). 350–67.

"A Symphony in Lavender." In *A Humble Romance and Other Stories* (1887). 37–48.

"A Tardy Thanksgiving." In *A Humble Romance and Other Stories* (1887). 49–59.

"A Taste of Honey." In *A Humble Romance and Other Stories* (1887). 92–106.

"The Tree of Knowledge." In *The Love of Parson Lord and Other Stories* (1900). 85–140.

"Two Old Lovers." In *A Humble Romance and Other Stories* (1887). 25–36.

"The Underling." In *The Fair Lavinia and Others* (1907). 257–308.

Understudies. New York: Harper and Brothers, 1901.

"An Unwilling Guest." In *A Humble Romance and Other Stories* (1887). 330–49.

"Up Primrose Hill." In *A New England Nun and Other Stories* (1891). 305–20.

"The Vacant Lot." In *The Wind in the Rose-Bush and Other Stories of the Supernatural* (1903). 167–98.

"A Village Lear." In *A New England Nun and Other Stories* (1891). 268–87.

"A Village Singer." In *A New England Nun and Other Stories* (1891). 18–36.

"A Wayfaring Couple." In *A New England Nun and Other Stories* (1891). 121–39.

"The White Birch." In *Six Trees* (1903). 41–65.

The Whole Family: A Novel by Twelve Authors. Mary Wilkins Freeman, William Dean Howells, Henry James et al. New York: Harper and Brothers, 1908.

"The Wind in the Rose-Bush." In *The Wind in the Rose-Bush and Other Stories of the Supernatural* (1903). 3–37.

The Wind in the Rose-Bush and Other Stories of the Supernatural. New York: Doubleday, Page and Company, 1903.

"The Winning Lady." In *The Winning Lady and Others* (1909). 3–32.

The Winning Lady and Others. New York: Harper and Brothers, 1909.

The Yates Pride: A Romance. New York: Harper and Brothers, 1912.

INDEX